THE GIRL ON THE HILL

THE GIRL ON THE HILL

"WHEN YOU'RE NOT WHO YOU THINK YOU ARE, EVERYTHING'S POSSIBLE".

SUE MACKENDER

Crooksbury
Publishing

Published by Crooksbury Publishing

ISBN 978-1-5272-7355-9

Typesetting services by BOOKOW.COM

For: Bradley, Joshua, Emily, Maddie, Oscar, Devon,
Kenzie and Phoebe
Play hard, dream big and it will happen.

ACKNOWLEDGMENTS

This book has been a long time coming and probably wouldn't have made it to these pages without my exceptional editors *Caroline Vincent and Justin Carroll*, who have painstakingly ironed out the wrinkles and tucked in all the loose ends. Thank you both so much.

Sidmouth Devon
Firstly, thanks to the ladies of *Sidmouth Museum who assisted me with my research and gave me the* perfect inspirational setting of Mutters Moor (above Peak Hill), a great place to hide the secrets for two of my characters.

Sidmouth is a beautiful Regency seaside town nestling between the red clay of the Devonshire Cliffs. It took me three visits to nail my settings (mainly because I fell in love with the place). Although my characters are purely fictitious, everyone I came across was charming, warm and friendly – the same that Mia experienced

Editing in lockdown wasn't so easy – home had too many distractions, so I had to look elsewhere. I'm sending never-ending thanks to the wonderful author *Rosie Dean a.k.a. Jan Sprenger* – for my Isle of Wight retreat that helped me nail my final draft and fed me excellent dinners.

Closer to home, *The Red Lion Horsell – Callum Hawkett, Annie Porter and Richard Brown,* who kindly let me take up residence in the pubs glorious garden while on lockdown; occasionally providing me with a warming cup of coffee.

Thanks also to *Squires Garden Centre Littlewick Road[* prelockdown, who kept me fed with jacket potatoes or speciality salads, always managing to find me a quietish spot to pour out my chapters.

"Diamonds are forever" never a truer phrase, it's tough being a

writer and it's great to have co-authors as friends to discuss plots, characters and any hiccups along the way. We call our little group the diamonds – and they truly are.

Denise Barnes, best-selling author as *Molly Green* - brings a wealth of knowledge - I cower waiting to hear her shout tautology alert! I know she despairs at me at times, but I'm a better writer for it. *Terri Fleming*, author of the most wonderful book *Perception*, if you haven't read it you should do. Terri is the one who turns my frown upside down when I felt like throwing in the towel. She'll give me a good talking to and send me on my way. *Tessa Shapcot a.k.a. Joanne Walsh* wearing her editor's hat who looks at things from a different perspective in more ways than one, and on so many occasions for being the butt of the laughter this year, it's kept us all going. Don't mention the sausage!

Last but never least to my wonderful readers forever pushing me for the next read, I promise it won't be so long next time.

And last but not least – also, my long-suffering, tea making, bacon sandwich providing, a glass of wine pouring husband. I couldn't wish for a stronger, more supportive man behind me – same goes for my ever-growing family. Thank you.

CHAPTER 1

1997 – Chartley Independent School, West Sussex

I wish I were someone else...

Maureen sat on the grassy bank; knees raised. From her viewpoint on the hill above the school buildings, she observed a procession of cars arrive at the school gates, collect a child or two, and then head back the way they'd come.

She watched her friends as they were picked up to be taken on their holidays. Sophie's family, so blonde and perfect, gathering her into their arms before whisking her away to Greece. Or Cassie's dad, throwing her the spare crash helmet before she clung to his back on the motorbike as it roared away from the school. Leaving Maureen alone. On the hill. As always.

Her arms hugged her body against the wind that grabbed her coal-black hair and whipped it against her face. How would it feel? To be that girl, wrapped in her dad's arms, the biker jacket probably smelling of his aftershave and old leather. To be Jenny Chung, to have a family who fussed over you, checked your cheeks, shepherded you like a prized lamb into the car, arms draped affectionately around your shoulders? Someone who gave a damn.

Most of her fellow students would travel to summer destinations she could only dream of. Some had careers lined up, their lives shiningly mapped out. Others were destined for university, to read subjects such as law, or politics. Here she was, eighteen, and supposedly with her life ahead of her. But she had no plans for a great career, all she wanted was to escape. She'd envied the phone calls her friends had with chatty parents and giggling siblings. Talks of "when I get home" and messages of "I love you" returned before hanging up. In truth, though they didn't know it, these girls had been her family, a yardstick to measure a sense of belonging that now had ended.

The only thing set in stone was that she couldn't go back to that awful house, to her hateful father, her ever-obedient mother, and her sister Georgina with her snide remarks. She had to get away – if not, she'd be swallowed up into an empty, meaningless existence, just like her poor mother.

What made her so different from her friends, Cassie, Grace and even Sophie? Cassie with her bright wit that never failed to draw people's attention. Maureen lifted her darkly bronzed arm to return a wave from Grace, who sheltered her eyes from the sun with one arm, whist extravagantly blowing kisses with the other. Maureen slowed her wave. Her eyes stung as Grace dipped inside the silver Volvo, peeling away another layer of isolation. What would become of them all? Grace would probably marry a farmer or a vicar, someone respectable and safe. She raised her eyes to the call of a skylark. If only she could fly away. If only she could follow the fleeing exodus of friendship and mimic their existence, have their unlimited possibilities.

'Keep in touch,' they'd chorused. Sophie had even packed her bags for her. *She* would no doubt end up married to some dogooder and have six identical children.

Over the years, this hill had been her place of sanctuary, her retreat when she'd needed to distance herself from Miss Viner and the world outside. This place always welcomed her, allowed her to breathe and think. Up here, she didn't need to pretend. Now her school days were over, she had the chance to begin a new life so why not do it today? She could go someplace where no one knew her, reinvent herself, make her dreams reality – start again, far away from her father and men like him.

The bells that had echoed throughout the school cloisters fell silent. She'd sketched the grey stone walls with the robust turrets and cawing crows, her real home since childhood, so many times.

The sound of a whistle and her name floating on the wind broke her reverie. Her stomach clenched. Oh God, Miss Viner. In panic, she squinted into the sunlight towards the school's pillared entrance but it was Matron, metal whistle in her hand. Without realising she'd been holding it, Maureen breathed again.

Maureen patted the windswept grass, feeling the tickle of the blades as they sprang free of her grasp. 'Well, this is it. Goodbye hill, you've been a good friend.'

She rose to her feet and made her way down. Matron was impatiently tapping her watch, but Maureen ignored it.

'Croxley-Smith, why are you still here?'

'No need to shout,' she muttered.

'What did you say?'

'That my taxi should be here any minute.'

'It had better be. I haven't got all day, Maureen.'

She cringed at the mention of her name. She planned to change it to *Mia* as soon as possible. It would be part of her new identity.

Matron was a crusty old tyrant, who all too often expressed her disapproval by pressing her lips together strongly. Maureen couldn't even remember ever having seen her in a happy mood.

In the distance, a taxi made its way down the poplar-flanked driveway. Thank God she'd soon be free. She could feel her temper blazing like a forest on fire. Maureen feared she couldn't control it much longer. She wanted to have the last word. Just once. To finally put bloody old Matron in her place. In her head, she heard a voice daring her. *Go on. Let the old bag have it…*

'Ah, here's my lift now,' she said, relieved that she wouldn't have to stay much longer.

'I should think so too. I've better things to do than wait around for you, Croxley-Smith.'

The driver got out and loaded Maureen's belongings into the boot. As she opened the rear door, she hesitated.

'You know what, Matron? I should introduce you to my father. You have *so* much in common. He makes my life a misery, just as you have the entire time I've been at Chartley.'

Matron's jaw fell, her palm slapped against her chest. 'Why you
—'

Maureen wagged a finger.

'Uh-Uh, I'm talking, and it's rude to interrupt. Now, why don't
you get rid of the fifty denier tights, buy an underwired bra, and
get laid? It'll make you a much happier person.'

Matron's face turned a puce hue as her mouth opened and shut
like a dying fish.

Maureen closed the taxi door with an elated flourish. It was
Mia and not Maureen who'd given Matron hell. From now on
she'd be Mia. She liked the name – *wished-for child*, according to
the definition in the book of girls' names. Well, she was far from
that, but it was pretty cool all the same.

She coughed a laugh. 'Goodness, did I just say that to Matron?'

The driver grinned in his rear-view mirror. 'You sure did, love,
made me smile.'

Sitting back, she smiled too. From now on, she'd take no prison-
ers. Her mother might be subservient to the Major, her so-called
father, but she owed him nothing. The world was out there waiting
for her, for Mia: she could do it if she tried.

Her good humour faded the nearer she got to Willow House,
so much had happened there she couldn't just pretend it away.

CHAPTER 2

1985 Surrey

Maureen peeked through a gap between the sofa and the armchair, knowing he couldn't see her. If she didn't make a noise, he wouldn't find her and lock her in the cupboard.

Mummy was crying again. It didn't seem right, and Maureen wanted to give her a hanky but didn't dare.

'It's done, woman! Don't argue with me! You know better than to disobey me.'

'But, Charles—'

'I said enough. She's been nothing but trouble since the day we adopted her. The one time I let you have what you wanted, look at what happened. You're not capable of making decisions on your own. You brought home a darkly-brat; were you blind woman? Couldn't you see she had a touch of the tar brush? I have my position to think of. I won't have her here a minute longer. Do you hear?' He'd grabbed Mummy by the shoulders and shook her.

Maureen wished he'd leave. Everything was horrid when he was home. It was his eyes that frightened her the most. His eyes, and what he did to Mummy. His face was red, very red, and he looked all hot and shiny, spit spraying from his mouth. She hoped it wouldn't land on Mummy's face.

The row had started yesterday after Daddy had called her into his study. She'd almost wet herself then. She hadn't broken Georgina's doll. Gina had lied like she always did. She'd thrown the doll at Maureen when she'd stepped into her room. It'd missed and hit the wall but, of course, he hadn't believed her. He'd said stuff, those eyes bulging at her, saying she was from unsavoury stock. What did that even mean?

How much longer was he going to shout at Mummy? If she were a boy she'd tell him to stop being a bully. Was it because she was a girl? Had he wanted a boy?

His voice thundered off the walls. 'Stops snivelling, woman! She's going, and that's an end to it.'

Hurry up and go! I need a wee. Maureen crossed her legs as tightly as she could.

'Get to my study now and sign the papers.' Her mother flinched as he slapped his fist against his open palm.

'But, Charles, please—'

'I'll not stand for insubordination.'

No, Mummy, please don't make him angrier. You know what he'll—

The open hand slapped twice across her mother's cheeks. Maureen put her hands over her ears to block out the sound of Mummy's scream, shrinking further behind the couch, her eyes squeezed shut.

'Understand this, woman. You don't defy me.'

Maureen flushed the chain and washed her hands, peering around the door to check it was safe to come out. She released the breath she was holding as she saw her father through the window loading his luggage into the car and driving away. As she stepped further into the hallway, a voice from behind made her jump. *Gina!*

'There. I've finally got rid of you.'

She turned to see her sister hanging over the handrail of the stairs, with eyes cold and cruel.

'Daddy's sending you away.'

She jutted out her chin. 'He's not. Don't fib. Mummy wouldn't let him.'

Gina gave a slow smile. 'She can't stop him, and it's all down to me because *you* made me angry. You're going away *forever.*'

'*No!* I'm not your—'

Lisa, their nanny, came from the kitchen.

'Girls, girls! Stop this arguing at once.'

'She's being sent away, she's being sent away,' Georgina sang triumphantly. Maureen hated it when Gina taunted her in that singsong voice. It made her want to slap her hard, but she didn't dare.

'That's enough. Stop being nasty to your sister, Georgina.'

'I'm not being nasty. Daddy *is* sending her away, he told me. You ask Mummy.'

Lisa ignored the comment. Moving close behind Maureen, she gathered up her long black hair.

'We really must get this cut, young lady. It's got far too long.'

'I don't want mine cut,' Gina said sulkily, stroking her frizzy mane.

'Yours doesn't need it. It doesn't grow as quickly as Maureen's.'

That was a good thing, wasn't it? That her hair grew quicker. It was something she was better at than Gina. Knowing this made Maureen puff out her chest and stand a little taller.

She liked their nanny. Like Maureen, she had black hair; Lisa gave wonderful cuddles and read Maureen stories when *he* was home and she was made to stay in her room while he yelled at Mummy.

She didn't mean to listen; she was only going to the kitchen for a glass of water when she overheard Lisa and Mummy talking.

'She's too young,' Mummy said.

'I know, but what can we do? We should *try* and see the positives. You never know, it may be a blessing in disguise. At least she'll be out of harm's way. I dread to think how it feels to be locked in that dark cupboard. At least she'll be spared that. Don't cry, Constance. Chartley might be the making of her. She'll find new friends, and we can write long, newsy letters. She's a survivor. She'll surprise us all.'

'I hope you're right. I wish I could do something. I just feel so trapped. He'll never agree to...'

'It's rude to listen at doors.'

The voice sent a chill down Maureen's spine. Gina crept up behind her grinning a twisted sort of grin, her doughy white face framed by frizzy blonde hair.

'Don't tell…' she pleaded in a small voice.

Gina poked a rigid finger into her chest. It hurt. 'No need to, you'll be gone soon.' She bent nearer. 'And you're *never* coming back.'

Maureen's breath came in little gasps. 'You're a liar.'

'No, I'm not. You ask Mummy.'

Maureen put her hands over her ears, pushed past Gina and ran into the garden. If she didn't listen to Gina's words, they wouldn't come true.

She ran to the far end of the garden, squeezing herself between the shed and the wall, squatting down, sobbing into her lap.

'I thought I'd find you here. Come on,' Lisa held out a hand and Maureen took it, wiggling free of her hiding place, 'look at your pretty dress all covered in cobwebs. You shouldn't take any notice of Georgina. Sometimes she's not nice.'

Once Maureen had stopped crying and her hiccups had subsided, she felt brave enough to ask about the things she didn't understand.

'Lisa, when you get adopted, what happens?'

Lisa pulled a face that Maureen didn't recognise. It was like a thinking face but with a different shaped mouth.

'How do you mean?' Lisa said, stroking Maureen's hair from her brow.

'Well. Is it like a shop with all the babies lined up and you walk along until you see the one you want?'

Lisa smiled. 'Not quite, but you were chosen, both of you.'

Maureen plucked a daisy from the grass and counted its petals.

'Then why didn't they pick two the same and not one with a touch of the tar brush?'

Lisa jolted her head back. 'Maureen. Where did you get that expression from?'

'Daddy said it to Mummy. Is it a bad thing, having a touch of the tar brush? Is it because my skin is not the same as Gina's? And if Daddy doesn't like it why did Mummy pick me, and not one that matched Gina, with yellow hair and blue eyes? Then he'd play with me and push me on the swing like he does Gina, and Mummy wouldn't cry anymore.'

Lisa made a tutting sound and chewed her lip. 'Now let me think. Mummy chose you because she thought you were a special baby girl. Sometimes, daddies get a bit cross with people. Being a major in the army means he keeps our country safe. It's an especially important job. He has hundreds of soldiers to look after and tell them what to do. He doesn't mean to shout so much.'

'But he doesn't shout at Gina, only me and Mummy.'

Lisa patted the back of Maureen's hand, frowning. 'It just seems like that, poppet. It will get better as you get older, I'm sure.'

That night, Maureen cried into her pillow. Gina wasn't lying. Her mother had come to her bedroom and told her she was going to go to a new school. Mother had said it in a strange sort of wobbly voice.

'You'll have lots of *lovely* new friends, a *big new* bedroom and *wonderful* things to do.'

'I don't want wonderful things to do or a big new bedroom. I want to stay here with you and Lisa. Can't you send Gina instead?'

She stretched out her arms for a hug, but Mummy's face had gone all twisted and funny.

'I'm sorry,' she'd said, backing out of the room, leaving Maureen to cry herself to sleep.

Maureen stood by the crack in her bedroom door listening for Gina's footsteps going downstairs to breakfast; once she heard Gina talking to Lisa, Maureen rushed to the bathroom to get a towel. Pulling back the bedcovers she placed it over the wet patch. Her lip began to tremble. What if she wet her bed at the new school? Would the children laugh at her? Would there be others like Gina to make her cry? I need to be a big girl, not a boo-baby, she thought as she scrunched her small hands into fists.

The worrying feeling inside her tummy felt like a balloon getting bigger and bigger. She squashed her lips together tightly in case it burst. She *had* to be strong, act brave like a big girl. Could she be like Gina? She pulled the bedclothes over the towel and pummelled the pillow, pretending it was Gina. The thought made her tummy wobble. She bit her lip. There were girls like Gina at her school too but that didn't matter because Maureen's teacher had said she was good at drama, so at the new school she'd pretend she was in a play and be the one that got booed. Fee-fi-fo-fum. Like Jack and the Beanstalk. Jack did a silly thing with the beans, but his mummy still loved him. Could she pretend to be brave? She flopped onto the bed, her knuckles pink and sore. Tears came, she hugged her pillow to stifle the sound of her sobs. She didn't want to be a bad girl, but she had to, or she'd end up just like Mummy.

CHAPTER 3

MAUREEN stood on the doorstep of Willow House and wetted her lips. She didn't want to go in; this was the last place she needed to be. Sadly, she had no choice. Her hand hovered above the knocker; she closed her eyes rapping it, listening to the sound of footsteps approaching. *Please don't let it be him.*

The door opened. A young woman wrinkled her nose in disapproval.

'Oh, it's you.'

Mia felt the sudden rush of heat through her body. Gina, the grinning Cheshire cat. The one who got the cream.

'Is he here?'

'No. Lucky for you he's away.'

Maureen pushed past, averting her eyes from the under-stairs cupboard and all it represented.

'Don't worry – I don't intend to stay one second longer than necessary.'

'Good. No one wants you here,' Gina muttered, as Constance came into the hall.

'Hello, Mummy.' Mia said, desperately wanting to throw her arms around her neck, but that had never been appropriate. Just like her mother, she'd been a shadow in this house, submissive to the dominant personalities: her father, the Major, and spiteful Gina.

Constance didn't move. Her eyes gave a flurry of blinks as her frail hand touched her temple.

'Maureen. I wasn't expecting you. Has school finished?'

Mia put her bags at the foot of the stairs. 'Yes, Mummy, all done. By the way, I don't use the name Maureen anymore. It's far too old-fashioned. From now on, I'd like to be known as Mia.'

Gina snorted. 'Always pretentious. Nothing quite good enough for our Maureen.'

Both Constance and Mia ignored her.

'Yes, all done. No more school, Chartley's no longer my home.'

'And neither is this,' Gina hissed from behind.

Panic flashed across her mother's eyes. Mia wondered why. It was years since she'd had been allowed home and even though she hadn't expected a brass band, it was clear her mother wasn't too pleased with her arrival. Then she noticed her mother's dishevelled appearance. Her ever-immaculate hair, rouged cheeks, a broach, always a broach, were absent. She was thinner – much thinner, almost as if her body had shrunk inside her clothing, she'd aged beyond her fifty-odd years. The cardigan and skirt looked as frumpy as the ancient knitting bag with the peacocks she carried around with her. This wasn't the image of the perfect army wife anymore. Was this *his* doing?

Mia was jolted from her thoughts as Constance uttered a single 'Oh.' She hadn't expected a joyful reunion, but her mother's 'Oh' stung like the twang of an elastic band. Constance turned to Gina.

'Georgina, would you please make us all a hot drink. Maureen let's go into the lounge. I'm not feeling so good today. Nobody told me you were coming.'

'I'll just put my bags upstairs first.'

'Don't bother,' Gina said without looking at her as she walked towards the kitchen. 'You won't be staying.'

It was the first true thing Gina had said. Mia wouldn't be staying; she'd be away from here as soon as she had what she'd come for.

Mia followed her mother into the lounge. She waited for Constance to settle in the winged-back chair by the window before perching on the edge of the settee opposite. Constance was doing that hand-wringing thing she always did when agitated.

Strange, Mia thought, as she took in her surroundings. *You'd expect some change over the years, new wallpaper perhaps or curtains, but everything is the same.*

'How have you been, Mummy?'

Constance's eyes glistened with tears. 'Much the same, Maureen. You've grown into such a beautiful young woman.'

'Thank you,' Mia said, smiling at the compliment, 'but you weren't expecting me?'

'No, I wasn't. Your father does everything and tells me nothing, but you know that. I don't see any correspondence, I didn't know if he'd allow you to come home, so I have no idea what's been arranged.'

Mia shook off the sensation that she was shrinking – shrinking back into her childhood. She was something to be "arranged" not welcomed. A cold shiver ran down her spine, she tried to shrug it away. 'Mummy, really, arranged?'

Constance sighed, removing a lace hanky from her sleeve to dab her eyes.

'You remember what he's like.'

'How could I forget.'

'You wouldn't want to stay here. The rages you know…'

Mia felt hurt – there it was again, the rejection, knowing she was unwanted. She felt her heart harden, stronger now, no longer a child.

'I don't know why you ever bothered adopting me in the first place. It was obviously a mistake.'

Constance's lip trembled as a cat-like cry escaped her lips. This was all wrong. Mia felt sorry for Constance but could not suppress a rising anger; with Gina out of sight, there was no one else to challenge.

'What do you suggest I do, Mother – sleep on the streets?'

Before Constance could reply, Gina returned making a great show of pushing through the door with the tea tray. Constance looked up at her hopefully.

'Georgina, dear. Did Daddy give you any instructions about Maureen before he went away?'

There it was – Georgina dear. Georgina darling. Georgina, Daddy's favourite, and Mummy's too, by the look of it. Any hope of change faded to dust. Mia briefly closed her eyes, fighting to stay in control, only to find Gina's mouth kicked up in a sneer.

'Yes, Mummy he did. He doesn't want *her* here.'

'I am in the room you know,' Mia said angrily.

Gina didn't look up as she poured tea. 'But not for long.'

'*Georgina.*' Her mother scolded, 'Be kind to your sister. Why must you always be so cruel?'

Mia bit the inside of her cheek. 'Not a problem, Mother. I'm used to it. Gina, fetch me a pad and paper.'

'Don't order me around. I don't need to fetch you anything. Daddy gave clear instructions, it's all organised.' She handed Mia a brown envelope before dragging her chair and positioning herself between Mia and their mother.

Mia remained poker-faced sensing Gina's glee as she opened the envelope, giving the contents only a cursory glance, and nodded.

'Not quite everything… I shall require my adoption certificate.'

This time, there was no mistaking the fear etched in her mother's eyes. Constance raised a trembling hand to her mouth, cagey eyes averting to the floor. She fidgeted and fussed with her cardigan before fanning herself with a flapping hand, mumbling, she made as if to stand, then sank back into her chair. Mia was confused by her mother's peculiar behaviour but carried on regardless.

'There are legalities I need it for.' Mia jutted her chin expecting an argument, but her Constance was studying her lap.

'Legalities. What legalities?' Gina said, slapping the arm of the chair.

Mia savoured the blissful moment of riling her. If only her situation wasn't precarious, she'd have celebrated that fact alone.

'I intend to change my name officially,' she said addressing Constance, 'by deed poll, and I want a passport. For both, I need my adoption certificate. Then I won't be bothering you again. I've no intention of staying in this country any longer than necessary. I have plans.'

Gina folded her arms across her chest. 'Hah! Plans. I hope you do because Daddy's washed his hands of you.'

Constance shuffled to the front of her seat – her fists opening and closing as if trying to grasp something.

Gina half raised from her seat. 'What is it, Mother, what's wrong?'

'This has nothing to do with you, Georgina,' Constance snapped, surprising both her daughters. 'Maureen, your adoption certificate is in safekeeping. It's with my private papers at my solicitor's,' her eyes flickered. 'Your father wasn't interested in the legalities at the time.' Mia knitted her eyebrows together in askance, but if Constance saw it, she didn't react. 'Georgina will give me the details of where you are staying. My solicitor will organise everything for you. Naturally, you need these things.'

'Daddy won't like it, Mummy,' Gina interrupted, 'I have full instructions on what to do with *her.*'

'For once, Georgina, you will do as I say. If Maureen is to be sent away *again,* then she needs to be allowed to have what she needs to make her way in life, and I'll see that she does.'

Mia watched the exchange thinking how odd it was that her documents were at her mother's solicitor, she didn't even know her mother had one. Mia desperately needed her adoption certificate. Was she being fobbed off? The thought stung but she wouldn't show it. She had no choice but to believe her mother would keep her word.

Without once looking back, Mia left the family home that had never really been hers. As she climbed into the taxi, she promised herself that she would never again put herself through that. There was no one to miss her, no one had marked her birthday, not even with a single card, but none of that mattered now. Who she was, was now down to herself. They could all go to hell.

Mia gazed out of the taxi window, a feeling of excitement building as she read the road-signs with names of places she had only ever heard of. Hyde Park corner – they'd discussed the soapbox politics held there in civics lessons at Chartley. Her father was paying for the cab so she told the taxi driver to take the long way round so she could get her bearings. He pointed out places she knew, Trafalgar Square, Westminster, and Buckingham Palace. Mia imagined herself roaming the streets taking in the noise and bustle, sitting at a pavement café, in Covent Garden watching, learning. It made her fingertips tingle.

The traffic grew slower now, the view not so enticing. She glanced at the address in Tottenham that meant nothing to her. It didn't look as inviting as Harringay. She knew next to nothing of London. Only what she'd seen on TV or gleaned from the other girls at Chartley. The thought of Chartley and what had happened there made her shoulders tense, but that was in the past. She paid the taxi driver and shrugged the rucksack onto her shoulders. Her worldly possessions now consisted of that and a nylon holdall.

Tottenham was a lively area, buzzing with people, traffic, and noise. Mia stood where the taxi had dropped her off surveying her surroundings. A smell caught her nostrils, a mix of frying onions, spice, coffee. The gutters held the detritus of boxes and cabbage leaves, of squashed tomatoes.

'Any bowl a pound,' a stallholder called out repeatedly. The scene was lively. Cackles of laughter filtered through sounds of car radios, blasting horns, revving engines. It was intimidating and exciting at the same time. Mia thought that every race in the world had gathered in this one street. Passers-by jostled around her as she gazed in the opposite direction at even more stalls selling shoes, clothes, and bags. Bright arrays of women's clothing hung from hooks swaying in the breeze – a glittery sheath dress caught her eye. She'd investigate it later; priority now was to find where she'd be living. Her expectations weren't high, but that wasn't a bad thing; if your expectations were negative, the results were often positive.

Turning, she glanced once more at her new address. A homeless man was lying in her path, his life packed around him in carrier bags. What was his story, she wondered as she entered the narrow alleyway leading to her room above a kebab shop. She knocked on the only door she could see. A man who spoke little English showed her up a flight of stairs. He pointed to a badly painted door, handed her the keys, and left. As she opened the door, the dank musty smell of stale tobacco assaulted her nose. With a sense of foreboding her hand searched for a light switch. A single bulb illuminated the room. The space was cramped, grubby, with stained carpets and worn furniture. A curtain separated the bedsit from a toilet. The kitchen consisted of a two-ring burner and a toaster. The Major's disdain was more than evident in his choice of accommodation. It made her smile. If he thought this would break her, he'd be wrong. She would survive this; she'd buy cheap things from the market and make it liveable. The rent, his letter had said, was paid up for the next six months. After that, she was on her own.

CHAPTER 4

THE glittery dress from the market had long gone, replaced with a black sheath from Karen Millen. Yet another layer of the onion peeled away, her cheapness and sense of being unworthy. Soon, she would shop in the boutiques of Mayfair, the ones with black-suited doormen to discourage any riffraff; doormen who'd nod politely as they let her in.

The men who visited the casino fell into several groups. Mia assessed each one as they arrived at her blackjack table. Business types on expenses, cheap suits, flirtatious, hoping for some company, a one-night stand. Then there were the celebrities: flashing the cash to impress a group of friends or a breast enhanced wag dangling from their arm. Next was the Old Money, who didn't care if they lost a few thousand on the turn of a card. These she found exciting. These were what she was after, a classy rich man to take care of her. Not as some cheap thing to be picked up in the casino, no, she only wanted the best: stylish and sophisticated to feel good about herself. She'd seen what happened to some of the girls who'd gone home with the big rollers – too much cocaine numbed a girl's brains and sullied their looks. Stability was what she craved for. Sometimes she could almost smell the military background, they were a definite no. Public school, or self-made – gentleman, these were her favourites, they treated her with respect.

Occasionally, elegant, bejewelled women with beautifully manicured hands joined her table, sometimes accompanied by husbands or partners who stood supportively behind them. The intimacy quietly restrained. The touch of a shoulder, a refilled glass. These were the women Mia envied and aspired to be.

Her manager, Inika, could have been mistaken for a Greek Goddess. She towered over Mia and over half of the men in the casino, her tight, blonde curls a wreath of platinum that shone above the crowds.

'I have to say I admire your nerve. I suggest we start again. Have you worked in a casino before?'

How could she have been so naive? She'd lengthened her neck and looked Inika straight in the eye.

'I've done my research. I know the rules of each game. I've watched YouTube and online games. I can do this. I want this job and I think I'll be incredibly good at it.'

Inika's lips pursed and tweaked in amusement.

'Well, you have some nerve; I'll say that for you.' Mia held her breath waiting for Inika to end the interview but instead, she opened a drawer in her desk, selected a document and passed it to her. An application form. *Cocktail Waitress*.

'I think you have potential and you certainly have the right attitude, but I run a professional business. If you want to start at the bottom, I'll train you until I think you're ready.'

Mia's heart sank, she didn't want to be a cocktail waitress, but she needed a job and it was certainly a way in.

'If you want it, you can start Friday. You need to be able to handle yourself. With those looks you'll be popular. Where are you from, Italy, Greece, Spain?'

'I wish I knew. I was adopted.'

Inika gave a long slow nod. 'You get a basic salary, and the tips are good. All our girls wear a uniform.'

Mia couldn't hide her despondency.

'It's up to you,' Inika said, flipping a hand dismissively, 'That's what's on offer.'

Mia had to accept though she didn't want to appear too keen, which wasn't difficult because it wasn't the job she had been after.

'So how long would I have to do this for before I get trained as a croupier?'

'You're certainly keen I'll give you that, but first you need experience of working in a casino. It's not all glamour. It's hard work to keep a smile on your face on a six-hour shift and learn to deal with a drunk without upsetting them. If you can do that for six months and still want to work here, we'll give it a try.'

Mia loathed the job no matter how moneyed the clientele. The men still mistook her for some sort of merchandise to be handled. As she glided between them with trays of drinks, they pushed folded banknotes into the cleavage of her skimpy uniform, but she'd been through worse, hadn't she. Nothing was going to stop her making her place in the world.

The pigeons outside her window cooed and trilled to each other. She glanced at her watch, a quarter after two, most people would have just finished lunch. She'd finished her shift in the early hours. Inika had a driver drop the girls off home throughout the night for their safety.

Mia threw back the covers, swung her legs off the bed and sank her toes into the soft rug she'd got from the market. She hugged herself, stretched, and took the two steps to the shelf where she kept her toiletries. Having washed and dressed she ran her brush through her hair addressing herself in the mirror.

'Happy birthday to you. Happy birthday to you, happy birthday dear Mia, happy birthday to you. Nineteen not so wonderful years, but it will change.' She winked at her reflection and grabbed her purse. Locking the door behind her, she started down the stairs.

The ledge on top of the meter cupboard was where the landlord left any post. It was as empty as it had been yesterday and the day before that. Wouldn't it be wonderful if there were a stack of birthday cards waiting for her?

Huh, who are you kidding.

At the end of the alleyway, Paddy, the homeless man, had also just woken. His cardboard shelter had been folded to one side.

'Perhaps you're not so badly off Mia,' she mumbled to herself as she dodged the traffic and headed through the market stalls to A Cuppa Char.

Squeezing herself between two empty stools, she nodded to her fellow diners. Freddie rubbed his hands together when he saw her. A Cuppa Char was a great place to start the day. It always made her feel less alone.

'Ere she is, the prettiest girl in Tottenham. Mornin' darling, usual as it?'

'Er, no not today thanks, Freddie. I'll have a BLT on brown and double-decker bacon and sausage on white and two teas.'

'Someone's hungry this mornin',' he said, piling lettuce and tomatoes onto a slice of brown bread.

Mia smiled. 'It's not all for me.'

He gave a cheeky grin. 'Two for breakfast is it?'

'Yes, but not in the way you think,' she said, chirpily opening her purse.

'Well someone put a smile on your face, anyone'd fink it's your birthday or somefin.'

'Actually, Charlie, it is.'

'Nah really. Well, happy birthday love.' He reached over to the confectionery shelf selecting a KitKat. 'Sorry I ain't got no cake, but that and the teas on the 'ouse.'

'Thank you, Freddie, that's lovely of you.'

Mia made her way back to where Paddy sat in the empty shop doorway looking dejected.

'Here we go Paddy, I thought we might have breakfast together.' He frowned and looked at her through rheumy eyes. She often wondered how old he was. With the dirty hair and greying beard, it was hard to tell.

She lowered herself to the step beside him and handed him one of the two paper carriers. He peered inside mumbling thanks.

It was strange the way the world walked past them unseeing. Paddy wasn't much of a talker, but then who *would* he talk to – apart from the odd charity worker or the Salvation Army he was invisible to most. She finished her breakfast, got up and brushed herself down before handing him the KitKat.

'Pudding, enjoy,' she said, 'I'll see you later.'

Paddy looked up at the sky, 'It's gonna rain later.'

Back in her room, she filled her rucksack, ready for the weekly visit to the launderette. Her phone was on its charger; she unplugged it and switched it on.

Wouldn't it be nice if she'd a missed call from Constance? Perhaps Mia should give her a call, but then, perhaps not. The conversation would be a miserable one and worse for her mother if *he* is there. Still, at least she'd kept to her word, her mother's solicitor had provided everything Mia needed to start her new life.

Peter, the liveried doorman, greeted her with a smile as she entered the casino.

'Don't you ever sleep?' he said, grinning broadly.

'Not while there are things to learn and opportunities to take,' she said with a wink as she slipped into the lift alighting on the fifth floor. The staff changing room was unusually deserted today.

Opening her locker, she changed into her uniform and was just applying lipstick when she became aware of someone watching her. Inika stood in the doorway.

'When you've done that, come to my office.'

'Yes, sure.'

The door swung shut and Mia heard the opening and closing of Inika's office door at the far end of the corridor.

'Shit. What have I done wrong?' Saliva drained from Mia's mouth. Had Inika sounded annoyed? Had someone complained about her? She racked her brains but couldn't think of a single thing. Was this the end? 'Bugger, I'd better not keep her waiting.'

Locking her things away, Mia rehearsed her speech as she headed along the corridor hallway. *This time I do have the experience. I can shuffle a pack as well as the best of them. I can accurately cut the chips, deal cards, collect chips, and make pay-outs. I deserve this and I'm going to fight for it.* Sucking in a breath she tapped on the door.

'Come in.' Inika yelled from inside.

Mia wobbled on her heels and pushed the door open. Inika sat at her desk.

'Take a seat,' she gestured, smiling, 'and don't look so worried. I just wanted to give you this, that's all.' She held out an envelope.

Mia sat down and tore it open. Before she'd had a chance to see what was inside, Inika spoke again.

'I thought today would be an appropriate day to promote you. That's your new contract. Congratulations, you're no longer serving cocktails. Happy birthday, Mia.'

'Oh my God,' Mia sighed with relief. 'I thought you were going to sack me.'

'No. Why on earth would I do that? You certainly proved yourself, you're one of my best workers. Who else would turn up two hours early to work without getting extra pay?'

There was a light tap on the door behind her, Mia turned as one of the barmen entered carrying an ice bucket, a bottle of champagne, and two glasses. Mia's eyes widened as she beamed a smile.

'You didn't think I'd let your birthday pass without celebrating, did you?' Inika said, making room on her desk.

Mia bit on her lip, overwhelmed, trying to control the urge to rush around the desk and hug Irina.

'Oh, and you're not working tonight. I'm taking you to supper, then an early night.' Mia went to object but Inika shook her head and poured the champagne. 'No arguing. Make the most of the evening, see friends, have a good time. Your first shift starts at 9.00 p.m. tomorrow. I'll start you on the quieter tables, but you're now officially a croupier.' She raised a glass to her lips; Mia did the same. 'Happy birthday.' Mia breathed in and felt a sense of belonging. Would everything go her way from now on?

CHAPTER 5

MIA picked up the few belongings she had and carried them to the waiting taxi. A chance conversation with Inka over her birthday supper had revealed that she lived in a large Edwardian house owned by Inika's lover Anton, who spent most of the year abroad. Several girls from the casino rented a room there and one was vacant. Perfect for Mia.

The room overlooked a park and was light and airy, with an own en-suite. It was twice the size of Mia's former dreadful bedsit, but she'd miss seeing Paddy. She was glad she'd left him the duvet; that would keep him warm.

Mia was wary of Inika, she seemed too good to be true, a sort of guardian angel to most of the girls. It made her suspicious as to why Inika acted so generously – would she want something in return?

Inika had laughed when she'd posed the question.

'Darling, if you're wondering if I'm going to sneak into your room one night forget it. You won't be the first to think I'm bi, but I can assure you I'm a strictly one-man woman. When you meet him, you'll understand why. And if you're wondering, I never ask personal questions of my house guests. House rule is that any overnight visitors, of whichever sex, leave the building when you do.'

'I won't be having visitors.'

'Not even family?'

'Especially not family.'

Inika hadn't pressed her, just shrugged her shoulders, and squeezed Mia's arm.

Since then Mia had celebrated a further two birthdays with Inika.

The gambling tables arced around the room with wide sways of plush carped forming a natural pathway. The high ceilings were illuminated by crystal chandeliers interspersed with ceiling mirrors over each table. It was a respectable establishment with a restaurant one floor down and a spa in the basement. Any overzealous patrons often only needed a quiet word with Inika to back down. She was a fair boss, and all the girls felt safe when Irina was around.

'Stop daydreaming and take a break,' Inika said. 'I hate it when it's quiet. Let's make the most of it before the two-a.m. rush.'

'I thought I'd stay, there's a large group in the restaurant and the maître d' has notified us they'll be arriving shortly.'

'Okay. But until they do take the weight off your feet.' She looked down at Mia's shoes. 'Alistair McQueen's. Nice!'

Mia laughed. 'Yes, I love them. They're worth every penny I paid. They're gorgeous and so comfortable.'

'Good. It's nice to give your body nice things. Now take a break. You can watch the screens from the staff room and see when it gets busy.'

Mia obeyed, considering her good fortune, and made her way to the staffroom. There were CCTV monitors alerting staff to sudden rushes of gamblers, or the need for more cocktail servers.

One man caught her eye. She'd seen him before. She squinted trying to make out what he was like. The camera view was from above, but she recognised him anyway. She remembered he was tall enough that, when he was sitting at her table – as he had been last time she'd seen him – he could look her in the eye from his chair. His hair was thick with a bit of distinguished grey at the temples. She remembered his tanned skin that was blemished probably from some adolescent virus-like chickenpox. And he had nice hands. Hands said a lot about a man she read somewhere.

He was never flash with his money; just pleasant, polite. Something about him was appealing. He was probably ten to twenty years her senior, often usually in the company of the same group of men, occasionally a woman. He didn't wear a ring but that didn't mean he was single.

She was put off by married men. Being someone's bit on the side wasn't for her. She recalled he'd spoken softly. She had no immediate plans to make herself known to him but found something quite fascinating about him. Many of the girls dated customers even though Inika had strict rules. However, Mia didn't want to be thought of as the type who could be picked up for a few gaming chips.

It was time to get back to work. She put on her shoes, reapplied her lipstick, and took the lift down ready to take her place at the blackjack table.

Inika was reprimanding a waitress for spending too long at one client's side. Mia waited until she'd finished and was alone before moving closer.

'Hey, you see the guy over there, white open-neck shirt? Dark grey suit. The one on the end facing out.'

Inika frowned, turning to look in the direction Mia had indicated. 'Trouble?'

'No, not at all. I just wondered who he was, that's all.'

Inika took a step back and glanced over the sea of heads, smiling at the room but to no one in particular.

'Well done, little one. You have good taste. That's Rufus Stone. Self-made, unmarried. He has houses all over the world. Anton knows him. I've been to his villa in Sardinia, and Anton has done business with him. He is what you would call one of the "good guys." Do you want an introduction?'

Mia was tempted to say yes but hesitated. She was far too young and inexperienced to carry off a conversation with a man like that; she would only make a fool of herself.

'No thanks, I just wondered who he was. He seems nice.'

Inika twisted her mouth into a wry grin. 'They all do darling when you first meet them. It's when you scrape the surface you find most are bastards. Although I have never heard bad of Rufus Stone, who can tell. Be careful what you wish for.'

'Oh, I will.' Mia said as the face of her father came to mind. Had he ever been a nice man?

CHAPTER 6

Sardinia

Teresa, her housekeeper, stepped out of the shadows of the villa to greet her and followed her inside.

'How was your afternoon, Madam?'

Mia, draped in carrier bags, was already climbing the sweeping marble staircase.

'Good, thanks,' she shouted over her shoulder.

Teresa followed her into the coolness of the entrance. 'A letter came for you, Madam, from England. Shall I bring it up?'

Mia turned. 'From England?'

'Yes, Madam.'

Who would write to her from England? It could only be bad news.

'Yes, Teresa, if you would.'

Mia dumped her shopping by the dressing room door and kicked off her shoes. Her bare feet paced across the cool marble floor, as various scenarios came to mind. Perhaps it was the cruise-liner she'd worked for after she left the casino. Weren't they based in England? Apart from them, Gina, and her mother's solicitor, she couldn't think who'd write to her and for some reason, she felt uneasy.

Teresa returned a few moments later and handed her the letter. 'Would you like your shopping put away?'

Mia turned the envelope over, corner to corner. Teresa repeated the question.

Mia nodded. 'What? Oh, yes, please.'

The envelope was typed but the contents were written in Gina's loopy handwriting. Mia was tempted to take it straight to Rufus's office and shred it. Anything from Gina could only be trouble. She'd been ringing on and off for a while but more often recently and she'd ignored her calls knowing it would only be more of the same – about how unfair it was that she was left to care for their father, now severely disabled by a stroke, and Constance. Gina had implied their mother had mental health issues. Mia wasn't surprised; their poor mother had taken so much over the years. Was she as bad as Gina made out? Gina liked to make herself out to be the heroine. In truth, it suited her to have Mia out of the way.

Mia lowered herself onto the bed, watching as Teresa, oblivious to her apprehension, proceeded to carefully unpack Mia's purchases, and hang them on padded hangers before slipping a transparent sleeve over the top. Mia watched the way the older woman held the cashmere scarf against her hand, caressing the soft fabric. It stirred some long-forgotten memory. Lilac had been a bad choice of colour.

'Do you like the scarf, Teresa?'

'Oh, yes, Madam, very much. It's beautiful. It reminds me of the fields of lavender back in Cork and the heather on the common I played on as a child.'

'Lavender?'

'Yes. A farm nearby grew it. I love the smell. It masked the stench from the pig farm.'

Mia wrinkled her nose in disgust.

'Don't you like the smell of lavender? It's very relaxing.'

Relaxing? I think not. But Teresa was right about one thing. It had been incredibly good at dulling the smell of stale urine. A shudder of revulsion went through her as she recalled how she'd picked handfuls of the stuff from the garden to push under the ill-fitting cupboard door – her prison.

'They're all done,' Teresa said and left her to read the letter.

Dear Maureen,

I know you are avoiding me and wrapped up in your own life, but it's time to be less selfish and think of others. Daddy is gravely ill and not expected to last the month. I've promised him I'll get you home so that he can make amends. He's desperately sorry for the way you were treated and wants to apologise – die with a clear conscience, knowing that you forgave. He regrets sending you away. It's pitiful to hear him crying and asking for you. Find it in your heart to forgive. No matter what you think, we were both linked by circumstance and adopted into a good family. How many people get the opportunity to go to such an expensive boarding school? Please, Maureen. You must come before it's too late. Mummy is desperate to see you. It's been too many years, she can't go on forever and she's very frail. If you don't want this on your conscience for the rest of your life, you'll do the right thing.

Don't worry about me – you don't need to see me. I'll make myself scarce while you're here.

Please call me.

Gina

Mia shook her head, balling a fist ... *"become less selfish and think of others"* and *"we were both adopted into a good family! Do the right thing."* How dare she? Gina wasn't the one locked away for doing nothing more than meeting his eye. Mia's eyes slid from the page She was worried about Constance – mental health issues. What had Gina meant by that?

The thought of him wanting to apologise was tempting. Would he apologise for setting a clear divide between Gina and her? She doubted it. She re-read the letter with mixed feelings. The mere thought of him made her feel dirty, tarnished as Miss Viner had. The only interaction they had was to punish her. *He* never stroked her hair or placed a caring arm around her shoulder. He'd made his disdain for her plain but despite all that Gina's words trickled through and gave her a sense of guilt, as if she, Mia, owed the bastard.

She stripped off her clothes, searching for a sensation of untethered freedom but there was none. Only the vision of the hateful cupboard sprang to mind — like being buried alive in a lidded coffin, squashed and airless with the odour of urine and lavender. A shower, she needed a shower to feel clean.

The warm water coursed through her hair and over her body. She scrubbed aggressively at her scalp; it didn't help. Her mind was in overdrive as it came up with reasons to return to England, followed by a dozen others why she shouldn't. What she needed was company, a cold glass of wine, and a moan. Inika would listen, as always. Not that her friend could ever appreciate how Mia felt, living in her loved-up, perfect world with Anton. The day Inika was leaving she'd called her into the office.

'Now remember, you are welcome to stay with us whenever you like for as long as you like. I'll be on my own a lot as Anton is always traveling, so you'll be doing me a favour. The villa has nine bedrooms, you can take your pick.'

'Nine! Only nine - how on earth will you manage?'

'I know darling, but one will learn to cope.' Irina splayed out her hand admiring the diamond ring Anton had given her.

'I'm sorry I'll miss the wedding.' Mia said, genuinely disappointed

'Me too, sure you can't get off?'

Mia shook her head, 'Afraid not, apart from staff orientation it seems I have to learn everything from how to operate a lifeboat to put out a fire.'

'Sounds a bit worrying.'

'Yep. Don't mention the Titanic.' She said, buttoning her coat.

'Do you know Mia, somehow I don't think you'll like it.'

'I know, but your leaving made up my mind. I want to travel and working as a croupier on a cruise ship is the easiest way to do it.'

'As long as you come to visit if you ever sail into Cagliari.'

'I promise.' They hugged their goodbyes.

She was just completing her third season, she'd marvelled at the crystal seas of the Indian Ocean, the ice-blue of the glaciers in the fjords of Norway, had roamed the streets of picture book Venice and experienced the opulence of wealth in Dubai. But now, it was becoming a trial. She missed someone to share her experiences. Inika was the closest thing she had to family since her schooldays. Mia missed her.

In the morning, they'd sail to Sardinia, Inika's home. The draw of a familiar face so close was crippling, but time ashore was limited. Mia'd woken suffocated by the cramped conditions of living below deck – the constant nose of different languages tangling together. She'd had enough. She'd retrieved her suitcase from storage and while the bustle of the crew prepared to unload its passengers in Cagliari, Mia slipped ashore.

As the taxi had whizzed past towns and villages, Mia'd begun to smile. Sardinia felt like a hug, it warmed her. Its honeyed ancient buildings felt welcoming. The vegetation was lush and colourful, and she knew she'd not be leaving here for some time.

Inika had shown her off like a debutante, included her in all the social outings, taking great care to introduce her to all the right people. It wasn't long before Mia found herself in the company of Rufus Stone and this time, it had felt more equal. He was as Inika mentioned – one of the good guys.

CHAPTER 7

MELANCHOLY hovered as she steered along the twisting roads. The air was full of nature's perfume - soft, like warm amber. The Macchia scrubland and granite – covered hills on one side, the translucent sea Mia barely glanced at on the other.

Slowing on a tight bend, she tried not to let her vision fall on the shrine, erected to honour Teresa's husband, Luigi. Mia's only experience of death was Pippa. The intense sorrow Teresa showed after Luigi's death she'd found incredibly painful to witness. Had she, Mia, felt that sense of loss about anything?

As the road flattened to a plateau, she pulled hard on the steering wheel. The car obeyed, bumping its way along the rocky pathway. It came to rest in its usual place under a juniper tree.

The foot-trodden path led through the rough scrubland. Ahead, a large flat boulder – a natural dip in its surface – made an excellent seat. In front of her miles of aquamarine sea met the turquoise sky.

The letter was making her reassess everything.

Rufus had given her a good life. But *love*? That was still just a word. She examined her feelings; surely she should know what love felt like but as much as she thought she loved him, she wasn't *in* love with him. If she truly loved him, infidelity wouldn't enter her head. Yes, she missed him when he was away, but only because the house seemed so much larger when he wasn't in it.

Villa Calasetta, their home, snuggled into the cliff below her, its stone walls dazzling white against the formal gardens. To the right of the building, the glistening topaz of the pool interrupted the lush green lawns. When she'd first moved into the villa, the garden was quite an uninteresting space. She'd drawn sketches and plans, thrilled when Rufus had let her go ahead with the project. She should have loved every inch of it, but ... she traced the pathway from the terrace to the summerhouse, that glistened at night under a thousand white fairy lights.

The night she finished its creation they drank champagne and celebrated. Teresa had joined them. She wasn't much of a drinker and had soon returned to the house.

Rufus had stirred, then risen from his seat to move towards Mia. She tilted her head for a kiss, but instead, he dropped to one knee.

Her jaw fell open. Telepathically, she begged him not to say it. The message didn't get across.

'Mia, you are the most beautiful woman I have ever met, you make my life complete. I want to spend my life with you. Will you do me the honour of becoming my wife?'

Holding out a crystal box, he lifted the lid to reveal the most stunning champagne diamond she'd ever seen. Time stalled on his hand; it seemed to move in slow motion as he plucked the ring from its velvet cushion and slid it onto her finger before she'd had chance to reply. The fluttering in her chest flattened and tightened like a buckled belt as he gazed at her expectantly.

She shouldn't accept it. She knew she'd never be faithful to him, she was certain of that. Even if she'd always be discrete, he deserved more. That much she owed him; she'd never intentionally hurt him.

'God Rufus, what a surprise. The ring's gorgeous but ...'

He withdrew his hand and got to his feet; his jaw set hard.

'You don't wish to marry me?' he said, in a voice laden with disappointment.

'I-I – you took me by surprise. I wasn't expecting it.' The silence stretched and pulled as she stuttered to find the right words. 'It's just a bit soon, that's all.'

'Is it? I knew the moment I met you. I'm sorry you don't feel the same.' His voice was harsh as he turned back to his seat.

She held out her hand, admiring the fabulous oval stone, aware of his eyes drilling into her, studying every reaction in her face. She could just say yes, but it would seem false because it hadn't been spontaneous as he'd expected, and now the moment had passed.

She got up and went to him, positioning herself at his feet, sensing his thigh muscles tense as she laid her head in his lap.

'Can we just be engaged for a while and let me get used to the idea?'

She closed her eyes with relief as his hand rested on her head, his firm fingers gently stroking her hair. She felt disloyal and wretched; wanted to weep when she should be dancing with joy.

'If that's what you want? I thought you'd be pleased.'

'I am. Honestly, I am, but I'm also just a little bit scared. You don't know me.'

'I know enough to know that I love you, that I want you to carry my children and spend the rest of my life with you. I thought that's what you wanted too.'

By way of reply, she pushed herself up and knelt, circling his neck with her arms, and kissed him deeply.

Since that night, how many times had she put him off? How many years was it since it stopped asking?

The breeze disturbed her hair, Mia shivered and rubbed her forearms fighting the idea that no matter how stunning and luxurious their house was, in a way it bore little difference to Chartley or, for that matter, Willow House. They were all places where she felt compelled to escape from. She craved to climb higher, to experience a sense of control over her life. A time to be calm – able to think. Villa Calasetta wasn't a place of fear or punishment, far from it, it was a magnificent building. The trap she'd built herself.

CHAPTER 8

Inika was on the terrace, bikini-clad, dancing to music playing through her tiny earphones.

Mia untied her wrap dress, revealing a shocking-pink bikini as Inika bent forward to receive a *mwah-mwah* kiss. Then removing earplugs, she lowered herself onto the sunbed next to Mia.

'So, come on then, sweetie, tell me what's worrying you. Judging by your text, you need to talk.'

'I've had a letter from England.'

'Ah. I see. This calls for Pimm's. It's too hot for wine. I'll go and make a jug.'

'Yes, yes, but in a minute, please? Just listen, I need to unload I'm so mixed up.'

Inika swept her long legs to one side, adopting an attentive pose.

'What am I doing with my life, Inny? And please don't roll your eyes, I'm serious.'

Inika opened her mouth but quickly shut it.

'How much longer can I keep up the pretence? It's not fair on Rufus. He doesn't deserve it. I just don't know how to love him. It's not in me.'

Inika readjusted her sunglasses. 'What's brought all this on? You don't usually have a conscience.'

Mia tilted her chin. 'The letter says the Major's dying. They want me to go home. He wants my forgiveness,' she flung her hands in the air. 'Do I even grant him that? Does he deserve it? And that's another thing. I've never told Rufus about them – how I was treated. He knows their names obviously, but not much more. Christ. Everything's a mess.' She held out her hands weighing them in the air.

'What, never? And he hadn't asked? Why not?'

'He never pushed me because it upset me. I don't want him to find out I'm not the person he thought I was. I'm a lie. I invented the person he wanted to be with, not the horror of me as I was then, or where I came from.'

'Do you think a man like Rufus would not have had his lawyers check you out?'

Mia wasn't listening.

'It's difficult to accept that this is it. You have no idea what I'm talking about, have you? Of course, you don't; you and Anton are so in love with one another. But I'm, I'm –' Mia pursed her lips. 'I feel like I have to pretend to be someone I'm not or I'll lose everything I have here. And, without that lie I've created for Rufus, I'm nothing.'

Inika sighed with exasperation. 'Look, okay you're a bit of an oddball, you have a thing about hills and hate having your picture taken but you have a good life.'

Mia shook her head sadly. 'When I left England, I set myself a goal. I was convinced if I got exposure to wealthy men, my life would change for the better.' She felt cheap even saying it. 'But it's not the answer.'

'Then what the hell is? You think you can return to England and do what? Work as a croupier again? You'd hate it. You bagged your millionaire, even if he is…is, you know, not exactly what you wished for. He is very, very generous.' Inika raised a finger. 'Darling, hold that thought. I'm dying of thirst.'

Inika left her, Mia got up and strolled to the railings running alongside the terrace to gaze across the vista of twinkling sunlight dancing like scattered gems on the crystal blue waters of the Mediterranean. Inika was right; meeting Rufus had changed her life, but it wasn't enough.

Perhaps if I do go home for a few days things will be clearer. What do I have to lose? But will an apology from him do it – wipe out the

emptiness inside? The very thought of seeing him again makes me want to gag, so why do I feel obliged to go? It's not just that, is it? If I go, what then? Do I just come back here, and marry a man I don't love? Will he even want to marry me now that I kept him waiting so long? Isn't marriage for normal people, people who can fall in love? Not an emotional cripple who is incapable. Oh God, please tell me what to do.
Her gaze dropped to her feet and the view of the rocks below – the sea angrily rolling back and forth, spewing giant foaming crests of white that surged between them. *How easy it would be to climb over and let the sea take her away. Wash away her past, her problems, her guilt.* She gasped, terrified by her thoughts, and stepped away from the railings. What was she thinking? *Perhaps I should see a therapist, psychiatrist even. I know I'm depressed and if I don't do something to sort out my head this could end badly.* She rubbed her forearms for comfort. *I can't keep blaming everyone else, perhaps I was born this way.* But could an apology from the man who broke her somehow… fix her?

A vision of her father, eyes bulging – his spittle spraying her face as he scolded her. What had she ever done to make him hate her so much?

Movement on the horizon caught her attention. A lone catamaran sailed around the headland, its puffed-out canvas stark white against the blue. It distracted her momentarily. She padded back to her sunbed. She wasn't a nice person, look at how unfair she was to Rufus. He was kind and loyal and put up with all her demands.

'I'm such a bitch. Rufus doesn't deserve it and I don't deserve him.' As soon as the words left her lips, she acknowledged that it was his kindness that bound her to him – like a spider's web clutching on from every edge of her, invisible but as binding as a jailer's key. He'd been so patient. He wanted stability, a family, things she couldn't – no, wouldn't – give him. Rufus's demands on her were not excessive. None of her illicit affairs had been constant; none had made her feel any differently. The only constant *was* Rufus.

'Here we are.' Inika appeared with a tray. 'This will cheer you up. Pimm's. Alcohol for the soul, fruit for the body,' she giggled, pouring two substantial measures.

'So, what *am* I going to do Inny?'

'You have to ask? Not go to England for a start. You'd be mad too. After all you've told me about what that man did to you. I'd send him to hell, begging. He certainly doesn't deserve absolution. Forget about him. You've managed this far without either of them.'

'But I'm so confused. I feel I've been given a chance.'

'You don't need a chance, darling. I don't know what your problem is. You have lovers and as much money as you need. Poor Rufus is hardly ever home. He doesn't beat you and gives you all the freedom you want.'

Mia fished the mint leaves from her Pimm's and slid them back into the jug. Without realising it she'd emptied the glass and placed it back on the tray. She wrung her hands together, then stopped as she thought of Constance doing the same. She reached into her bag for a bottle of sunscreen and sprayed it liberally on her taut limbs, then lay back and closed her eyes.

As brown as a berry. Or a touch of the tar-brush?

Inika rolled over onto her front. Mia opened her eyes and watched her settle. How could her friend ever really understand her problems? There was so much Inika didn't know about her. Not even that her real name had been Maureen, let alone what had happened to her at Chartley. Thankfully, the nightmare of the deed rarely sought her out nowadays unless someone forced a camera in her face.

'Why don't you just take off?' Inika said lazily. 'Do some shopping, take your mind off things in London, and if you want, pop in on the old folks. Make it an hour's visit. Just don't torture yourself. Then on the way back go via Madrid, take a holiday, and make up your mind about your future with Rufus.'

'Oh, right, and won't that just go down like a bucket of cold gravy, I've only seen Rufus six out of thirty-two weeks this year. I won't get away with it.'

'But, darling, do you honestly care?'

'Yes, I do. I don't want to burn my bridges.'

Inika sat up and examined the jug. 'Oh dear, we're running on empty. More Pimm's or a G&T?' Mia didn't reply. 'Great. I'll just go get another jug then.'

Mia was annoyed that Inika didn't take her seriously. 'Just bloody shout for a maid. What are servants for?'

'Can't,' Inika said, loading the tray. 'She's visiting her sick mother.'

'Really? See what I mean?' Mia ran her fingers through her hair. 'It's a sign. A necessity. Perhaps I'll feel better about it. It might not be as bad once I get there.'

'Mia, you make my head hurt. You are like windscreen wipers, on, off, on, off. Do what you must… I think you're making a dreadful mistake. You're too fragile now. I certainly don't think chasing ghosts in England will make you feel any better.' Inika's mouth stretched to a smile. 'And Rufus wouldn't be too happy after a long trip away to find you've gone shopping. But a trip to England to see your ageing parents he'd think perfectly acceptable and I suppose it would give you time to assess your options.'

'That's what I mean. It won't seem like I'm avoiding him.'

'Even though you are,' Inika looked at her knowingly.

'Stop it. You know what I mean. I didn't even go home when the Major had his stroke.' Mia got to her feet, hands-on-hips, and paced up and down. 'You're right. I have to do it.'

'Pleased to find a solution for you, my dear. Drinkies, then a swim, I think. I'm saying no more on the subject.'

Three hours and much alcohol later, they moved inside. Indecision tied in knots but Inika was having none of it.

'Mia, I could slap you. It's only a visit. It's not like you are going to live with them. God's sake, woman, it's decided. You're going to hear the bastard's deathbed confession. Pat your mother's hand and come back again. If he pops his socks before then, you could bring Constance here for a holiday and everybody will be happy. Now eat something.' Inika pushed the bowl of prawn salad she'd prepared towards Mia. 'You're making such a fuss. It can't be that bad.' She forked a morsel into her mouth. 'What are they like, really like? I mean not just the harrowing stuff.'

Mia pressed her lips together. 'I honestly don't know. Both Georgina and I were adopted. She came first – I was the afterthought. Did I tell you that?'

'Numerous times, and don't be silly. They wouldn't have gone through all of that red-tape fandango that comes with adoption if they hadn't wanted you. Of course, they wanted you. Our memories play tricks on us. I'm sure it wasn't like that. You always select the negative. Lighten up.'

Mia pushed her plate away, a lump squatting in her throat. She waited for it to pass. Something was happening to her and it was happening too often, slowly wearing away her protective coating.

'Negative, huh? Nothing wrong with *my* memory. At Chartley —'

'Yes, yes, we all hated school, but what about your mother, what was she like?'

Mia huffed out a breath. 'Hard to tell really – she was overshadowed by him. He was a bit rough with her. I saw him slap her once and he used to grip her so tightly you could see the bruises on her wrists. She was subservient. That's what I'd call her. She wasn't cold, just sort of buttoned up. I felt sorry for her.' She paused, thoughtful. 'You know, I haven't set foot in the house since I was eighteen.'

'Hm.'

'Inika, what are you thinking? You're making that face.'

'I am not. I was just thinking that it's sad that you have such bad memories, and it explains why you are so acidic at times – why you can't give love. If you never received it as a child. how can you give it as a woman? That's why you have no friends, only me because you're so bitchy to everyone. You think that's how you should behave.'

Mia squirmed. Even though the alcohol had made her more open, Inika's comments, no matter how true, were unwelcome.

'I've had enough of this. I have lots of friends and lots of people around me. Stop making me out to be an oddball.'

Inika shrugged and rose. As she passed around the back of the sofa, she placed her hand on Mia's shoulder. Mia felt the warmth Inika emitted, wishing she could be more like her. Their conversation bothered her. Inika *was* her only friend and she knew it. Suddenly, she felt numb. *What if this feeling never went away? Ever?*

CHAPTER 9

MIA swung the car onto the villa's forecourt. Giuseppe, the gardener, stopped hoeing when he saw her as he always did when she'd stayed out overnight. She left the car and entered the villa, feeling his black eyes boring into her back. She was sure he was spying on her. There'd never been much love lost between them. However, Rufus was a great fan of the way he kept the grounds.

Teresa appeared from the kitchen, her apron spotted with baking remnants, speaking quickly in her rich Irish accent. 'Madam, Mrs Evans has been calling since yesterday.'

'Gina? What did you say?'

Teresa's eyes darted nervously. 'I said you were out, and we had no idea when you might be back, but I'd pass the message.'

'And what did she say?'

'That she would be calling you on the mobile telephone, I hope it was fine for me to give her the number. She said she didn't have it. I was worrying, as she'd said it was urgent.'

'Good, good,' Mia nodded. 'When did she call last?'

'At breakfast time.' Mia turned to go to her room but changed her mind.

'Teresa, the cashmere wrap I bought yesterday. I've decided I am not keeping it.'

Teresa's eyes widened. 'Really, why it's so beautiful?'

'The colour is better on you. Please accept it as a gift.'

'Wha— no, I couldn't. It's too beautiful and much too expensive a gift – and when would I be wearing it?'

'Any time you want – when you go to mass, see friends. Please, it's yours.'

Teresa's face beamed with happiness. 'Well if you're sure.'

'I am. Thank you, Teresa.'

Mia's mobile rang the moment she entered her bedroom. Tension knotted through her shoulders. Could she face one of Gina's vengeful monologues?

'Maureen, thank God.'

Mia rolled her eyes. 'Hello Gina, being melodramatic as usual, I see.'

'I'm not being melodramatic, and I haven't got time to argue. It's Daddy. You need to come home.'

'Why, has he died?'

'I wouldn't have bothered calling if he were. No, he's not dead, not *yet* anyway, and don't be so bloody callous. He's asking for you.'

A vision of the fearful man on his death bed made her tremble.

'Are you sure about that? It doesn't ring true. He hates the sight of me.'

Gina huffed. 'That may have been true in the past, but not now. You wouldn't know him now. He's mellowed.'

Mia couldn't keep the bile from her voice. 'Really? Next, you'll be telling me he's taken up priesthood.'

'For God's sake, Maureen, he knows he's not got long – he just wants to make amends. I told you all this in my letter. Can't you just do the right thing for once? You need to come home. They are both so frail. Archie was saying only the other day you'd never, *ever* forgive yourself if you don't…'

Mia zoned out. Refusing to be emotionally blackmailed, she didn't care what Archie Evans, Gina's husband, was saying. He was a moron, wore knitted cardigans and socks with sandals, and worse, he was an active member of the Boy Scouts.

'Gina, shut up. All right, I'll come but only for Mummy's sake. Don't say another word. I'll text you as soon as I've booked flights.'

She ended the call. Her conversation with Inika about returning to England had been more of a thought process, but this was real and now, she'd better set things in motion. She pressed the direct dial to Rufus's PA, Monica. Rufus had once said that Monica was at her disposal and she took that literally.

Monica rang back shortly after receiving Mia's request, 'I'm sorry, there aren't any first-class seats available until the twenty-first.'

Mia hesitated, but only for a second. 'Have you checked every airline?'

'I have.'

'Then the twenty-first it will have to be.'

Monica's air of superiority never went unnoticed - anyone could see she was in love with Rufus. Strange that she had what Monica desired, yet didn't cherish it.

It was late afternoon; Mia had come to her room to shower and change for dinner as Rufus was due back today.

The sound of a car pulling up in the drive brought her to the window. She wrapped a towel around her wet hair and watched Rufus's suit-clad legs appear from the rear of the car. He stood for a moment, resting his hands on his lower back and arching into a stretch, before dipping back inside the car to retrieve his briefcase. She tapped on the window, but he didn't look up and vanished under the porchway and into the house.

She dressed quickly, concerned that if he came looking for her and found her naked, he'd want to bed her, and she wanted to talk first. But instead, he went straight to his office without even bothering to come and say hello. Perhaps he was tired. She'd talk to him over dinner.

An hour later, Rufus joined her on the terrace for a pre-dinner drink. She tilted her head to accept his greeting, but his lips barely brushed her cheek.

Puzzled by his quietness and indifference, she frowned. She'd changed for dinner, donning the shell pink floaty dress he'd bought her in New York. He usually commented on how lovely she looked when she wore it, but not tonight.

'How was the trip – successful?'

Rufus eyed her over the top of his glass. 'You don't usually en-quire about business matters.'

'That's because you usually give me my present before dinner, but you went to your study instead.'

His eyes fixed on hers, she shifted nervously, something didn't feel right.

'The gardens look marvellous, don't you think?' she said, hoping his mood might change.

'Giuseppe does a great job.'

She leaned in towards him. 'Rufus, is something wrong?'

His face held no expression – his voice flat. 'Why? Should there be?'

'No, no of course not. It's just that you seem… you seem a bit weird, that's all. You usually share a few jokes.'

'I had always been under the impression you found my jokes tedious,' he said stiffly.

Before she could reply, he called out to Giuseppe who was trundling a wheelbarrow across the lawn, and left her. The two men shook hands. Rufus had his back to her, so she couldn't see his expression nor what they were saying. This was not going as planned. Had something happened? Perhaps the deal had gone wrong.

Teresa gave a polite cough. 'Excuse me, Madam, would you like dinner on the terrace or the dining room?'

'Inside please, and Teresa, once you have laid out supper, we don't want to be disturbed.'

Dusk was falling and the light from the house cast an eerie glow across the lawn as Rufus came back into view.

'Ah, there you are,' she rose and linked her arm through his, steering him inside. 'You must be hungry.'

'Actually, I ate earlier. I think I'll go to bed. It's been a long day.'

She swung to face him, placing her palm over his shirt pocket. 'Oh no, can't you stay up a little longer? I need to talk to you.'

'I'm sure it can wait 'til morning.'

She pouted. 'Actually, it can't.'

'Just for a short while then.' The heave of his shoulders was not lost to her as he held out her chair, before seating himself. Did she detect a hint of sadness in his eyes?

Teresa served the supper of poached fish and vegetables. As the housekeeper picked up the serving spoons, Rufus touched her arm.

'Nothing for me, thank you, Teresa, delicious as it looks. I see you've even made your delicious soda bread, but I have no appetite this evening, and I'm sure Madam can serve herself.'

Teresa smiled warmly and took her leave.

Mia helped herself to a little of the fish, pushing the bread away. She never ate it or the potato farls or the Irish stew Rufus favoured.

'So, was the trip successful?'

'Mia, I'm tired. I have reports to read and decisions to make. We both know you have no interest in my business.' He raised his hand to his mouth stifling a yawn. 'What was it you want to talk about?'

She lowered her knife and fork. 'It's my father.' She paused, expecting Rufus to say something. He didn't. 'My sister Georgina phoned. You know Daddy had several strokes, well, he's deteriorating rapidly and asking for me. And–'

'If your family needs you then go.' He tilted his head to one side. His scrutinising her made her feel uncomfortable.

'Rufus, you're acting very oddly.'

He looked away. 'If you need to go, then go. You usually do exactly what you want, without my blessing.'

'I just thought as you've been away and we haven't seen each other,' she lowered her eyelashes. 'I missed you.'

Unexpectedly, his bronzed face came to life, a smile playing his lips. Was he toying with her?

'So, when are you going?'

'The day after tomorrow.'

'That's fine. Now, if there's nothing more, I'm going to bed. Oh, and I'll sleep in the end room. I just discovered I've picked up something nasty.'

'Oh, you poor thing. Goodnight then, sleep tight,' she called after his retreating figure. What an odd thing to say she thought; not that he's picked up a bug but something *nasty*.

CHAPTER 10

Mia took her morning swim alone, unusual, as it was something they would normally enjoy together. She walked across the lawn to shower and dress, to notice the table on the terrace was only set for one.

Teresa was at the sink hand washing Mia's silk underwear as she wandered in.

'Teresa, why's the breakfast table only laid for one?'

Teresa dried her hands on her apron. 'Mr Stone wanted a working breakfast, so I took him a tray in his study.'

Mia rubbed the back of her neck as her shoulders tightened. Was she imagining it or was he avoiding her?

As the hours ticked past her concern grew. She pushed open the door to his study, it was empty. There was no sign of him anywhere in the house. Mia hovered in the kitchen doorway keen not to walk on Teresa's wet floor.

'Have you seen Mr Stone, has he gone out?'

Teresa put the mop to one side. 'He went out with Mr Calder; said he'd be back late.'

Not unusual, Mia thought, Sandy was one of Rufus closest friends and business colleagues, but what was unusual was that Rufus hadn't brought him out to see her or said goodbye. She filled her day convinced there was some dire business problem distracting him and that she was being paranoid.

The thought had never crossed Mia's mind that Rufus wouldn't be there to drive her to the airport. According to Teresa, he had risen early to go fishing with Sandy. Rufus's phone was switched off when she tried it. Was he avoiding her? It all felt a bit precarious. She shooed away the thought. It wasn't unusual for him to switch off his phone when he went fishing, but she wished she'd had the chance to say goodbye. He didn't realise how daunting this visit would be and one of his hugs would have given her courage.

Rufus's driver dropped her off outside Olbia Airport. It made her feel strangely adrift.

With time to reflect, thoughts of visiting her family disturbed her, and an uneventful flight found her mind wandering constantly in that direction. Gina, do-gooder, Women's Institute member, hospital visitor, Neighbourhood Watcher, she even made her own jam! She recalled Gina's sneering face. *They're getting rid of you. Not me, I'm the one they want to keep.* Well, Gina wasn't in a position to lord over her now and Mia wasn't frightened of her snide remarks. She could give as good as she got. The playing field was now level.

It took forever for her cases to appear on the conveyor belt. The trolley was unbelievably heavy to push. Gliding through the sliding doors of the arrivals hall, she scoured the waiting drivers, looking for a plaque with her name. There was none.

Really! She pushed a trolley through the exit and waited amongst a gaggle of family and friends scouring the faces of passengers. Still no sign of her driver. Wishing she hadn't worn heels, she switched on her mobile. It took a few moments to pick up a roaming signal. Stabbing at the quick dial, she waited for Monica to pick up. The phone purred unanswered. A glance at the airport clock made her disconnect the call – Sardinia was an hour ahead Monica would have left for the day. With a sense of doom, Mia headed towards the taxi rank.

The driver got the sharp end of her tongue when he didn't get out of the cab quickly enough to load her luggage.

'Where to, luv?'

'Esher,' she replied, 'and I'm certainly not your love.' She closed her eyes as a nerve twitched to the left of her mouth. Seconds later, her left eye came into play, twitching in unison.

She'd forgotten the intimacy of London cabbies and her head throbbed. Was she having a stroke, just like her father? *Don't be stupid, you idiot, you're not even a blood relative. But then again, what if my real father suffered strokes – heart attacks, did I have inherited inflictions?* She coughed. *Stop being so ridiculous, it's probably just dehydration.*

As they moved away from the airport, her mobile began to ping as it picked up messages from her network. The first from Monica to say the car hire company had called; their driver had been involved in an accident and had been taken to the hospital. They had dispatched another, but he would be at least ninety minutes, she enquired if this was okay? Or should she try another company? Would Mia let her know?

Mia blew out her lips. *Didn't she know you have to switch your phone off on an aeroplane?* Becoming more agitated by the moment she scrolled through the increasingly angrier messages from her sister and deleted them. Strangely, none from Rufus.

The closer the taxi got to her destination the more her nerves were screaming at her. She wasn't ready for this. She leaned forward.

'Driver. I've changed my mind can you take me into London instead? I'll tell you whereabouts once I booked a hotel.' After a couple of calls, she'd secured a room and sent a text to Gina saying she wouldn't be there that afternoon and switched off her phone. The journey into London was exhausting. The taxi stuttered through endless roadworks and it started to drizzle, reflecting the mood of the miserable faces who rushed to keep dry. She closed her eyes and cupping her hands in her lap. What she needed now was a massage, a good meal, and a night's sleep, in that order.

The next morning, although physically revived, depression set in. She opened the curtains to reveal an ice-blue sky, an overnight frost had dusted the rooftops trees and shrubs. England seemed smaller somehow. She groaned yearning for her balcony view across the bay.

The spa had been fully booked the night before, so she booked herself in for a massage later before she left for Willow House. Another few hours wouldn't matter.

Gina was almost hyperventilating when Mia finally rang her.

'You're a selfish bitch, Maureen. You could at least have phoned to say you weren't coming until today. I didn't receive your text until much later. Archie and I were going to take the children to Pizza Hut. You disappointed mummy and daddy who were looking forward to seeing you and I had to go back and get their meal ready.'

Mia rolled her tongue around her teeth, she doubted her parents were looking forward to seeing her, even if the major had requested her presence. If there was one thing she was clear about, she'd hear him out before getting back to Sardinia as quickly as possible. She'd give them two days. That's all.

'For God's sake, Gina, you always make such a mountain out of a molehill. And don't call me Maureen! You can go for pizza anytime. I'm here now, aren't I? I'll be there by four,' she sighed. 'Stop making such a fuss.'

'Fuss?' Gina exploded. 'You try looking after them *and* juggling a family and hospital visits.' She listened unsympathetically as Gina choked out her grievance.

'Stop being a drama queen. You know you love playing the dutiful daughter, getting all the pats on the head. I didn't leave of my own accord, *remember.* And no doubt they look after you on the cash front.' She knew she was being cruel but wasn't she entitled to? 'It's always about you, isn't it, poor little creep-arse Gina? I thought you'd like staying at home with Mummy and Daddy playing happy families.'

'You absolute bitch, Maureen... Mia... whatever you call yourself. Well, you can try it for yourself. It's your turn now.'

Sod Gina. It couldn't be that bad, she'd be able to cope, wouldn't she? After all, she'd only come to visit.

As the taxi made its way along the A3, Mia's nerves were getting the better of her. Logically, she knew that this time, she was mentally stronger as well as physically fitter than him. She'd been told his stroke had been particularly debilitating. If he couldn't even walk, he could hardly throw a punch and his days of ordering her into a cupboard were over for good. She pondered when she'd last had a proper conversation with him. Had she *ever* had a proper conversation with him, or just endured a succession of lectures? No wonder Constance never contradicted him, but often slipped her an extra biscuit when no one was looking – did that constitute love? Adrenaline pumped through her veins, reacting to her growing apprehension. Was she really going to do this?

CHAPTER 11

As the taxi pulled up outside Willow House, Mia was tempted to ask the driver to take her back to London. The very thought of entering the house shook her.

The taxi pulled up several feet short of the gate. 'Can't you drive me to the door?' The driver ignored her and began unloading her luggage onto the pavement. She paid him without adding the tip.

The willow tree on the lawn beside the house hung with the mist between its branches, branches that, long ago, had been one of her hiding places. The long tendrils spewed like a fountain from the top, spilling to the ground like the ribbons of a maypole.

Steeling herself, she hovered outside the gates and stared up at the place she'd once called home but could find no comfort in her memory. The house looked unloved – sorry for itself. Neglect showed on every window frame, where cracked putty edged the glass. The pebble-dash on one side of the building ballooned away from the wall, exposing brickwork. A drainpipe, rusty and dislodged, dripped into a camellia bush. Only the front garden looked tended. The path had been swept clean of leaves and the hedges were neatly trimmed. The shrub's foliage drooped and damaged with the frost crouching its branches. She looked up at the house silhouetted against a dreary sky as evening crept in.

What the hell am I doing here? She looked from her cases dumped untidily on the pavement and back to the house. They were heavy; she'd over packed as usual. Surely there must be someone who

could carry her luggage, but who? She searched the arc of the cul-
de-sac – empty, there was no one in sight, but across the road, a
man was up a ladder doing something to a tree. He would do.

'I say, hello, you there up in the tree.'

He ignored her.

She tried again, raising her voice an octave. 'Hello, there. Can
you come down, please? I need help.'

The man fixed her with a stare. 'What?'

'I need help. My bags.'

'What about them?'

He took his time descending the ladder and crossed the road,
unsmiling. Mia was beginning to feel the chill of the climate.

'Hurry up, please. It's very cold and I need to get indoors.'

He glanced from the cases to Mia and back, blew on his hands
and rubbed them together.

'Well, I have to admit you've got some cheek.'

'You're very rude.' Although annoyed by his manner, she
couldn't help but notice how very tall he was and that, on inspection, he was rather good looking in a sort of rough, uncultured
way.

'Rude? You take the cake lady. I wonder what your last servant
died of?'

'Oh no, Teresa's not dead —' He threw her a sideways look, a
smirk registering on his lips. 'I mean, thank you. They are very
heavy.'

'I presume you're the prodigal daughter - Maureen, isn't it?'

'What?'

'Georgina said you were coming to stay.'

I bet she did. 'I don't know who you think you are but—'

'Me?' he touched his chest, 'I'm the man who just climbed down
a twelve-foot ladder *and* crossed a road to carry your bags.' Shaking
his head, he plucked her cases from the pavement and deposited
them on the doorstep. Mia fished in her bag for her purse to tip
him, but he waved her away and strode back to his task without
another word.

Her eyelids blinked several times, exhausted by her conversation with Gina, the dread of entering the house, and now this man with such an offhand manner. What else could today throw at her?

As she stared at the door, her breakfast threatened to return. Two more steps and she'd be inside.

The doorknocker was the same brass cannon she remembered being fascinated by as a child. Her hand went to her bag, faltering as she realised she didn't have a key. The temptation to turn and see if the man was watching was great, she denied it and steeled herself to rap the knocker, unnerved. Her insides buckled, contracted, like the stretching and releasing of a rubber band.

A small blurry figure could be seen through the frosted glass, approaching slowly.

'Who is it?' came the soft but educated voice from behind the door.

'It's me, Mum, Mia.'

'I'm sorry you'll have to speak up, I'm a little deaf.'

'It's me, Mia,' she pushed the letterbox open and shouted through it. 'I said it's me, Mia. Oh, bugger, it's Maureen, Mum.'

'There's no need to swear, dear. Okay then, hold on a moment while I open the door.' Metal clanked as her mother fumbled with bolts, locks, and chains before finally peeling open the door. 'Maureen, ah yes, that is you, isn't it?'

Constance looked frailer than Mia could ever have imagined. She seemed shrunken and shuffled her feet in ill-fitting slippers. Mia held her arms out expecting a hug, but Constance was already making her way to the living room.

'Lock the front door properly, will you, dear. You just can't take chances anymore. All the awful things you see on TV.'

Mia did as she was told; having dragged her luggage over the threshold she set about replacing the bolts and chains.

'I'm glad you're here. Your father will be expecting his tea soon. Georgina said you'd be here to prepare it. He likes something hot at this time of the day. She's left everything in the fridge, ready. He gets very grumpy if it isn't ready when he wants it.'

Mia was a bit put out by her mother's matter-of-fact manner. she was 18 when they last met. Surely, there should be more by way of welcome. It appeared not, as Constance settled herself in the chair by the window to gaze out into the garden. Bloody hell, she hadn't expected this. 'Mummy, I'm not a very good cook. We have a housekeeper.'

'Do you dear, that's nice,' her mother's eyes following a squirrel skirting the fence. 'Georgina's left everything written down.'

'I expect she has but— what's that God-awful smell!' Mia held a finger against her nose as her gaze fell to the skirting boards. Every power-point contained an air purifying unit. Lily of the Valley vied for position with Forest Pine. It stung her nostrils, attacking her senses on several levels, irritating the back of her nose. She thought she might sneeze and pinched her nostrils as she fumbled for a tissue.

'What time's Gina coming, Mother? I'm sure you'd prefer her to make your food the way you like it.' Constance mumbled a reply that she didn't quite catch.

'Sorry, Mummy, what did you just say?'

'I said, Georgina's not coming. She's taking a little rest.'

'A little rest?' Mia said a little too loudly, making Constance flinch. She softened her voice. 'When, Mummy? When is Gina coming?' she asked, adding a forced, 'I just can't wait to see her.'

'I think she's back on a Wednesday, I can't remember the date.'

'But today's Thursday,' Mia said in distress.

'Yes, that's right, dear. Now, if you don't mind, perhaps you'd better get settled then you prepare a meal. We don't want Daddy angry, do we?'

Mia left the room fearing what she'd say next. Her bag was in the hallway. Locating her phone, she speed-dialled Gina. The phone was switched off, and there wasn't even a personal message, just an automated voicemail. *Bitch*, she thought, but there was nothing else she could do for now.

Where to start next? She glanced at the stack of matching luggage; this would take several journeys. Taking the weight of the larger Louis Vuitton, she stepped on the first stair riser. But there was a problem, a stair-lift affixed to the wall was in her way, she could neither lift her suitcases over it nor squeeze past it. After tugging for several minutes, she had a brainwave. Flipping the seat into place, she stacked her cases side by side on it and pressed the green button. She was delighted as it ascended, carrying her suitcases with it. All she had to do was keep them balanced and keep in pace. Easy! At the top, she slid the cases onto the landing carpet. Pleased with herself, she dragged them along the corridor.

The flowery patterned carpet leered back at her. Good God. They still had the same awful flooring, an orange, purple, green, and red pattern; it looked like someone had thrown up. Nothing matched, certainly not the raspberry colour of the walls. Dragging one case toward her old bedroom, she nudged open the door. She could just about make out her bed by the window; buried underneath the two-seater settee which had once lived in the front room. Some of the dining room chairs were there too, stacked upside down on each other. Mother's treadle sewing machine sat in the corner beside Gina's doll's house. Whichever way Mia looked there was junk, boxes full of books. Black bags stuffed with old clothing were piled by what was once her dressing table. She closed the door crossing the landing to Gina's room. Turning the handle, she pushed open the door. She shook her head in disbelief feeling winded by the contrast between Gina's and her own.

The room was lovely. It had been redecorated. It was all coffees and neutrals. She felt the duvet; it was duck down. The drapes were the same shade of mushroom as the carpet. An en-suite shower room had been constructed where the wardrobe had once sat, and a new closet built. Fluffy white towels were stacked in the shiny white unit.

Beside the bed in front of the window was the framed photograph of Gina and Archie on their wedding day. Two goofy-looking kids grinned out from another identical frame. The more she looked, the more the eyes appeared to be mocking Mia. Opening a drawer beneath the dresser she swept her arm across the top, shooting their images inside before she slammed it shut. Crossing the room, Mia opened the wardrobe doors expecting to see more of

Gina's belongings but it was empty. The bathroom was the same, there was no evidence of Gina's recently having been there.

Now to tackle her suitcases, how wonderful it would have been to have Teresa here to unpack and organise her. Her unpacking complete, Mia put away the suitcases, stretched out on the bed and checked her watch. *Rufus should be home by now. I wonder why he hasn't called.* Pushing herself up on her elbows, she checked her phone.

No messages. Confused, she swung her legs off the bed and speed-dialled his number. A weird pulsing sound greeted her, followed by, 'Your call is not accepted.'

Not accepted, what the...? She redialled; the message was the same. Scrolling through her contacts, Mia located Monica's home number.

'Hello, Monica speaking?'

'What's wrong with his phone?'

'Sorry, who is this?'

'You know perfectly well who this is. Where's Rufus? I can't connect to his phone.'

'Ah, is there anything I can help you with while he's unavailable?' Mia thought she detected a hint of pleasure in her voice.

'Unavailable? Well, where is he?'

Monica's voice came back with a more confident tone than usual. 'As I said he's unavailable.'

'Not to me, he isn't.' Blood began pumping its way around Mia's temples – like a boa constrictor's vice tightening by the second. 'Get hold of him and get him to call me *immediately*, Monica.' Mia's voice had registered a pitch that shocked her.

There was a long pause, she thought she heard a stifled laugh but dismissed it.

'I'm afraid I can't do that. You see —'

'What do you mean you can't? You bloody-well better had for your sake, when he hears about this, he'll fire you.'

'Oh, I don't think he will,' Monica retorted, with smugness to her voice.

'Look you—'

'No, *you* look,' she spoke over her, 'Mr. Stone instructed me personally that he didn't want any contact from you.'

'*What*? You're lying.'

'I think you'll find I'm not.'

'Monica, I won't put up with this. There's going to be hell to pay!'

'That's similar to what he said after he read the file I gave him.'

'File? What file?' Mia was panicking now – sucking air into empty lungs as her bowels liquefied and constricted.

'The one from the Rafi inquiries,' Monica sighed. 'Let *me* finish this conversation and explain to you very clearly. You see, you haven't been very smart, have you? Mr Stone has a full portfolio of your, shall we say, house guests?'

Mia's mind raced, she thought she'd been discreet; she'd only brought two men back to the villa this time and thought she'd slipped them past Teresa without her knowledge, but that creepy Giuseppe was always watching her. Perhaps it was him.

'But I can explain…' Mia protested.

'All of them? I don't think so,' Monica continued, her voice sickly with pleasure, 'the tennis coach was very loose with his talk of your… encounter, as was Mr Bolognini's chauffeur. Do you want me to continue?'

Mia's voice came out in a whisper. 'No, I get the picture.'

'Mr. Stone will arrange to have your belongings from both houses delivered to wherever you want them. You may keep what jewellery you have with you but nothing else. He will deposit some money in your bank account to tide you over. Very generous under the circumstances, but your credit cards have all been cancelled.'

Mia let the phone drop from her hand. Her vision blurred as she sought some way to rectify this, desperately hoping to find a survival route – there was none. Rufus was hurt, she'd betrayed him. what more did she expect. Bile rose in her throat. The last words he'd said to her returned, he'd picked up something nasty. He wasn't referring to his health at all but to her. The icy chill of reality cut through her. Twenty-four hours ago, she had an exclusive lifestyle, two homes, money, and staff. Now she had nothing.

CHAPTER 12

MIA slumped back on the bed and closed her eyes trying to comprehend how she'd ended up in this situation. This was all a horrible mistake. The cloak of depression expanded. There was no escape, no luxury hotel to run to, no flight back to the sun and the sea. She must try to make it work here – for the next few days at least, but then what?

Pulling on a cashmere sweater she became aware of buzzing sound coming from the bedside table. Further inspection proved it to be some sort of intercom. The buzzing grew more agitated and Mia slid the small red button to the receive position.

'Maureen, what on earth are you doing up there? Daddy will want his snack. Gina never keeps him waiting.'

A sharp click told Mia her mother had disconnected. At her mother's behest, she wiggled past the chairlift and down the stairs. The kitchen was exactly as she remembered it. The fridge held lots of fresh ingredients that Mia had no idea what to do with; she wasn't a cook. There was chicken, fish, fruit and vegetables, and bottles of assorted medications bearing her father's name on the chemist's sticker. Several sorts of milk and something that looked like wet sawdust. She shut the fridge door and leaned against it.

'There had to be something easy to cook around here.' Mia muttered. What's in the larder? She almost cheered. Ah, ha. Beans! The old metal bread bin held two sorts, one uncut loaf and something called gluten-free. She brought it up to her nose and gave it a quick sniff. Yuck. Then Mia sawed off a slice, switched on the grill, and set about making beans on toast.

She had almost finished when she heard a commotion coming from the dining room. Hurriedly, she prepared the food.

Her lips pressed together as she steeled herself to enter what had once been their dining room. Should she knock? She balanced the tray precariously on one hand slopping the glass of squash. She could do this. After all, he had asked to see her. It was his request she came here. She opened the door gently with her free hand.

'Hello, Dad...' She almost whispered, her voice constricted in her throat. Her feet refused to move. Could this dribbling mess really be her father? She focused, not on the man, but on what he was sitting on. It resembled a child's highchair, only larger in proportions. One arm dangled loosely at his side, the other rested on the tray. He wasn't looking directly at her. A string of saliva escaped his downturned mouth. His bloated body slumped to one side

She'd been duped. This man was incapable of conversation. There had been no request to see her, it was all just a lie – Gina's ploy to get here. Anger bubbled. She spoke his name through gritted teeth.

'Hello, Daddy?' She waited, unsure if this creature could even reply.

His head jerked backwards at the sound of her voice. His gaze fixed on her; his face turned puce. He made a sound that resembled growling. 'GRRUSE, GRRUSE.' Interspersed was the odd word she recognised but bore no relevance to anything. 'HAT, HAT,' he growled. 'TWIS! Akfaaast.'

What the hell was he on about? A memory of a thrashing, being locked in a cupboard and her father's red face pushed up close to hers, popped into her consciousness. She stepped back, relieved that he couldn't come near her, but this enraged him further. So, taking a deep breath, Mia stepped closer. He waved his good arm in the air in jerky, random motions, his face growing redder and redder. He yelled, 'PURRRATS! GRRUSEE.'

Mia put the tray in front of him and fled the room. Her mother could obviously hear the commotion but sat calmly in her chair looking out into the garden, her bony hands folded neatly in her lap. On top of her knitting bag.

'Mother, did you know about this?'

'About what dear?' Her mother's bony chest rose as she gave a deep sigh. 'I said he gets very agitated dear; Gina never keeps him waiting.'

'Never mind about that. Gina told me that he wanted to see me and make amends for the way he treated me in the past. She said he wanted to square things and that he was dying. That's the only reason I came back.' *To this dreadful place.*

Her mother's eyes teared up. 'Gina was naughty to do that. Daddy can't talk, he can hardly communicate at all. It would have been kinder if he died. Gina wasn't lying about that; he is dying, it's just that it's happening very slowly.'

Unable to speak, Mia slumped into an armchair. Gina had conned her. God, this was hell. Her father was a dribbling mess and her mother in La-la land. God, or someone like him, was punishing her.

Sweat dampened her palms as she realised that her only hope of refuge was no longer available to her.

'Did you find the diet sheet and preparation instructions dear? Gina left them for you. And may I have my snack now? I'm a little peckish.'

Robotically, Mia got to her feet and, moving slowly on unsteady legs, made it to the kitchen. Gina's handbook was propped up against the kettle. She was about to toss it into the bin when she noticed it was subdivided into two sections, His and Hers. Mia read quickly. One-half was about her father; well he had his lunch, so she didn't need to bother reading further. The other section was for Constance, who was due soup and a fresh piece of fruit "cut into dainty pieces." Even in her zombie state, Mia could manage that.

'Here we go, Mum. Chicken soup and pear all cut up the way you like it.'

The old lady examined it. 'Thank you, Maureen, but you didn't core the pear.'

'What?'

'The pear, you didn't remove the core, Gina always takes it out. Never mind dear, I'm sure I can manage. I'll see you later.'

Mia clamped her teeth together to stop herself saying something she'd regret. As she passed her father's door she hesitated, she could almost feel his eyes boring through the wood at her. The TV murmured in the background. She gulped another deep breath, opened the door without looking at him, and turned the volume up.

'Now I can't hear you, you horrible old man.'

She took refuge upstairs. Gina's phone was still going to voicemail. *Of course, it was.* She lay back on the bed, overwhelmed by Gina's cunning and her own gullibility.

She jerked into consciousness by the sound of raised voices from downstairs. She wiped the sleep from her eyes. It took Mia a moment to realise where she was and who the voices belonged to. Odd words came floating up the stairs, *outrageous and irresponsible.*

Mia vaulted off the bed, located a pair of flat shoes, and started down the stairs. She halted, one foot hovering above the second step. Below the head of a grey-haired woman, dressed in a navy-blue uniform. She was waving her arms around in front of someone Mia couldn't see. Mia lowered herself gently and perched on the top step, listening. Eventually, the nurse vanished inside his room.

'Poor Charles,' she cooed, 'this is outrageous, let's get you out of those clothes. I can't believe your daughter could just abandon you with a plate full of totally unsuitable food. It could have choked you; such a shock. Dear, dear.'

The Major could be heard mumbling something indistinguishable. Mia tiptoed back upstairs. *Great, some hired help. No need to interrupt and I can have a quick shower.* After all, the nurse was being paid for whatever it was she did.

Much later, a voice called out her name. She rose on stiff legs and made her way downstairs.

'Oh, there you are, I've cleaned your father up and fed him. You should be ashamed of yourself, leaving him like that. It's disgraceful. Now, listen to me. You are to follow my instructions to the letter.'

Mia watched the woman's mouth working, fascinated by a large hairy mole that grew above her lip.

'You will not feed him anything that is not on the list. You will not —.'

Something in Mia snapped, as a memory of Miss Viner came into her head. Mia flew into a rage.

'Out, do you hear me, get out! How dare you speak to me like that.'

Shock registered in the nurse's eyes, and the previous high colour drained from her face. She retreated backwards, colliding with the coat rack, flinched, jerking her hands up to protect her face, almost as if expecting Mia to strike her. Mia calmly reached past her to lift a navy-blue mac off the hook.

'This yours?'

The startled woman nodded; her eyes fixed on Mia's hand. Mia stepped past, opened the front door and hurled the coat up the path. The nurse flattened herself against the wall to escape, then half-trotted outside and picked up her Mac. With space between them, she retaliated.

'This is despicable behaviour,' she said, her bottom lip trembling. 'I shall report you to the authorities.'

'Same here for your arrogance and rudeness. Now bugger off and don't come back. I'll get a proper nurse for my father, not some supercilious old bitch like you.' Mia slammed the door shut and turned to see her mother standing in the lounge doorway.

'Oh, dear Maureen, I don't think you should have done that,' she wrung her bony hands together. 'What will we do now? Daddy takes an awful lot of looking after.' Mia lay a hand on her shoulder.

'Don't worry, Mum, I'll sort it. Now how about a nice cup of tea? I'll make us one.' Constance nodded, and Mia guided her back into the front room.

Mia flattened herself against the closed kitchen door, struggling to bring her breathing back to the right tempo. Adrenaline was still pumping through her veins, both at what she had done and what she needed to do. The nurse had certainly focused her mind. While the kettle was boiling, she read Gina's handbook, then found a copy of *Yellow Pages* and made a few phone calls. Two hours later and dead on time for her father's catheter to be emptied, the doorbell rang. She rushed to open it before her mother did.

A salmon-pink palm was thrust towards her, she shook it. The gold tooth amongst its white brothers and sisters was the next thing that caught Mia's eye.

'How-de-doody?' he bobbed, 'I'm Josh and I'm here to be your fairy godmother.' He winked and pushed past her, peeling off his jacket, revealing a white buttoned top, the sort that dentists wore. It was almost blinding against the darkness of his skin. He smiled and wagged a finger. 'Now where's this naughty boy who needs me?'

Mia indicated her father's room wordlessly, stifling a giggle, as she watched him mince along the corridor. He was as gay as a pride parade, and just what she needed. She ignored the roars from her father as Josh introduced himself. Mia slapped a hand across her mouth to contain her laughter. The major was the worst sort of bigot, a racist and a bully to boot. His list of unjustified hate probably included homophobia. She vaguely remembered a person of colour – she refused to use his words. Indian, Asian? There'd been a big commotion when he'd returned unexpectedly. He'd screamed his outrage at the frightened woman. Gina, oblivious to the row, had been standing behind him opening purple tissue-paper — was it a doll, a dress, something nice for the golden child?

Constance had a worried look when Mia brought in the tea tray. 'Who was that?'

'Oh, just the new nurse, Mummy.'

'What's her name dear? Will Daddy like her?'

'It's a man, Josh, Mum.'

Constance didn't look convinced. 'Oh dear, I'm not sure he'll like that.'

'They'll be fine; listen, it's peaceful now. Now, what would you like to do tomorrow?'

'Do dear? Oh, I don't *do* anything.'

'Well, you do now. I tell you what, how about we go somewhere nice for lunch?'

The old lady beamed. 'Really, can we? But I don't think Georgina will like it. She likes to know where I am.'

'You just leave Georgina to me, mother... I'll sort *her* out when she gets back on Wednesday. I might just wring her neck.'

Constance was staring at the wall with a puzzled expression as if trying to work it out in her head. She gave a little nod when it seemed she'd come to a conclusion.

'Did I say Wednesday? Oh dear, I hope I got that right, I'm not sure which Wednesday and you certainly can't kill her, she's not here. She's gone to Australia.'

CHAPTER 13

Outside the cold rain beat against the windows, the wind rattling the glass. Mia's nerves rattled with them. She mustn't panic. Mother was old and probably confused. Gina had said there were mental health problems. Australia indeed.

Settling into a chair opposite her mother's, she glanced around the room, squinting to place the items that were familiar but somehow previously unseen. The black marble clock that pinged on the quarter-hour, the military paintings that hung each side of the fireplace. The furniture and curtains, wallpaper and knick-knacks and the tapestry bag that lay by her mother's feet.

'Is your tea all right? I'm not sure if it's how you like it.'

Her mother glanced her way, frowning, seemingly searching Mia's face for the words to reply. The frown faded, and Constance sought out a handkerchief from her sleeve.

'Hey, come on, I didn't mean to upset you.' Mia said as she reached out to place a hand on her mother's knee.

Constance dabbed at her eyes, squared her shoulders, and composed herself.

'I'm sorry to make a fuss, Maureen. It's just that everything is so different since you arrived.'

'I know but things will get better I promise. That nurse just had to go. Josh is doing a great job.'

Her mother nodded. 'He seems nice but it's not that, it's you.'

'Me?' Mia said, pointing to her chest.

Constance nodded. 'I don't know you.'

'Of course, you do, Mummy, I'm your daughter.'

'Yes, I know that. What I mean is; I don't know you. Daddy sent you away before your tenth birthday and you hardly ever came home for holidays. Oh, Maureen, you were a lovely baby and such a pretty toddler,' Constance said in a voice that carried a tremor. Mia felt the world slow down around her. She turned her head as her own eyes moistened, unable to reply. At last some words of honesty. Neither of them was responsible for having spent most of their lives apart. What was the point in going over old ground? No need to cause Constance more distress.

'I didn't expect to ever see you again.'

Mia gulped. 'I'm sorry. I didn't think I was wanted. Needed. You had Gina.'

Bright eyes fixed hers. 'You were always wanted. Things just happened.' She leant forward and picked up the tapestry bag, clutching it to her. 'Daddy could be very forceful in those days. I'm afraid he took a dislike to you.'

Mia squirmed, wanting this conversation to end. It was too emotionally challenging, her mother was elderly, and with that came nostalgia, but also less inhibitions in speaking the truth. Mia thought she was ready for. It turned out she was wrong. She changed the subject.

'What about your hair, where do you get it done? We should make you an appointment. That would be nice, wouldn't it? Always makes me feel better.' *God listen to me. How bloody condescending am I?*

Constance picked up her cup and saucer and sipped her tea. Her eyes focused on something outside that Mia couldn't see.

'He's a nice man,' she said. Mia didn't turn to see who she was referring to; her mind was on other things. 'He carries the garden furniture out in the summer and places the patio umbrella in just the right place to shade me, such a kind man. Did you know he won an award at the Hampton Court flower show? He does a nice job of the lawns too. Gina often makes him a cup of coffee. But I expect you're too busy today,' she gave a little wave towards the window smiling and, with hardly a change of breath, returned to their earlier conversation.

'I don't have a hairdresser anymore. Well, not one I go to. I used to enjoy that, a trip out, different faces, a bit of chit-chat, but since Georgina took up the hospital visiting, she couldn't take me. I'm a bit of a silly old thing. Too afraid to go by taxi or bus on my own. Gina found Nikki, a home hairdresser. She's from Birmingham. Or was it Manchester? Anyway, she talks through her nose, and smells of cigarettes.'

Mia's jaw tightened as her molars ground against one another. It seemed she wasn't the only one railroaded by Gina.

'Still nice to have someone to chat to,' Mia said, cheerfully.

'Mm. Not really dear.'

They sat in silence finishing their tea while Mia studied her mother's appearance. She'd never been a beauty. Her features were small, her skin downy with the hint of a darker line on her top lip. Apart from a wedding ring, her mother wore no jewellery and was traditional in her dress; sensible skirt and shoes, twinsets in lilac or blues, which now hung from her shrunken frame. The conservative obedient army wife, Mia thought. How had she accepted this life, why had her mother never left him? He'd always been a hard taskmaster, he treated them both badly. Had her parents ever been in love? Mia doubted it.

'Nikki used to talk a lot.'

'Did she? Well, at least it gave you some company.'

'Not really dear. You see she spoke *at* me. Each visit I got chapter and verse on what happened in her life, from her useless boyfriend to fussy customers and the cost of perm lotion,' Constance fiddled with the corner of an embroidered handkerchief. 'Never once did she ask if the water was the right temperature, or rollers too tight. Oh dear, now I'm talking too much, I seem to have got out of the habit of making conversation. It's quite exhausting.'

Anger paired with an image of strangling her sister came to Mia's mind. Constance had been given the barest consideration, starved of company, time, and affection, but she could sort this, make it better.

'Well that's in the past, and while I'm here things will change. I promise. We'll get you a proper hairdresser, one that also does manicures. I'll get the phone book.'

Mia swore under her breath as she dislodged a pile of old newspapers to get to the telephone directory. She flicked to the appropriate section and returned to Constance.

'There's a choice of two locally, or we can make an appointment in town, what do you think?'

'I don't know. I'm not accustomed to making decisions.'

'That was in the past, Mummy. You're a grown-up, not one of Gina's brownie troop. From now on, you call the shots. Understand?'

Constance raised a hand. 'I do dear but it's all very exhausting. Do you mind if I have a bit of quiet time now? My voice is quite hoarse with all the chatter. I need to get used to using it again.'

Mia left her, as she passed her father's door thinking what an odd sensation it was to wander around freely knowing *he* was incarcerated behind that door, and couldn't harm them, but could the same be said for Gina?

CHAPTER 14

THE precariousness of her situation troubled her. Without Rufus, she had no money and no home, so first thing on the agenda was getting a job. That sobering thought found her showered and dressed by six-thirty a.m. A time she was more used to arriving home by.

The study was the only room that hadn't been rearranged, it too had deteriorated. The red and cream flock-wallpaper was yellowed with age, peeling away from the skirting boards. Mildew blackened walls showed beneath curled-up edges. Gina had neglected the place. Dilapidations featured in every room except, of course, for her own, lavishly modernised

A noise from the hall startled Mia.

'Morning. How's the naughty boy been in the night?' Josh met her midway and handed her the post.

He was just a tad too cheery for Mia at such an early hour, plus the gold tooth flashing in and out of his plump lips made it impossible not to stare.

'I never heard a thing from him. Is that good?' She cocked her head to one side offering an apology of a smile.

'Course it is sweetie, that's just how I like 'em. Sound like a baby.' He flipped a crooked hand up and down in her direction. 'Better go and make sure he's still breathing.' He nudged her, 'Only joking, bring you a coffee?' She nodded clamping her lips together to suppress a giggle. He was a breath of fresh air in this musty old house.

Mia returned to her father's study, balancing the post on the minimum space available to her, a pitted leather shelf just a few inches deep. The roller-top section of the desk was still locked, and she hadn't located the key. As she sorted the post, she was intrigued to find that two of the three were addressed to her. The first, she recognised as Gina's handwriting. She took the paper-knife from the pot and opened it.

Dear Maureen,

I expect that you're enjoying your time with Mummy and Daddy. Your visit was long overdue. Nurse Bates is excellent and will see to everything Daddy needs. Mummy is quite self-sufficient as I'm sure you've noticed.

Mia rolled her eyes. Condescending as always Gina. I've noticed more than that, she's

neglected and bored shitless.

It has been incredibly stressful, having to cope with them by myself over the years, as well as running a home, being a mother and of course a wife.

La-la-la-la. Same old, but rather flippant. Mia acknowledged an uneasy feeling spreading beneath her ribcage.

We are taking a six-month trip to Australia. Archie has a cousin who runs survival treks in the outback. It will be an enjoyable experience for us all. I am confident that you will do what's right by Mummy and Daddy in my absence, and I'm sure the six months will just fly by. I mean it's not like you have commitments or anything. We depart on the 17th and will be back by the end of ...

'No! You can't do this to me. You absolute shit, Gina.' Mia dropped her hands to her screwing her eyes tightly shut. 'This can't be true. I'll kill her, I'll bloody kill her. She can't do this to me.'

'Kill who, dear? Not Gina, I told you she's in Australia.'

Her mother stood in the doorway resplendent in a lilac twinset and pearls. On her head, a purple felt hat, and her winter coat draped over her arm.

'Mother where are you going?' Mia tried to calm down, forcing breath to her diaphragm.

'Out. Did you say lunch or tea, I can't remember?' Her small eyes twinkled above her downy cheeks freshly powdered and with just a hint of rouge.

'Mummy it's only just turned nine.'

'But I wanted to be ready. Georgina hates it if I dawdle.'

Mia was suddenly and very unexpectedly overcome with a rush of affection for her mother.

'Well, I'm not Gina, so please don't worry, I won't be cross. We'll go out to lunch instead of tea. Would you like that?'

From behind her desk Mia looked into childlike eyes, swallowing back the obstacle forming in her throat.

'Can we? Shall we go to Claridge's? I haven't been for such a long time.'

Mia smiled at her, crushing the thought that she had no income.

'Does Daddy still have an account?'

'I think so, dear.' She looked thoughtful. 'Gina will know, she's sending you a letter.'

Constance turned and shuffled out, stopping midway.

'You are staying with us, aren't you?'

'Yes, I've no other plans,' Mia answered honestly.

Satisfied, Constance hummed her way out of the room and left Mia to finish her letter.

I have arranged for power of attorney to be transferred to you in my absence for emergencies, paying bills et cetera. They will send you the appropriate forms to sign and return, even better if you can put yourself out and drop in with your proof of identity.

The second envelope contained the papers Gina referred to, from a Mr Mead at Tomkins, Timpkins and Mead Solicitors. Automatically Mia found herself completing the documents and placing them back in the envelope. She would call at their offices this afternoon on the way back from Claridge's. The major did indeed still have an account, and it appeared that Gina often took advantage of it, judging by the statements Mia had unearthed. There was a lot she was learning about Gina, mainly that she'd been extremely good at feathering her own nest.

Mia was looking forward to taking her mother out, Constance's excitement had rubbed off on her and, after all, it was Claridge's. However, a wave of despondency floated above her – was this the best she could hope for by way of social life?

Josh appeared from nowhere. 'Here you go girl, get that inside you, sounds like you're having a bad day.'

Mia moved the stack of papers to make room for the cup of coffee.

'You have no idea just how bad the last forty-eight hours have been. I can honestly say they're the worst of my life.' It was true, she'd realised: she had no friends in England. She could try to stay in this damp decaying old house with its putrid smell and ghostly memories if Josh would help her out.

'Josh, I know it's not the sort of thing you do but could I ask a massive favour?'

Josh leant against the wall. 'Depends, try me.'

'Well, I'm taking my mother out later. And this might seem a strange request, but if I left a hammer and nails in the kitchen, would you see to it the cupboard in the hallway never opens again?' Josh's eyebrows linked suspiciously. 'I'd do it myself, but the banging would probably upset both my parents.'

He pushed himself off the wall flashing her a blinding smile.

'Ours is not to reason why, or each to his own. Take your pick. I'm no handyman but consider it done. Now drink that coffee before it gets cold.'

'Yes sir,' she said, surprising herself as she mocked a salute. Turning back to the desk she picked up the envelope containing the power of attorney documents and as the bud of an idea began to bloom, a smile lifted her face. She licked her lips; this could just turn out to be an incredible opportunity.

'Oh Gina, you are going to regret this.'

CHAPTER 15

THE days flew by – Mia's plan took shape. Motivated to clear the desk in her father's study, she purchased a shredder and worked her way through the piles of papers, all neatly filed by Gina. Most of it was outdated rubbish until she noticed one stating Gina took a monthly allowance and even a Christmas bonus.

'Huh, so it's not all charity begins at home then. Daddy's little darling takes a monthly cut. Well, that's stopping right now.'

What this study needs is light and fresh air, Mia thought as she tried to open the curtains. She tugged, taking a curtain in each hand, but the brass curtain rings didn't budge. Another tug and the fabric disintegrated in her hands. A loan spider clawed its way up the wall at speed detached from its web. A cloud of dust filtered around her. She covered her nose stifling a sneeze. The tepid winter sunlight did its best to filter through the filthy windows, dust motes swam around her. The windowsill was littered with insects' corpses. She puffed to open the window skeletons the sudden draft wafting the lifeless skeletons to the floor. She jumped back as a chunk of plaster separated itself from the wall, hit the metal curtain pole and bounced past her.

'That's all I need, another bit of exposed brickwork. Gina, why did you let this house get in such a state? The place is falling. Were you saving the money for something – a nest egg perhaps? Georgina Evans, upright citizen, a saviour of the people, Brown Owl – care in the community and kind to animals. It's laughable. And everyone thought I was the black sheep of the family. Oh, Gina, you are a sneaky little cow.'

It was too cold to work in here even without the window open, the dampness chilled your bones. Mia felt the radiator – cold, she tried to turn it on, but the cap wouldn't budge.

So, the choice is another jumper or put on the stinky paraffin stove idling in the hall. A stench that cloyed the air. No contest, jumpers it is. She squashed away past the chairlift to her bedroom, layered some tops and returned to the study, carefully closing the windows so as to not cause further destruction.

There was nowhere to sit and work other than on the floor, which wasn't ideal, but easier to sort the files of paper into an order of importance. She knelt in the middle of the semicircle and fanned them out around her; reading, organising, shredding or labelling she went.

Pleased with her efforts, Mia pushed herself to her feet, her nose, hands and feet were marble cold. She stretched her limbs, stamping her feet to chase away pins and needles. Rolling the sleeves of her jumper to cover her fingers, she banged them against the tops of her arms. The curtains windows threw shadows around the room, antiques collected over time dominated shelves thick with dust. Military paintings flanked the fireplace, the walls either side hung with smaller oil paintings arranged in groups. On the mantelpiece were photographs of…she leant forward to read the inscription.

"*Major Charles Reginald Croxley-Smith and…*" she couldn't make out the rest, but he was either accepting or giving a medal. The last two shelves of the opposite booklined wall were hidden by wallpaper parting from its join.

God, it's like a mausoleum. Everything dead even the wallpaper-paste. Her glance once again settled on the locked desk. What was so important that it had to be hidden away behind lock and key? Curiosity challenged her.

'What are you guarding so protectively? You will not beat me, little lock.'

She needed something to force it. A paper-knife wasn't strong enough but the kitchen drawer held a pair of scissors. All it loosened was a varnish.

Grrrr. She'd searched everywhere you could think of, even considered phoning the useless cleaner Mrs Flynn but got no joy there either. Could it be in her father's room? *Worth a try.* She braced herself for the assault on both her ears and her nostrils. Her timing was bad. First, she was hit by the contrast in temperature, it was stiflingly hot enhancing the cloying smell of bodily waste mingled with surgical spirit and deodorant. It made her gag. Josh had just given her father his wash, a bowl lay on a giant changing matt, she shied away from the sight of soiled bedding as Josh became aware of her presence.

'You've picked a bad time to come visit. Hasn't she, Charlie boy?'

There was a trace of shaving-soap near one of her father's ears, his hair was uncombed and stood in tufts. He was wearing a pale blue pyjama jacket with a paper bib attached on a strap hung strategically to catch his drools. Her father dangled ungainly mid-way in a hoist hovering in between the bed and the man-sized highchair made ready to receive him. Mia recalled the photograph of him smart in his military uniform with its ribbons and medals standing on the mantelpiece next door. She felt something, pity perhaps. Unsure, she shook away the thought.

'I don't suppose you've seen any keys lying around in here, have you? It's a small one that would unlock something like a drawer.'

At the sound of her voice, her father began to thrash wildly, a guttural roar escaped his twisted lips. It startled her, she winced.

'Oh, he's pleased to see you. I've never seen him so excited. Hey Charlie, isn't this nice that your daughter's dropped by?'

Jumbled valves and uncompleted words poured in outrage. Wildly thrashing his good arm, the hoist began to swing dangerously. Josh struggled to control it.

Repulsive as the sight was, she grabbed the side of the hoist to assist. It took the two of them to steady it. Her father was dead weight, and though Josh was strong, he was slight. Gradually, they managed to lower him into his day chair, Mia held on, her head turned away aware of the proximity to her father's head while Josh undid one set of harnessing straps and connected another.

'There you go Charlie boy, sorted.'

Mia wasn't sure if it was the sound of her voice or the fact that Josh had dared to call him Charlie, that threw him into another fury, his eyes goggled, his face turning the shade of ripe pomegranate.

'Shut shipshuck, gruuu talk. Geeet owwt mmmma.' He raised his head high enough to meet Mia's eyes. A draught of bitter cold swept head to toe at the sheer hatred he emulated. Common sense knew he couldn't hurt her, but she jolted back anyway. Josh clipped the lock on the tray front securing him.

'There we go, all nice and clean, safe and sound.' He flipped a finger to his lips and tapped it. 'Now what did you ask? Oh yes - keys? There's a bunch in that bowl on the windowsill.'

They both ignored the violent head rocking and screeching, as Mia searched the pottery dish and found what she hoped was the right key. All the time, she felt her father's eyes boring into her.

'Thanks, Josh,' she said, her eyes following the patterns of brown and green swirls in the carpet, only daring to raise them when she reached the door.

Back in the study, Mia faced the locked desk, clutching the small, metal key in a faintly sweating hand as she tried to shake off the image of his hatred; the yellowed whites of his eyes, wide and staring, the spittle sliding down his chin as he roared obscenities at her. She pulled in the chair to sit resting her head in the hands until the trauma of him subsided. Sucking in a breath, Mia felt emotional, her hands still shaky. She tried the key listening for the click of metal. The brass bar holding the desktop flush gave way…A long slim drawer ran half the length of the desktop. Mia pulled out the contents, a bulky cream envelope. She squished it.

I wonder what secrets you've got lurking in there, Daddy.

The anticipation was intense, but so was the cold turning her fingers blue. Gathering the envelope, she turned off the light and went to her room. Once inside she switched on the electric blanket, kicked off her shoes and slid under the covers.

The stamp on the envelope read 1993. She turned it over: two small metal arms stuck through a tin brass hole. The points flattened back against themselves, opening it. Whatever was in here was important. Dizzy with excitement, she tipped the contents onto the duvet.

Share certificates of unknown companies. So many, she only briefly scanned them. All were in her father's name. Stretching for a notepad and pen, she inadvertently caused some papers to slide to the floor. They could wait, she'd be moving on to them later.

Balancing the notebook against her knees she wrote:

– envelope – locked drawer; stocks and shares – seek financial advice; bank/accountant?

Leafing through she had expected to come across at least something bearing her name, but no and there was no mention of her mother either, only endowment policies in favour of Gina's children, payable on their eighteenth birthdays. That was fair enough, they were, after all, legally his grandchildren, but nothing for Constance?

There must be a will. Or perhaps he'd thought she wouldn't outlive him, he'd ignored her as he had done most of their married life? The papers she'd examined so far gave no mention. Mia rested the papers on her chest staring at the wall.

What a strange life her mother had chosen, a loveless marriage with a domineering husband, permission needed for every move she made. What had made her accept the status quo? Had something happened while she, Mia, was at Chartley?

Better check what I dropped on the floor. A slim brown envelope had rolled towards the edge of the mattress and Mia had to reach a bit before she caught it.

Last Will and Testament of Charles Reginald Croxley-Smith

Her fingers fumbled to pull out the document, her eye scanning the will for the named beneficiaries. Disgust devoured her. Neither she nor her mother featured – not anywhere, but Gina did. Smug conniving Gina had played a blinder *sole beneficiary* to the whole estate, Gina Evans, nee Croxley-Smith. Although it shouldn't have shocked Mia, it did. As her hand brushed her cheek it discovered wetness. Normally she'd not succumb to such nonsense, she'd not cried properly in years but now the time felt right, now the frailty and precariousness of her situation hit her like a blow to the chin. She had no home, no man, no money, and Gina had everything. For all these reasons, Mia permitted herself to cry. Later, as the tears of despair abated, she replaced them with anger. Anger and a need to make things right. Avenge her mother – revenge, her father, but perhaps he'd already had his comeuppance, his was enduring sufferance, but Gina? Gina had no idea how she'd played into Mia's hands.

CHAPTER 16

CONSTANCE was hovering in the hallway clutching some letters as Mia came downstairs.

'Here,' she said, 'I kept these for you. I'm sorry, I can't remember when they came. I put them in a drawer and quite forgot about them.'

'Thanks, Mummy,' she said, taking them, 'I'll just open these then I'll make us some lunch and come and sit with you.' Constance gave a bright smile, turned and shuffled back into the lounge. 'I'll get you some slippers that fit, Mummy, otherwise, one of these days you'll be tripping over the damn things.'

Constance stopped and looked down at her feet. 'Georgina bought them for me for my birthday, I like them they're quite pretty.'

'Pretty they may be, but they're too big. She should have checked.'

'She got them bigger so that I could wear socks in the cold weather.'

Mia tutted, and made for the study halting outside her father's door. Josh was humming a tune she recognised, it was *Hey Fatty Boom Boom*. She stifled a giggle, thankful that he wasn't singing the very dubious lyrics, and steered herself back to the study.

With the desktop open it was easier to work. As she sifted through the assorted envelopes it was obvious that Constance had got a bit muddled as several were addressed to "the occupier." An expression Mia found peculiar, it reminded her of the war. Countries being occupied, people without freedom. Perhaps that's how her mother had felt, all these years.

The cream envelope caught her attention. She turned it over. The script was strong and bold, the postmark eight months earlier. It didn't have an airmail stamp, and it wasn't in Gina's handwriting. Intriguing.

'Only one way to find out,' she said out loud. She tore open the envelope, read, blinked, and read it again.

Calling all former pupils of Chartley Independent School. Would you be interested in attending a reunion of leaving years 1993 to 1997?

Celia and I are looking to see who would be interested in attending. Many of us have kept in touch, many haven't. We were thinking of a weekend in July or August next summer allowing plenty of time to work out travel plans for those of you who live abroad or have other commitments to organise. Hoping for a fun-packed weekend full of laughter and the nostalgia …

Nostalgia! Hardly that. Mia couldn't possibly…No, not for her. Too many ghosts, far more than she was able to handle. Forcing the invitation back into the envelope, she held it between both her thumbs and forefingers ready to tear it up, but then changed her mind. Instead, she placed it in the drawer and took herself off to the kitchen to prepare her mother's lunch.

Distracted by the letter, she opened a tin of tomato soup, buttered slices of bread, and de-stoned a peach. In her head, a battle commenced between nostalgia and fear. Wouldn't it be lovely to see everyone, catch up on gossip – find out how they'd all fared? Who would surprise the most – who would be most disappointing? Long forgotten memories came forward; Mia remembered when they'd all cut their hair in the same style looking totally ridiculous. The restyling of the dreadful dress Grace's mother had made her for the end of year prom. All of them kissing Michael Barrett and scoring him out of ten. So many laughs and good times shared, but who'd bring it up - Sophie? She could hear her squeaky voice even now and imagine her giggling – glass of wine in hand recounting how they'd fixed Miss Viner's little game. Would they all laugh?

Would she? Would the nightmare be ignored, swept under the carpet? The elephant in the room. Pippa O'Keefe hanging from a tree. Click, click, click. They thought it would put an end to it. For days, it looked like it worked. Miss Viner had avoided her, but as the weeks and months went on, Mia felt her eyes on her again every time she changed for a shower after sports. One day Miss Viner found her alone in the library and hissed, 'Don't you think I gave my friend copies? You caused me lots of problems Croxley Smith, and I'll make you pay before you leave this place.'

Constance was listening to the Archers when Mia took in her lunch tray. She looked up and nodded thanks holding a finger to her lips to indicate she was listening. Mia nodded and, unable to stomach lunch herself, left her mother.

Mia needed to keep busy, clear her mind. Gathering some cleaning materials from the cupboard under the sink she went to her room.

Clothes hung off the open wardrobe doors where she'd been too lazy to put them on hangers, others discarded on the back of the chair. Her night table – a stale cracker, a dirty cup and an empty soft drink can.

Bloody hell. Just because you don't have Teresa to clean up after you, doesn't mean you have to live like a pig, she scolded herself. *I should be ashamed of myself and what would Mummy think if she ever came in here?* Somehow that thought spurred Mia into action, she collected the dirty washing and made a pile ready to take to the utility room. Next, she tackled her dressing table replacing tops and stacking bottles in neat rows. Polishing the layer of dust from the vanity mirror.

Only left to do was changing the bed and give the room a good airing. Armed with clean sheets, Mia pulled the bed away from the wall. As she moved around the gap, her foot met something; she knelt and retrieved a shoebox. Settling on the edge of the bed, she felt her heart thumping, warning her that whatever was inside wouldn't be good news. Gingerly she lifted the lid, tipping out dozens and dozens of unopened little blue envelopes. The minute she saw them, she knew what they were. Her childlike handwriting stared back at her. He teeth caught her lip as she opened one.

Dear Mummy,

Today we had rice pudding with strawberry jam, and I got ten out of ten in my spelling test. I fell over in PE and cut my knee; Matron put a plaster on it for me. I didn't cry. Later we watched TV...

Tears splashed onto the pages.

'Why?' Mia sobbed, watching the ink blur. The letters home, the ones she'd written with care. Unopened. Who would do such a thing, her father? Gina?

All those mornings, days, weeks, years at breakfast where the names of pupils who had mail were called out, but never hers. No one questioned it. Not Grace, not Cassie, not Sophie, they shared their newsy letters from home while she stared at her plate willing her name to be called. She hid her pain, *nobody likes a cry baby,* and took herself off to the top of the hill to cry – with only the wind to dry her tears. When she got older, she'd written letters to herself – disguising her handwriting so that she could feel part of something.

Had Constance written to her? There was a shelf by the front door over the umbrella stand, where anything to be posted was left until the end of the day. *Gina.* It had to be she who always walked the post to the post-box.

What a despicably cruel thing to do. It can only have been through jealously, but why? Mia didn't understand. Gina had the love of both parents and everything she asked for.

Mia's vision clouded; the emotional pain hung suspended – the final hurt. Gina had been careless. Why hadn't she destroyed them? Did she intentionally want Mia to find them in a hate-crazed moment? Mia's forehead hardened. *Gina, you may not realise it, but you've just given me your stamp of approval. Tomorrow, I will start my plan.*

CHAPTER 17

Mia woke early, eager to set her plans in motion. It was time to rebalance the books – undo the wrongdoings, not just for her, but for Constance as well. With no idea how to go about valuing a property, Mia plucked three names from Yellow Pages, two who came were not to her liking, the third recommended she spoke to an associate, a property developer named Grant Langley of Oakridge Properties.

She watched from the window as the Range Rover drew up outside. The door opened; Grant Langley stepped out. Mia took in his appearance. Fair hair, tall, over six foot she assessed, meticulously dressed in a pale-blue shirt and navy striped tie – she would enjoy this meeting, he was handsome as hell. She watched him opening the back door to unhook a dark blue jacket from the rear of the car, and shrug into it. She stepped back from the window as he straightened his tie. She checked her appearance in the hall mirror before opening the door to greet him.

They exchanged pleasantries as Mia explained there were some parts of the house she couldn't show him. There was no way she was going to inflict her father on this nice man and Constance too was to be avoided, she'd only get confused.

Mia opened the kitchen door into the rear garden. Their footsteps crunched on gravel puddled with weeds as they made their way to the rear of the property.

'So, you see Mr Langley...'

'Grant, please.'

'Grant.' He was exceptionally good looking even better, close up. She breathed in the citrus, cedar and earthy leather as if it were a drug; such a change from the horror of smells inside the house.

She'd missed the company of men, someone, to talk things over with. Rufus, of course, would have had all the right advice, but Rufus wasn't an option, she batted that thought from her mind. It was unfinished business and she hoped there would be time, one day, somehow, to apologise for her behaviour.

'As you can see it's all very rundown,' Mia nodded to the jungle of garden.

Grant scanned the whole of the garden.

'I'd love to have seen this in its heyday. I bet it was stunning.'

Almost as stunning as you with your hazel-green eyes, she thought. He was at least a foot taller than her. His face was honest and open, his teeth white and natural, not the bleached white of the inflated egotistical men she usually came across. He was the whole package.

As if reading her thoughts, Grant fingered his wedding ring. She gave him her best smile.

'I just don't know what to do for the best.' She indicated bare patches on the outside walls, that had once been white, in some distant era. 'The place is falling apart; it will cost a fortune to renovate. Do I sell it as it is and take a loss, or give it a bit of a fix-up and go for more?'

Grant considered her words. 'There is another alternative. It's a good-sized plot with excellent access. The land is probably worth more than the house. What's through those trees? May I look?'

'Sure.' She led the way on tiptoe, wishing she hadn't been so vain and had opted for flat sensible shoes. 'Mind how you go. There's a paved path here somewhere under all this grass. I'll get the gardener to cut it. He only does the front, so my mother tells me.' Wet grass brushed against her knees. 'We'll both be drenched by the time we've finished. I'd forgotten how big the garden was. I haven't been down here since I was what? Eight -nine. I think, from memory, there's a shed.'

'I thought this had always been the family home.'

'Yes, yes it has, but I wasn't the golden child, that was my sister. I was at boarding school; I only came home a couple of times. I think I was about twelve the last time.'

'Sounds awful.' He sounded sincere. 'Were you homesick?'

'Often. I missed my mother and our nanny Lisa.'

'Not your sister?'

'Definitely not my sister. Anyway, water under the bridge or whatever.'

Grant's hand warded off a branch from a fir tree, allowing them to pass. Beyond the fruit trees, there had been a vegetable patch now overgrown, with arcs of brambles that covered where once neat rows of carrots and broccoli had grown alongside rows of summer planted peas she'd helped pick. To the left, beyond the rusty frame of the old swing stood what remained of the shed. It was hard to distinguish where the shed ended and the greenhouse began as they leaned and merged. She searched for the gap between the two – her hidey-hole. The place that she went to when it all got too much.

'So, this is it,' she said sweeping an outstretched arm across the space, 'What do you think?'

Grant moved his head up and down, in a slow nod, casting a professional view on the area space.

'It's a good-sized plot. That could be your best way of raising a decent sum – demolish the house, the area is big enough to make a good-sized cul-de-sac, three maybe four dwellings.' He took a photograph of the area and paced across from fence to fence. 'Look, let me get back to you after I've checked there are no nasty covenants.'

'Covenants, like what?'

'All sorts. Boundary issues, preservation orders, rare grasshoppers.'

'Grasshoppers? You're joking, right?'

'I wish I were – sometimes we come up against conservation people, with bats and things like that. Let me get back to you.' He led the way, Mia followed, she didn't want him to go. He was so nice that she couldn't help herself from a little light flirting and probing, as they retraced their steps.

'Tell me, Grant, I suppose you live in one of your Oakridge Homes with a Stepford wife, two-point four children and a Labrador?'

Grant threw his head back and roared with laughter. 'Not quite,' he said, as they reached the gravel path, 'but I do live with my wife, who could never be called a Stepford wife. Helen's very individual, as my bank balance could verify, but she'd hate me for saying that she has a career of her own. We have two daughters, two cats, and yes, a Labrador. I hadn't thought of myself as such a cliché.' She put out her hand and he took it shaking it firmly. 'I'll be in touch in a day or so. There's been a bit of redevelopment in this area, so outline planning shouldn't be difficult to obtain. Leave it with me.'

'Thank you. Perhaps we could have lunch or something, I could do with picking your brains.' His cheeks showed a light flush and she realised she'd overdone the familiarity.

He nodded politely recovery. 'Okay, about anything in particular?'

'Just where I go from here?' *Be professional Mia, this is business.* 'I hardly know a soul in the UK. I would like someone to advise me, like where's a decent area to live nowadays within my budget? Not sure I want London anymore and I'll need to support myself and get a job.' She shrugged. 'I didn't realise how everything had changed here, the prices, everything so expensive after living abroad.'

They had reached the gate; Grant stepped through it and smiled his twinkly smile.

'How long have you been away?'

'I left England when I was 21, did a couple of years on the cruise ships before settling down in Sardinia. Been there ever since.'

'Sounds like a charmed life.'

'Funny how I never appreciated that at the time but since being here, it sorts of puts it all in perspective.'

'And you won't be going back once you sorted out your family?'

'No. England is my home now, good or bad.'

'Good I hope, I'm sure we can sort out a few of those problems for you.' He checked his watch. 'Oops, I'm late. Bye for now. I'll be in touch.' Grant ducked inside his car, waved and was gone. She watched his car vanish beyond the bend and sighed, as a sense of isolation filtered in.

CHAPTER 18

'MAUREEN come, quick. There's a man in the garden fixing a sign to the gatepost. It says "for sale".'

Mis removed her rubber gloves dumping them on the draining board.

'Nothing to worry about Mummy; I have everything under control.'

Constance looked concerned, fluttering her hands like she'd lost track of what was happening. 'Is it a mistake?' Her voice quivered.

'No Mummy, no mistake. This house is far too big and draughty for you, now that you're older. I'm going to find you somewhere else to live that will be much nicer. I mean, wouldn't you like to see more people and have things to do instead of staring out of that window all day? Come away from there and sit down. I'll make you a cup of tea and then I'll explain my idea and you can have a look at some nice brochures.'

'I don't want any tea,' she said, sitting back in her chair and dragging the tapestry bag onto her lap.

'Okay then, hang on a minute. I'll go and get the brochures,' Mia went to the study and collected what she needed. 'Here you are. Let's have a look together, shall we?'

'What are they?' Mia read the panic in her mother's eyes.

'Just a brochure with pictures.' She placed the pile on the table at her mother's side. 'Mummy, can I make a request, please? Can't you just try and call me Mia? Maureen's so old fashioned.'

'I'll try, but Maureen is a perfectly nice name. It means dark, or dark-haired, and you certainly have that. Now let me look at the pictures.'

'Apparently, it also means chosen one, but I don't think I was that.' Constance wasn't listening she was already engrossed in the pictures. Mia realised she'd given her the wrong one. 'Sorry. That's one's not for you. That's for daddy. This is a home for retired service people. They have a thermal pool; everything daddy needs including daily physiotherapy. Much better for him than being stuck in that one room all these years.'

'I'm sure, if you think it's fine, it will be, but I don't know what Georgina will have to say about it.'

Mia tried not to sound annoyed. 'Gina's not here Mummy, I'm looking after you now.'

'Then you do whatever you think best.' Constance said, leafing through the pages of the Wycombe Manor glossy. 'This one looks nice, Maureen; everyone looks happy in the pictures. And what pretty bedrooms – oh and look at the gardens.'

Mia raised her eyes to heaven; her mother already had forgotten to call her Mia. *Oh well.* 'I thought we'd go out together and see what was on offer, what do you think? It's exciting Mummy, just like an adventure. I promise it will be your choice.'

Constance became unnaturally still. Mia wondered what she was thinking.

'You look worried, Mummy.'

Her mother spoke into her lap. 'If I go there, will you be leaving – go back to Sardinia?'

'No, I won't. I'm going to make things better for you. So that you can lead a happy life outside of this horrible old house and we can do nice things together.'

Her mother digested the words. A small smile pulled at her thin lips.

'You know I never liked it,' she confessed. 'Rambling damp old place. His choice, of course.'

Mia knelt beside her. 'Did you ever have *any* choices Mummy? How could you live that way?'

'Things were different in those days. Expectations were to marry a man who could provide for you. It wasn't all about romance and things like it is these days.'

Mia tucked her long hair behind her ears and leaned in. Constance smelt of the same Coty L'Aimant dusting powder she'd used for years. When she was young, Mia had put some on a handkerchief and taken it with her to Chartley, but the scent had soon faded – diluted by so many tears.

'But wasn't that in Victorian times? What about the sixties, seventies, eighties?'

Constance's eyes suddenly sparkled.

'It wasn't always as it seemed you know. I had my own life.'

Mia didn't want to contradict; she had little knowledge of what went on at home whilst away but was intrigued to know this other version of her mother.

'Come on then. Tell me, what did you do?'

'Danced. I danced a lot, barefoot.' Her eyes twinkled with excitement. Mia was in disbelief. *I never!*

'What sort of music?'

'Oh folk, blues, a bit of Motown. I bet you can't believe it, can you. I used to go to Sidmouth, for the folk festival each year. Thankfully. He...,' Mia had only recently realised that Constance had stopped referring to him as Daddy or your father. 'Was away, sometimes, a year or more at a time. I didn't really care.'

'You're a bit of a dark horse, aren't you? So, you didn't have such a sad little life after all?'

The smile slid from Constance's face. 'Only inside these walls.'

Mia knew exactly what she meant.

'Tell me more about the good times, and do you have any photographs? I'd love to see them.'

A shadow darkened her mother's eyes. Mia watched Constance press her lips together and visit someplace far away – out of reach.

'Most of the pictures are in my head. I look at them in the long hours when everything is still. No one can touch them there or change them.'

'Well. You are a dark horse, and there was me feeling sorry for you when all the time you had a secret life.'

Constance tapped the back of Mia's hand softly.

'Don't humour me, Maureen. I wish I'd been stronger, but I got my own back from time to time. One day I'll tell you all about it.'

'I'd like that – and will I be surprised?'

Constance slowly moved her head up and down. 'Oh, I hope so, I dearly hope so.'

The next few days were full-on. Together they viewed nursing homes, some better than others but Wycombe Manor was top of the list. They planned a second visit. It would be quite central for Mia to get to. Ascot wasn't too far away but she mustn't force her own opinion on Constance. It needed to be her mother's decision.

Unlike the others, Wycombe Manor was surrounded by beautiful countryside. Constance had even put on some lipstick for the occasion.

They were greeted by the residential manager, a smart woman in her thirties dressed in an immaculate grey suit. Mia trailed behind as Constance took the woman's arm, the faithful peacock bag in her other hand. Mia wondered why it was so precious to her. Perhaps it was like a comfort blanket.

They were led from one beautifully furnished room to another. Constance became alert and interested. She asked questions and nodded at the answers.

'Would my room be just like this?' Constance asked as she was shown into a bedroom dominated by a large bay window with exquisite drapes and matching soft furnishings. 'Maureen, look. I could look out at all that lovely countryside and that's the en suite.' She nodded to the open bathroom door.

Mia spirits lifted, reassured by the glow on her mother's demeanour that this *was* the right thing to do. With the tour concluded they were shown to the drawing-room. It was filled with the buzz and chatter of several residents. A grand piano stood to one side of the floor-to-ceiling windows, next to it an enormous vase of roses filling the room with a heady scent. Plump cushions chairs were arranged in cosy groups, several were occupied with residents enjoying their afternoon tea.

Mia touched her mother's arm. 'Are you alright if I leave you here and have a look outside? I think you've walked far enough for one day.'

'Yes, Maureen don't fuss. I'm going to sit there and have a nice cup of tea – have you seen the iced fancies?' Before Mia could answer, Constance had pointed to an empty chair and made for it. Mia waited until she saw her settled, she needn't have worried. Within seconds, her mother was making friends with two of the ladies.

Mia wandered the grounds discovering a music room, art room, a Croquet lawn that led down to an archery area and a lake beyond. It was perfect, but it wasn't her decision.

Retracing her steps, she re-joined her mother, feeling almost guilty at spoiling her fun. Her mother's eyes positively shone with happiness.

'Maureen these are my friends, Ivy and Joan.'

'Very nice to meet you, ladies.'

'We do hope Constance comes here. We got on so well together,' said the one Constance had introduced as Ivy.

'That's not down to me, that's up to Mummy. Have you seen all you want to?'

Constance beamed beckoning Mia closer. 'Yes. This is the one, isn't it? It's so nice.'

'Are you sure?'

'Positive.'

Ivy and Joan gave a polite clap. 'You'll be incredibly happy here; we are, aren't we Ivy?'

'Okay, I'll go and see to the paperwork and find out when you can move in.' *Fantastic news, it's expensive very expensive, but once the land deal has gone through, I won't have to worry about that, they'll both have plenty to live on.*

When she returned to the sitting room, she saw the women had been joined by a gentleman, who, it appeared, had said something amusing as all three were laughing.

'Come on Mummy, time to go.'

'Oh, do I have to? I'm having such a wonderful time. I haven't laughed like this in years.'

'That's good to hear, but you'll be back soon, and it looks like you've made friends already. Time to go now before it gets dark.'

Constance got to her feet and said her goodbyes. Mia went to take her arm, she shook herself free and glided along the hallway towards the exit, with almost a sashay, slowing only to acknowledge a gentleman with a walking stick and moustache, who was coming towards them. He stopped and removed his hat. Mia coughed a laugh as her mother gave him a wink. Did she just witness that? Surely, she'd imagined it.

Constance chatted the whole of the journey home. Mia had never seen her so animated.

'They have a hairdressing salon and a manicurist. Fancy that. And on Tuesdays, they have a bridge club and play with people from other nursing homes in some sort of league. And did you hear her say they'll get us tickets for the opera, arrange transport, for anything we want to go to and— '

Mia glanced at her. Constance sat rigidly tight-lipped, the tapestry bag clasped against her ribs.

'What's up?' Mia said, concerned. Had she changed her mind?

'Can we afford it? It looked awfully expensive.'

Mia chuckled. 'Yes Mummy, you can afford it. That's why we're selling the house so that you and Daddy can have somewhere nice to live.'

Constance gave a shrill cry. Mia slammed on the brakes.

'What is it, are you hurt? Just hang on a moment, let me pull the car over and let the traffic go by.' She guided the car to the curb, Constance was flapping, clenching and unclenching her right hand.

'What happened – tell me?' she said forcefully, immediately regretting the moment she noticed her mother's tears.

'It's your father, Maureen,' Constance let out with a rush of air, 'It just won't do. He wouldn't like it there and all those noises he makes. I think the ladies would find it most distressing.' A tear slid down her cheek. Mia reached across to comfort her, ignoring the blast of car horns as angry drivers were forced to overtake into oncoming traffic.

'No Mummy. Remember I showed you the brochure - the one that was for Daddy. I thought we'd find him somewhere else, where there are lots of military people. I know he can't join their conversations, but he would be able to listen. Some might even have served with him. And you, wouldn't have to worry about him because he'd be well looked after.'

'You mean he'd go somewhere else?'

'Yes exactly. Remember I showed you. Windsor, so he wouldn't be far from you. Would you like that?'

Mia got out a pack of tissues from her bag and blotted her mother's cheeks. Constance gave a faraway smile. 'You mean he wouldn't be with me at all?'

'Well, I could take you to visit, just now and then, if you wanted to.'

'No-no, he'd be much better on his own. What an excellent idea, Maureen; I'd like

that very much.' She turned and gave Mia a beaming smile, her bright button eyes aglow with excitement. 'You've been a good daughter, better than I thought you'd be. Gina is so bossy, and she spends all her time with Daddy, and I do get very, very lonely,' she raised a hand to stifle a yawn. 'Can we go home now? I'm a little tired.'

Constance was already nodding as they turned into their road. A removal van was parked outside the gate of Willow House.

'Stay there a minute, Mummy.' Mia got out of the car and met the man coming away from the front door.

'Can I help you?'

He looked at the clipboard in his hand then back to Mia. 'Croxley – Smiff?' Mia nodded. 'Delivery for yer. There's a lot so where d'yer want it?'

The man lowered the tailgate to reveal about half a dozen packing crates. Mia realised immediately what they were, Monica had said that she'd forward her belongings.

Mia returned the car having guided the man to the conservatory and left him to unload. Constance didn't show much interest in the delivery, she was back to shuffling, exhausted from the day's excitement.

After having sorted a light supper for them both, Mia settled her mother in for the evening.

The contents of the boxes held no thrill; it had been an exhausting day for her too.

Josh was putting on his coat ready to leave. 'How did it go?'

'Good thanks, she liked Wycombe Manor.'

'So, Mummy's sorted just Daddy to go?'

She sighed. 'Don't look so sad, you're doing what's best for both.'

'Thanks, Josh. I'm glad you agree.'

'Of course, they both have different needs and require different stimulation. It can only benefit them both.'

'Thanks, Josh. How would I ever have managed without you? You're amazing.'

'I know, they all say that,' he said letting himself out, 'I'm just remarkable.'

Mia placed a foot on the stair and hesitated before she raised the other. She wanted her bed badly, but would she be able to sleep with a job left undone?

With a knife taken from the kitchen block, she sliced through the sticky tape of the crate labelled 1of 7. Inside a neatly typed envelope marked in red felt tip pen, ONE.

Dear Ms Croxley-Smith,

This is the shipment of your personal belongings. You should receive seven boxes.

•Clothing, 4

•Shoes, 2

•Handbags, 1

There is no need to confirm receipt. The carrier's signature will suffice. Your mobile phone account will close at the end of the month, and to reiterate, all credit cards have been cancelled.

Mia crushed the note from Monica, letter in her palm in frustration. There was no one to blame, she'd brought this on herself. She lifted two of her favourite silk dresses, neither had been packed with care. There was no delicate folding, no tissue paper in the folds. She shrugged her shoulders; the packing exhibited the contempt that even Teresa held for her.

Can I blame her? Just who did I think I was to lord over her – criticise her food. She was loyal and caring. Oh God, things could have been so different – I could have been so different, but now it's too late.

The designer clothing looked amiss surrounded by chintz sofas and potted palms of the conservatory. Dropping them back into the crate, she switched off the light and went to bed. She lie on her back staring at the ceiling. Of course, she had to change – she'd made a start already, but the old Mia had to hang around for a little longer, just until her plan came to fruition. Teresa hadn't deserved her treatment, but Gina certainly did. Boy, was she in for a surprise.

CHAPTER 19

WOULD 2013 be the year to turn her life around? Christmas had come and gone, without celebration, gifts or cards, not even from Gina.

The New Year arrived wet and blustery with weathermen and Constance worrying about the likelihood of snow.

The January sales tempted Mia to buy a laptop, a printer with a scanner, she'd already got a new mobile with a new number. New Year, clean page, a fresh start, she told herself. Spare time was filled with study, PCs for dummies, Microsoft Word, Excel, and PowerPoint. If she wanted a job, she'd need the skills.

In the past she'd never bothered reading a newspaper or watched the news, now it seemed important that she knew what was going on in the world. BBC News was saved into her favourites as she caught up with current affairs, threats of a global wine shortage. The tragedy of a helicopter crashing into a crane in fog – the Duchess of Cambridge expecting a baby in July. She felt she ought to know these things – educate herself if she were to mix in more enlightened circles, at least she be able to converse.

Grant Langley stayed true to his word and had come up with a staggering figure that Mia could not refuse. The deal was done. It was official. Gina was stuffed.

Things moved more quickly than Mia could have imagined. Grant had his PA send her a list of contacts – one was an auctioneer. His remit was to assess anything of non- sentimental value that could go to auction. Mia appreciated the irony.

The piles of tat Mia had referred to, turned out to be either collectable or desirable. The value of one of the military paintings alone was enough to buy a very sharp new car, not that she needed one.

There would be nothing of worth left for scheming Gina to get her hands on. She couldn't inherit what wasn't there. It would be spent on her parent's future, for however long that may be, and if her father died first, at least Gina's children would benefit.

Helen Langley sent her the names of dress agencies that sold second-hand designer clothing and a dealer who sold pre-loved handbags. Mia kept little from the cache of belongings from her past life. Her life for the moment was here and now. She wasn't planning for parties on yachts just survival. Luckily, she'd made more out of her belongings than envisaged. The bulk of the money she placed in a building society, opening a current account for the remainder for when she needed a deposit and rent. Once the house had gone, she'd find somewhere to rent. Reality told her that her ideal was bigger than her purse.

Self-respect was a beautiful thing, she felt a glow of pride at her achievements, never having planned anything more demanding than dinner parties until now. Paper files of importance were scanned into her laptop. Spreadsheets itemising the household accounts that incorporated the precise details of care home costs and money expected from Oakridge Developments, were forwarded to Mr Mead to keep him up to date of her plans. Her meticulous organising was not just about getting her parents settled or getting even with her sister. It had matured Mia, given her values. A refreshing change to be in charge – the one calling the shots when up until recently she'd had no voice at all.

By May, Constance was settled and ecstatically happy in her new home at Wycombe Manor. Mia visited twice a week delighted to see the new woman Constance had become. It was like someone had waved a magic wand. Her step had a jaunt to it; her back was straighter; she was interested in life. And went on outings with Ivy and Joan and to the theatre with a gentleman friend called Richard.

There hadn't been much that her mother wanted to keep from the house. Like Mia, she had little to feel sentimental about. A few knick-knacks – a clock. Her main concern, as always, was the faded tapestry bag Constance without fail insisted on carrying herself. Which made Mia curious. Constance had always been evasive about its contents but whatever it was, it was certainly bulky.

Major Charles Croxley-Smith had been duly dispatched, by private ambulance, to the military retirement home. With Josh's help and advice, it had all been so unbelievably easy. Saying goodbye to Josh was hard. He'd been her saviour, his camp humour had lifted her, vanishing any darker thoughts. That and his continued reassurance that she'd done what was best for everyone even though undoubtedly Gina would disagree.

Everything was falling into place. Constance now had her own will, one that Mia made sure she was not a party to. She'd done what she could, what her mother did with her own money was her business. With the house sold, it was time for her to get on with her own life. The flat she'd moved into in Twickenham overlooked the river. It was modern, functional, with underground parking and a security man in the foyer which made her feel less vulnerable as she'd be living on her own.

Today she had time on her hands and was in a reflective mood. As Mia looked down out across the Thames thoughts of Rufus filtered in. What was he doing now? Would he be travelling, or at home. She imagined him breakfasting on the terrace. Did he still take his morning swim?

She contemplated the grey sky, over muddy brown water. The boats that passed were interesting but none as much as the sight of a yacht on the horizon, its white sales puffed by the wind. Her regrets were short-lived. As she moved from the window, she counted her blessings. *Yes, I've learned some painful truths but look what I've gained. I'd never have known my mother or discovered there was quite a nice person hidden inside me. Once I'd taught myself to stop being angry at the world.*

She forked her fingers through her hair. *It's good to be normal. Why did I ever think all that angst made me superior? Just look at me*

*organising life for myself. Looking after Constance, fulfilling her needs
– even his. Doing what normal people who don't have maids do is quite
rewarding.*

Thoughts of her old life brought Inika into her head. She'd been
meaning to ring her for weeks. The long-distance tone rang for
some time before it was answered.

'Inika? It's me, Mia.' A piercing squeal reached her ears.

'Darling, where the hell have you been? I tried to call you when
you didn't come back but your phone wasn't working, I thought
you were just going to London for a short trip. You've been gone
forever. Is Rufus with you?'

'No, long story, I'm staying here. I've been dumped.'

'Oh my God! Are you all right?'

'I am now. My loving bitch of a sister plotted against me. The
Major dying was all a ploy to get me here. She's in Australia.'

'No. You're kidding? You said you didn't trust her. You poor
darling. Is it awful?'

'Not awful. A bit of a shock at first but I have to say I'm quite
enjoying myself.'

It was good to have a conversation with someone who knew her,
well, who thought she knew her. They chatted for almost an hour
before hanging up with Mia promising she'd come out for a holiday
as soon as she could.

Mia made her bed and tidied up, feeling just that little bit more
complete. Talking to Inika had made her realise that she didn't
hanker for a luxurious lifestyle anymore, it seemed flimsy, empty,
and unfulfilling. She didn't belong there. In fact, Mia doubted
she'd belonged anywhere. Chartley had been the closest thing to a
family. At least the girls looked out for each other. A pang of guilt
wriggled in. Cassie, so willing to please. Forever offering to do
the things Mia hated, making her bed or doing her ironing, being
a princess again. Then again, before she came to Chartley, she'd
just been a little girl crying into her pillow. *Fe- fi- fo- fum,* who
thought her survival depended on being the pantomime baddie
when all she'd needed was to be herself? The real baddie had been
Miss Viner.

The mail was being directed from Willow House. Confirmation had been sent to say the Chartley reunion was going ahead. She put the date in the diary, perhaps the reunion would be Mia's final hurdle, she hoped so as she posted the RSVP along with her updated contact details. Wouldn't it be fun, would girls be shocked at how much she'd changed? She didn't want to be remembered as the bad girl or, for that matter, the victim.

Mia's next challenge was getting a job. She missed the juggling and organisation of the last few months. Would the lovely Grant Langley know of something? She dialled his number and left a message with his PA. Glancing back out of the window she felt, maybe it was her imagination, but didn't the view seem so much clearer?

CHAPTER 20

A<small>NY</small> day now, Gina would discover her allowance had been cancelled. That would ensure a phone call. As predicted, the tone of Gina's messages gained momentum the more Mia ignored them.

Maureen, will you please get in contact. I don't know what silly game you're playing but it's costing me a fortune calling from Australia. Call me. What have you done with mummy and daddy? Has something happened?

The phone number's disconnected. Why is it disconnected? There was plenty of money in the bank account to pay any bills. If I don't hear from you soon, I'll be contacting the police and social services! I will not be ignored. Call me or else! Gina

'Call me or else.' Dialling Gina's number, Mia was aware it was passed ten p.m. here which meant four a.m. in Perth. The phone rang for an exceptionally long time before Archie answered.

'Archie, it's Mia.'

'Have you any idea what the time is?'

'I have actually, it's ten-fifteen here now please get her.'

'It's most inconvenient. It's the middle of the night.'

'Not for me it isn't, now unless she wants to call me back at your expense...'

She heard a bang, the phone was being slammed on a hard surface, followed by shuffling feet and muffled voices. She waited.

'Thank you, Maureen, for waking up the whole house.'

'No problem, only you seemed kind of keen to speak to me, so I thought I'd better call.'

'Always a clever mouth, aren't you? Now, what's going on over there? What have you done with Mummy and Daddy?'

Mia wanted to torture her a bit longer but decided the news she was about to impart would have the same effect.

'Mummy and Daddy are perfectly fine and a lot happier than when you were supposedly looking after them.'

'What do you mean by that?'

'What do I mean? Well, Mummy has a completely new lease of life, going to the theatre, playing bridge. She's having a ball. I haven't seen Daddy for a while. They tell me there's no improvement but at least he has a change of scenery, physio, even a touch of swimming. Well, he bobs about in a harness thingy.'

'Wha— Maureen, explain yourself, what have you done with them? Mummy's not strong enough to go out on her own and Daddy needs specialised carers. If you've done anything—'

'I've done what you should have, got them out of that mausoleum you called home. I mean honestly, how you could expect them to live like that. Mummy sat vegetating all day with only Woman's Hour for company and Daddy, well, all he did was wait for Saint Gina to turn up.'

'Shut up, you always were a cow.'

'I doubt that. I was never there.'

'Shut up Maureen. I suppose you're back in Sardinia now you've got rid of your responsibilities.'

'Actually, I'm staying in London and will be working.'

'Working? You've never done a day's work in your life, just sponged off rich men on your back.'

Mia sighed. 'Let's stop exchanging insults. What exactly do you want to know?'

Gina was silent for a moment, thrown off guard by the fact that it was Mia who had called the argument to a halt.

'Gina, stop mucking about or I'll hang up. I said, what else do you want to know?'

'Where are they?'

'Safe.'

'Where exactly?'

'Mother's in Ascot, Father's in Windsor.'

'*What*, you mean they're not together?'

'Correct.'

'What? why?'

'They both have different needs, Mother still has a life, and Father doesn't. Simple as that.'

'Those places are expensive.'

'Very.'

'How did you raise the funds?'

'I sold things.'

'What things?'

'The house, the car, the antiques, daddy's stocks and bonds, that sort of thing.'

The gasp from Gina's end of the phone was almost deafening.

'But you can't,' her voice rose to a high-pitched squeal. 'You can't just sell everything without consulting me.'

'I can, and I did. All legal and above board, you gave me power of attorney remember?'

'Christ sake. You can't have spent it all?'

'As you said, this sort of care is expensive, and they may well live to a hundred, you didn't think of any of this did you, when you decided to con me and bugger off to Australia.'

'You just don't understand what you've done. You may not be academically bright Maureen, but there are laws. Daddy made a will and it says that everything goes to me and the children. Daddy showed it to me. It wasn't yours... to sell, any of it. I'll sue of course.' Her voice hid the quake of a sob. Mia hoped she didn't expect any sympathy, not after what she'd done secreting her letters.

'If there's anything else you want to know, contact the solicitors. They'll tell you what they told me. Daddy's will means nothing while he's alive, and after he dies, he can only leave what assets he has and that may be zilch.'

'WHAT. You won't get away with this.'

'I think you'll find I already have.'

CHAPTER 21

The days dragged. She'd scoured the papers for a job. Bad idea. If something caught her eye, she quickly discovered she wouldn't catch theirs. It seemed everyone needed a CV; each job required a minimum of two years' experience or fast typing speeds. How on earth were you supposed to get experience if no one gave you the chance.

Grant was still in regular contact, he had said he'd ask around, but so far nothing and she was beginning to wonder how she'd survive long-term. Strangely, at that moment, he rang.

'I don't know why I didn't think of it before,' Grant said, 'Zannah, a friend of ours, owns a recruitment company. If you got a pen, I'll give you the number.'

Mia dressed in a sharp grey trouser suit, cream blouse, and minimum jewellery. She sucked in a deep breath as she Her nerves were jangling. She gave herself a talking to. Where was the old Mia, the confident one, the one that would have said that it was they who should be pleased that Mia was walking through their door; offering her services, not the other way around.

The agency was in a quiet square surrounded by boutiques and coffee shops. She was greeted by a youngster who seated her in a reception chair.

'If you could fill in the application form? Ella will see you soon. May I have your passport please?'

Mia stared at the girl perplexed. *What is she talking about?*

'I want a job, not a holiday,' she barked.

The girl flushed and a woman Mia assumed to be her manager appeared from nowhere.

'It's okay, Jenna, I'll see to this lady. Ella's running late.' *At last, someone who knows what's what.* 'Would you like to follow me?' The woman was tall and attractive, probably around her age. The suit she wore was exquisitely cut. Her flame-red hair, like a lion's mane, swished across her shoulders as she walked. She ushered Mia through a door marked INTERVIEW ROOM 2.

'Please make yourself comfortable and if I can ask you to fill in the application form, I'll pop back and explain the process,' she beamed a winning smile. 'Can I get you a coffee? Water?'

'No thank you, I'm fine.' Mia unbuttoned her jacket, fighting back a feeling of being an imposter. The woman left her, it didn't take long to complete the form as there were more blank than filled-in sections. Perhaps she should slip out now before she embarrassed herself further. She should have been more honest with Grant about her tenuous experience, it was too late now; if she walked out, he'd probably get to hear about it. Mia pushed the form away and waited, terrified that when the woman returned, she'd laugh at her. She looked around noticing a pile of leaflets in a stand and took one, that explained what was expected of a temporary worker. There was nothing to be scared of, at least she knew what was required of her.

'All done?' The woman took the opposite seat positioning herself at right angles between Mia and the computer screen. 'I'm Zannah.' She slid a business card across the table. Mia glanced at it. *Zannah Farleigh FIRP Cert RP Managing Director.*

Oh, how embarrassing – it's Grant's friend, the owner. She closed her eyes momentarily, she must appear intelligent, she couldn't let herself or Grant down. She'd created a persona – and now she had to live up to it.

It took Zannah only seconds to scan the form before she put it aside.

'I take it you haven't sought work through a recruitment agency before?' Mia shook her head. 'Okay let's start again, shall we? We will need to see a copy of your passport to confirm your right to work in the UK. It's European Law, I'm afraid. I take it you have a passport?'

Mia nodded. 'Yes.'

'Good, but no CV – Is there any reason for that?' Zannah fixed her with her amazing green eyes.

'I've been living abroad.' *Obviously, Grant didn't tell her that when he made the introduction.*

'Ah lovely, whereabouts?'

'Sardinia mainly, but some time in Spain as well, we had two houses.'

Zannah gave an admiring nod. Mia decided to embellish. 'My partner,' she hesitated, what else could she call Rufus – boyfriend sounded so childish, 'was in the oil business. I didn't have a job title, but I ran the yacht hire, organised his diary and looked after the property management.' *Yeh in my dreams.* 'And naturally, I managed the household staff.' *Not a lie.* 'I'm not one for long flights,' she confided. 'So, I dealt with anything that came my way as my partner travelled a lot.' This was becoming easier than she thought.

'Sounds like an interesting job. So, what brings you to the UK?'

Easier to tell the truth. 'Well, my sister had been caring for our elderly parents, after our father had a stroke. She recently emigrated to Australia with her husband and children. That left me with their care.' *Time to name drop.* Her confidence was growing. 'Grant Langley has been dealing with the property side of things for me whilst I've been settling them into better accommodation. In fact, it was Grant who suggested you might be able to help.'

How amazing, she was almost telling the truth, but noticed Zannah's expression was guarded – she was being summed up.

'So, will you be staying in the UK indefinitely? Or are you just after temporary employment?'

Mia interlinked her fingers shuffling further back into her seat.

'I won't be returning to Sardinia if that's what you mean. My, err, absence put a strain on our relationship, so I'll be residing here. I need a proper income,' she laughed, 'unless I can find another millionaire quite quickly.'

Zannah's lips tweaked a smile as she turned her attention back to the computer screen.

'I hope you don't mind me doing this while you're here. It's easier to type into your record as we go.' Her fingers tapped adeptly at the keyboard. 'Nearly done now; just a couple of things. I'll need references - another legal requirement. Sadly, this industry is full of them.'

'I'm afraid I don't know anyone in England. The only people I've had much to do with have been Grant and the family solicitor. I don't know if either would do.'

'Grant will do nicely. He's a highly respected member of the community and your family solicitor, perfect.'

Mia studied Zannah, not her looks, stunning as she was, but her whole persona; business-like, professional, and yet approachable. The sort of person you could talk to. Someone to admire.

Zannah realigned her chair. 'Is there anything specific that you have in mind for work?'

'I have absolutely no idea. I'm good at organisation and I can use a computer – can think on my feet. That's about it.'

Zannah touched her cheek lightly as if removing an unseen flick of dust or stray eyelash.

'Well Mia, I'll be honest. You're short on experience, but long on having the right look, and confidence if you get my meaning. I have a client who has just finished a very impressive office conversion ...pool, gym, and - a ten-hole golf course in the grounds, that sort of thing. He needs someone reliable who can oversee prospective tenants; conduct viewings, take deliveries, monitor contractors, that sort of thing. There is a security man at the gate and cleaners, but other than that you'd be on your own. There's an office already set up. Mr Sahir likes a weekly update email on his project. He lives in Dubai, so it's mainly phone and email. What do you think? It would be using the experience you already have. Nothing you couldn't cope with.'

Mia could have hugged her. 'That sounds interesting. When would you need me to start? And I wouldn't have to wear a uniform or anything so tragic, would I?'

Zannah smirked. 'No nothing like that, just smart and business-like.' She shuffled the papers and handed them to Mia. 'Have a read through the duties and see what you think. The client's flying out tonight, which is a shame, as you won't meet him. He wants someone in situ by next Wednesday. Don't worry if it's not for you, I have calls out to some of our other temps. This booking had been allocated, but unfortunately, the person had a horse-riding accident. Trust me. It's nothing you couldn't cope with. The hours are from 10.00 to 4.00.'

Mia sensed someone hovering outside the glass-panelled door. Zannah rose.

'Sorry. Will you excuse me a moment?'

'Mm, no problem.' She studied the details, experiencing a rush of excitement. She wasn't useless after all. There was nothing on the job description that she couldn't deal with. She wanted it.

Zannah returned apologising. 'Sorry about that. So, what do you think? Is it something you'd be interested in?'

'It looks excellent, well interesting... a good place to start. I don't know the area, is it easy to get to?'

'You do drive?'

'Yes, but I don't know the area that well.' Zannah looked thoughtful and for one panicked moment, she thought she was going to change her mind. 'It's no problem, I'll find it.'

'I tell you what, 'Zannah said, still looking thoughtful, 'If you want to go and grab a coffee over the road while I finish up, I'll drive you out there in say,' she glanced at her watch, 'half an hour, so you can get your bearings.'

'That would be kind if it's not putting you out.'

'Not at all. I'd rather you see the location and get a better idea of the location to see whether you'd be happy working there,' she pushed away from the desk. 'If I could hand you back to Jenna, she'll talk you through the details. It's all pretty basic stuff, your bank details, copy of your passport for our records.'

Three people were sitting in reception, one didn't look that happy. It was only then it occurred to Mia that she might have needed an appointment. Had she put Zannah out?

'Jenna, can I leave Mia with you? Explain what she needs and draw up a copy of the details for the Sahir booking.' She turned her attention back to Mia. 'I'll come and find you as soon as. Is that okay?'

Forty minutes later, Zannah was driving them out of town and deep into the Surrey countryside. Mia caught a whiff of Chanel No 5; one of her personal favourites.

'So, would it be just me there? I read about the supervision of cleaning staff.'

'They all come under your instruction, oh and the gardeners as well. Your remit is always to present the property at its best. Fresh flowers in the entrance lobby, all the rooms pristine. If it's not right, you kick ass,' she gave a small laugh. 'I get the feeling that you can probably give me lessons in that.' There was a beat of silence between them, Zannah filled it.

'Once the place is let, there's a very impressive bonus payment on offer. You can use the facilities out of official viewing hours. I have to pass this way quite often, so I'll pop in and see how you're doing. That's if you accept the booking of course.'

Zannah turned into a tree-lined drive, the road sloping upwards. Mia gasped as the structure came into view at the top of the hill. The glass walls reflected the green of the lawns and the blue colour of the sky.

A security guard showed them in. They took the glass lift to the fourth floor.

'It can be a bit lonely, but providing everything's done, your time is your own. There's an indoor pool and a gym off the ground floor. Right, this is your office.' They didn't need to open the door; you could see right through the internal walls and into all the rooms on this floor.

Zannah pointed out the lake. 'I'll be envious of you taking a stroll around there with your coffee while I sit in traffic.'

Mia felt her excitement growing. Not just for the job but also because she felt she was bonding with Zannah and became more relaxed in her company as they chatted about Sardinia and places that Zannah had visited on the island – the shops in Puerto Chevro and the beaches along the Conca Verde. Zannah showed interest as Mia spoke of Constance's new lease of life. Mia thought how wonderful it would be to make a friend of Zannah Farley. A home, a job, and a friend. A fresh start on *her* terms.

CHAPTER 21

Today was her last day. The property had been let to an American software company. Mia had just completed a handover with the facilities team and come back to her office to clear her desk. The lake reflected the building and sky above, she felt reluctant to leave, she'd loved watching the wading birds and the squirrels play. Her appreciation of nature had grown since she'd been here. In the past, Rufus championed nature's beauty. How stupid and immature she'd been, what sights and opportunities she'd missed.

Imagine if this were a house, not a business premises, it would be glorious and if I'd asked, Rufus would have happily built it for me, but no point looking back, and no good pretending to love a man for a roof over my head. Either way, it's dishonest, and the more I think about it the more ashamed I am. I must take some responsibility. I can't blame everything on my childhood.

Dragging her eyes from the view, she turned back to her desk. Ella, from Zannah's agency, had already lined up her next assignment. There was nothing to do other than clear the computer files and collect her personal items. Mia quickly logged into her email account. Two new messages. The first was from Gina. She steeled herself for more abuse or argument.

Maureen – Mia smiled. Please reply to this email with daddy's current address. Her fingers moved quickly in reply.

The next was from Oakridge Properties; an invitation for their 12th charity golf day, of which the proceeds would go to a children's cancer charity. She read on through the long list of celebrities until she got to the part about the evening gala dinner. The fizz of excitement had her hoping this would be a stepping-stone, the start of her social life. She tapped out an acceptance. A few moments later, Mia's mobile rang.

'Grant, that was quick. I only just replied to your invitation.'

'Great you got it. I was ringing to see how the job was going. Zannah had lunch with Helen last week, she mentioned you'd been working. I felt a bit guilty for not calling.'

'Don't apologise. I can't thank you enough. Zannah's been keeping an eye on me, more so than her other temps, I suspect. She regularly finds an excuse to drop in. Not just the job though Grant. I have so much to thank you for. You have been a real Sir Galahad, my knight in shining armour. Helen too, helping me sell my belongings. As for the job, today's my last day and I'm ready for my next assignment. There, see - I've already mastered the jargon.'

He laughed. 'Zannah told Helen you've become an absolute asset. I'm pleased it worked out for you.'

'Thanks, I'd like to treat you both to lunch when you're free.' Grant's voice mingled with other sounds. 'Er, are you driving?'

'Don't worry I'm on hands-free. And no, there's no need, but I'll get back to you on that.'

'Please, and, thanks for the invitation. What's the format?'

'Celebrity golf during the day. The non-golfers, wives, girlfriends, partners arrive early evening for cocktails and mingle, dinner at eight - cabaret usually starts around ten. Oh. And an auction and anything else I can do to squeeze more money from their wallets.'

'Sounds great fun - will I know anyone?'

'Not sure, there are around three hundred for dinner, other than that, er well, me Zannah, Helen, I know you've not yet met in person, but don't worry. I'll make sure you're sat next to some nice bloke, or you can bring your own. By the way, how are the oldies doing? Are they settled in okay?'

'Nice of you to ask. I see my mother once a week. She seems incredibly happy if somewhat batty. She's thinking of taking up golf - at her age. Crazy.'

'Brilliant of her for wanting to try - well better go now. See you on the 27ᵗʰ.'

Mia sat for a while thinking about her father. She hadn't needed to drive to Windsor the previous weekend, but her conscience wouldn't settle. The whole experience had thrown her. He hadn't roared his undecipherable language, he'd been calm. There'd been a moment when he'd lifted his head, and their eyes met. Had she been mistaken – was it a look of gratitude?

Driving home she mulled over what to wear. Cocktails and mingle, he'd said. Easy when you know people. She wished she'd made more female friends. Inika had been an exception, much like Zannah, she'd also started out being her boss. What did that say about her as a person? She didn't want to mess things up, this event was important, but she'd be walking in on her own. It would be better with a partner, but she didn't know anyone. Perhaps Zannah could help.

They were having lunch together at a cosy bistro. Zannah had just finished telling her about the red-carpet affair she'd been to the previous night. Mia knew Zannah had once been married and had a son but hadn't mentioned any significant other.

'Oh no Mia, I sail single-handedly. I find men either a disappointment, heartache, or headache. I divorced years ago.'

'And which was he?'

Zannah peered over the rim of her coffee cup, measuring her reply. 'Royston was a philanderer, a liar, a drunk, take your pick. But he was also a Member of Parliament so that probably explains it,' she huffed out a small laugh. 'It was messy. One of his bimbos did a kiss-and-tell to the tabloids, it was horrendous.'

Mia noted a chink in Zannah's armour as she became serious.

'Jack had just started middle school. I couldn't have him in the middle of it.' She shook the unhappy thoughts away. 'And you? You're such a stunner, I know about the ex but no one else? What's your story – everyone has one.'

'Not as interesting as yours, I never married. Never found the right one. But I did have a good life, as I said when we met. I lived in Sardinia. My man, partner, whatever. He was in engineering, made a washer for everything from aviation to plumbing – not oil as I implied. Sorry.' Mia folded her napkin and placed it on her side plate. 'What do you do when you go to all of these grand functions - hire one?'

Zannah was cool as a chilled melon. 'That's exactly what I do. I have several favourites and book them in strict rotation, just so I keep control of the situation.' She leaned closer. 'It's my guilty pleasure.'

'Ooh tell me more,' Mia giggled.

'Well, I have a sporty one, Bradley. A young handsome one, Oscar. And Luca who's ideal if I need a dance partner or something, …you know, for balls and things.'

Mia had never been to a ball, but the idea that you could get a man on tap whatever the occasion appealed to her.

'But what do you do? Pick them from a catalogue or something?'

'Not exactly, it's all very tastefully done, a simple registration, what your requirements are. It doesn't always go to plan; they might not be available— works for me. Much better than the lies and bullshit of handsome men. And believe me, I've met a few.'

'What a fantastic idea,' Mia said, hooking her hair behind her ear. 'My goodness, I appear to have led a sheltered life.'

'It sounds brilliant. But knowing my luck I'd still pick a right Wally… Is that the expression? I overheard it being used recently.' Zannah grinned in reply. 'So how do you select them? It sounds ominous.'

'Not really. Basic stuff like how tall you want them, interests. That sort of thing, it's no good going to a Polo match with someone unable to hold a conversation on the subject. Or Cowes if they don't like sailing. I have lots of men friends,' she wiggled her fingers making an inverted comma sign with her fingers. 'I just don't want to be in a relationship, it suits me this way.' Zannah checked her watch then caught the waiter's eye for the bill.

'Oh no you don't, Zannah, this is my treat as a thank you for taking a gamble on me.'

'No way. It's me who is grateful. Mr Sahir is a very fussy client. He was delighted with you - in turn, that reflects on my agency.'

'You can pay next time.'

'But—

'But nothing. If we're going to be friends, we mustn't argue.'

Friends. That felt good. It meant she really was putting down roots.

They left the restaurant and parted company. Mia couldn't wait to get home and check out the website Zannah had mentioned. Her phone had vibrated twice during lunch, but she'd ignored it. As she settled in the back of the taxi, she retrieved it from her bag and listened to a voice mail. With trembling fingers, she returned the call.

'Hello, it's Mia Croxley-Smith. I understand my mother has had a fall.'

CHAPTER 22

THE corridors stretched out like endless runways. Signs for Outpatients, Pathology, X-ray, none of which Mia wanted.

'Wards, wards,' she called out as she dodged between the human traffic of people on crutches, wheelchairs, dawdlers – everyone was in her way.

A man in a plaid dressing gown overheard her. 'First left to the lifts, love.'

'Thanks,' she called over her shoulder. On the wall by the lift-doors was a listing of what was where. Forsyth Ward was on the third floor – but the lift was on the sixth. She couldn't wait, pushing open the swing doors she took the stairs arriving at the nursing station breathless and perspiring.

'Constance Croxley-Smith. I'm her daughter. How is she? What happened?'

The nurse gave a sympathetic smile. 'Take a moment to catch your breath. She's comfortable, she was fast asleep when I did her observations ten minutes ago. She's got a bump on her head and a bit of a shiner.'

Mia caught her breath and fisted her hands to stop them from shaking.

'They said she had a fall.'

'That's what the notes say from A&E when she arrived by ambulance. She tripped over a bag she'd left on the floor. A member of staff heard her cry out so went straight to her. She is in safe hands now, a concussion can be more serious in the elderly, so we are keeping a close eye on her.'

'Can I see her?'

'Yes, of course, it's this way.'

Constance was indeed sleeping, propped against starched white pillows, a plastic name tag attached to her thin wrist. Mia's eyes were drawn to a tea-stain on the blue and white hospital gown. It distressed her more than anything else. Why hadn't they changed her? Her mother always kept herself neat and clean. Taking a brush from her bag, she gently tidied her mother's hair, careful to avoid the large purple bump on her forehead. Constance stirred and opened her eyes.

'Hello, Mummy. How are you?' Mia reached for her hand, but her mother recoiled – she looked startled, alarmed. 'Don't be scared, it's me. How are you feeling?'

Constance sat forward trying to see past Mia. 'He'll be here any minute.'

'Who, Mummy? Who'll be here, the doctor?' Mia threw her a reassuring smile. It didn't have the desired effect.

'Who are you? Go away. I want Vikash. Ring the bell.' Constance looked around - searching – her hand tapping at the bedclothes.

'Mummy, you had a fall. You're in hospital, you're going to be okay.'

Constance swung towards her, nostrils flaring. 'I don't know you. Get out, get out of my house. Coming here to my bedroom. Who let you in? Where's Vikash? I want Vikash, not you.'

'I don't know who Vikash is, Mummy. Look, do you know where you are? You had a little accident and bumped your head.'

Constance clawed the bedclothes up to her chin, glowering at her. Her cheeks flushed. A nurse appeared in the doorway.

'I think maybe you'd better let her rest for now. She's a bit overexcited, probably best if you pop back later when she's had a longer rest and is less agitated?'

Mia got to her feet, fluttering her glance from her mother to the nurse and back again.

'Is this normal? She doesn't recognise me.'

'Perfectly in this instance. Don't let it upset you, she doesn't know what she's saying.'

Constance buried her face in her hands. 'You too, you can go as well. Where is he? Come back, please, don't leave me.'

Mia attempted to calm her mother, stroking her arm but Constance knocked it away, her rheumy eyes pleading in confusion. The nurse steered Mia away. All she could hear was the sound of her mother weeping.

Mia lowered into a chair in the corridor. 'Bumps on the head often confuse, change of surroundings as well.'

Mia rolled her shoulders, feeling washed out. This was beyond her experience.

'Can I get you a cup of tea, a glass of water?'

'Water, please.' Mia's voice gave way to emotion. 'She will be okay?'

'We just have to keep an eye on her.'

Hoisting her bag up to her arm, Mia reconsidered. 'Actually, no I'm fine. I won't have anything, I'll go to Wycombe Manor, gets her things – a clean nightdress,' she shuddered at the thought of her mother in the tea-stained gown. 'I think she'll be happier in her own things.'

'Good idea. Keep busy. We'll call if there's any change.'

As she entered the doors to Wycombe Manor, she was greeted by the manager who was keen for Mia to understand that this was an unforeseeable accident. As they were talking, Constance's friends, Ivy and Joan, came along, deeply concerned and hoping for more news. Mia spoke with them briefly before going to her mother's room.

The sunlight shone in through the high-set windows. Mia entered Constance's room rolling her head to release the tension in her neck and shoulders. Closing the door behind her she slid her handbag from her shoulders onto the bed. Constance's reading glasses were on the nightstand. They looked strangely adrift without their owner. The peacock bag was on the floor, probably as it was when Constance had stumbled over it. Mia picked it up. The leather handle was smooth and fitted easily in her hand. And it was heavy; it was amazing that someone as frail as her mother could have carried it around. The faded colours showed its age. Slowly, almost reluctant to touch something that was so absolutely Constance's, Mia was hesitant about loosening the leather drawstring. Should she be going through her mother's things? It felt intrusive. Perhaps just a peek inside, it smelt old, musty. There were bags within bags, silk and cotton ones, papers, and cards held together with an elastic band. A notebook with a girl in a sari on the cover, yellowed newspaper cuttings poked from its edges.

Frowning, she removed a gentlemen's spotted tie, and a delicate fan edged with mother of pearl. At the bottom of the bag was a tin box, the sort you kept petty cash in. The size of a paperback novel but deeper. She recalled seeing it somewhere in the past. The key was loose inside the bag, a thin lilac ribbon attached. Mia shook the box, it rattled. There was something inside, but not coins. She turned the box and placed the key in the lock; her chest tightened with excitement at entering her mother's secret world.

There were papers, sepia with age. She picked out a removed a cream envelope, inside it a photograph of a dark-skinned man. He was wearing a suit and a spotted tie. She glanced from the photo to the tie, was it the same one? She was about to delve further into what felt like Aladdin's cave of mystery when her phone rang. Pain gripped the back of Mia's throat as the nurse explained that her mother had taken a turn for the worse.

'I'll come straight away. Thank you.'

Blood pumped and swished a rhythm in her ears crowding her head with mundane thoughts, such as should she take her mother's toothbrush? Would she need her slippers? The gripping fear made her heart sink.

It seemed to take the taxi forever to find its way through the traffic pouring off the M3 motorway. Mia prayed to God to help her mother. Constance was kind, she'd been a victim for so long. Her life had just begun afresh, it would be cruel to stop it now.

She needed a familiar voice. Just one. She took out her phone. Gina was still in Australia. Her mother's solicitor had forwarded a letter from Gina, saying she was returning to England but in Mia's panicked state, she couldn't remember the date.

The taxi pulled up in front of the hospital. Thrusting a twenty-pound note at the driver – far more than required, but time was of the essence, she hurried along endless corridors.

The nurse got to her feet as Mia approached. Mia tried to side-step her in her haste, but the nurse stood firm. Her face read sadness – compassion. Mia looked away. Gently, the nurse placed her hand on Mia's arm.

Mia wobbled for a moment, unsure if she should just go into her mother's room, but as their eyes met, she realised it was too late.

CHAPTER 23

WHY didn't she cry? That's what most people did, wasn't it? Instead, Mia shuffled aimlessly around her apartment. Her body slumped at the overwhelming sense of loss, cold and numb, but no tears came. She had never lost anyone before. Short of buying anything in black, she just didn't know what to do or how to behave. Now she had a funeral to arrange. Automatically she rang Zannah, she had a booking scheduled. Briefly, she related her news. She had finally managed to speak to Gina, they'd exchanged voicemails, but that was it. Her other call had been to Mr Mead. Should she have her father notified, she wondered before immediately dismissing the idea.

There was little time to wallow in sadness, with so much to do. She scribbled down a list, not trusting herself to remember it all.

Collect Mummy's belongings from Wycombe Manor.

Collect Death Certificate from hospital.

Look up registrar of births and deaths which is closest? (Ask nursing home)

Notify people? Who? Find her mother's address book.

Discuss funeral plans with Gina.

The last one, she dreaded most of all. She knew Gina was back in the UK, staying with Archie's sister. They had a meeting scheduled with Mr Mead that afternoon, followed by a visit to the undertaker. Mia had taken on the unenviable task of choosing an outfit for her mother to be cremated in.

Mr Mead phoned to confirm that he'd spoken with Mrs Evans, who was keen to keep to the arranged appointment. Mia was surprised that Gina hadn't made direct contact. Surely now was a time to pull together.

Mia hired a car - taxis were too much hassle, and she needed to be in so many places at once. The secondary reason, more valid, was that driving would prevent her from drinking; four bottles of wine in two days only added to her grief.

The few personal belongings of her mother fitted inside one suitcase. Gina could have the job of going through the few trinklets and disposing of her mother's clothes, but the bag with the peacocks she put to one side. Something stopped Mia from seeking answers to the tie and photograph mystery. She was sure the remaining wad of envelopes and notepads would reveal all. But there was no rush.

Gina was already seated in reception when Mia arrived. There was no welcoming hug – no comforting one either to share their loss. Gina's mouth was pulled into an unforgiving line. She threw Mia a cold stare. Mia blinked; she hadn't seen Gina since the day she'd left Charley; nothing had changed but time. The frizzy hair was pulled out of her face and held tight by a floral, hairband. Mia had expected her to come in full black, not a fuchsia pink skirt and a navy print blouse.

'You can be bothered to show up then, after all of the trouble you've caused?' Gina spat.

Mia had promised herself she'd stay calm, but Gina's words made her bristle.

'Hello Gina, it's nice to see you too. No hug for your little sister?'

Gina curled her lip in a sneer, 'Adopted sister.'

Mia ignored her, took a seat, and smoothed down her skirt focusing on the reason why they were here and how Constance would have wanted her to behave.

Gina sat forward. 'You think you're going to get away with this. Well, you're not. I'll see you in jail first.' Gina's cheeks flushed, 'It's where criminals belong.'

Mia sighed, despairing, inwardly relieved as a man with gold-rimmed glasses on top of his head appeared from an open office door. Smiling he made his way towards them extending an out-stretched hand. He was different from how Mia had imagined him from their phone conversations and had neither height nor weight on his side.

'Ladies, Michael Mead,' he shook their hands warmly. 'I'm most dreadfully sorry about your mother. Please accept both my and the partnership's condolences. Constance had been a client here since I first started my apprenticeship, so many years ago. Shall we go in?'

They nodded, following him silently into his office. Mia took one of the two seats arranged in front of the desk, Gina the other. Mia thought about the proximity between them. It was about as close as they'd ever been, two adopted women - sisters in the loosest term, with truly little in common apart from the names on their adoption papers.

Mia's eyes roamed the room. The office was traditionally furnished, panelled on one side, and with legal tomes gracing high shelves on the other. Two sash windows flanked Michael Mead, the reflection of light surrounding his head like a halo.

Mr Mead settled to the task before him: he opened a bulky file and removed some papers before plucking his glasses from his head, placing them on the bridge of his nose.

Gina fidgeted in her seat, keen to get on. 'Mr Mead, I have written to you several times about my sister's underhand dealings of my parents' affairs. I want to know what you intend to do about it.'

Mia watched his chest rise and fall and the brief drop of his eyelids. He seemed old and tired, but Mia guessed he was only in his mid-fifties.

'Mrs Evans, I have explained, several times, that Ms Croxley-Smith has done nothing improper.'

Gina puffed out her chest, 'But—'

Mr Mead circled a finger to interrupt her, his voice calm. 'There is no but about it, Mrs Evans. You authorised full power of attorney to your sister. The document was drawn up by this very company.'

'Adopted sister and my father and I rued the day—'

'None the less Mrs Evans,' he interjected, 'Ms Croxley-Smith acted perfectly correctly on your *adoptive* parents' behalf.'

'But she sold off their assets and put them in a home! She split them up and sold the house, the antiques. She emptied the bank accounts —'

'Both your parents had separate needs, there is nothing illegal about that, and care homes cost money. Ms Croxley-Smith consulted our partnership throughout the process. It was the logical thing to do.'

Gina banged a fist on the table. 'Daddy left everything to me, in his will. This can't be right! Mummy didn't even have a will.'

The solicitor sat back in his cushioned leather chair, extending an arm to raise a document, for Gina to see.

'Firstly, your father is still alive – therefore that will remain in place until his demise,' his eyes dropped to the document in his hand. 'I have here your mother's last will and testament. I took the details personally.'

'Huh,' said Gina turning and nodding in Mia's direction, 'Now we'll see. Mummy won't have let me down. I always cared for her, whilst you just gallivanted abroad.'

Mr Mead gave a polite cough. 'Mrs Evans, can we try and be civil?'

Gina folded her arms across her chest and nodded.

'Good, then if you are both in agreement, I will read it.

'*This is the last will and testament of Constance Avril Croxley-Smith of Wycombe Manor, Petworth Road, Ascot Heath, Berkshire.*

'*On this day 22nd June 2013, I hereby revoke all former wills. If my husband Charles Winton Croxley-Smith shall survive me for the period of thirty (30) days, this will have no standing on my wishes in the distribution of property both real and personal.*

'I appoint Michael William Mead of Tompkins, Timpkins and Mead LLP as my executor. I appoint my daughter Mia Croxley-Smith (hereinafter called my "trustee") to be my executor and trustee.'

'*What* no. That's wrong, it's ridiculous.'

Mr Mead raised his eyes. 'Mrs Evans allow me to continue.

'I give the sum of three thousand pounds to Lisa Farrant of—'

'*What?* Lisa? The nanny? Why on earth did she waste good money on her?'

'If you please, Mrs Evans. Thank you.' He took a breath before continuing.

'I give my estate both real and personal unto my daughter and trustee Mia Croxley-Smith and—'

'*You what?*' Gina was on her feet, 'Let me see that.' Mr Mead flinched as she snatched the will from him. 'This can't be right; Mummy would never have done this to me.' She prodded a finger at the top of Mia's arm. 'This is your doing. Daddy wanted me to inherit, not you. After all the time I looked after them both, whilst you lay in the sun, under God knows who.' She paused long enough to wiped spittle from the corner of her mouth, before swinging her attention back to Mr Mead. Her lip curled in a sneer, 'That's it isn't it, she's been shagging you.'

It was Mr Mead's turn to get to his feet. 'Mrs Evans how dare you make such preposterous allegations. I assure you there has been no impropriety here,' he fixed Gina with a stern look, his face a burning red, '*and* no collusion.'

Gina gathered her things. 'I won't stay another moment and listen to this rubbish.' Her chair toppled as she pushed past, she didn't attempt to right it. 'You haven't heard the last of this. I shall take this to the high courts.' Leaning into Mia's shoulder she hissed, 'I don't know how you've done this, you little whore, but you won't get away with it.'

With a slam of the door she was gone, but not before loudly repeating her accusations to the receptionist and anyone else in earshot.

Mia held her hand over her mouth to stifle her sobs, but it was no good, the dike had burst.

Mr Mead slid a box of tissues towards her. 'Please don't take this to heart, Ms Croxley-Smith. People say things they don't mean in these circumstances. I'm sure it was all in the heat of the moment. Let me get you some water.'

Mia thanked him and smiled through her tears. It wasn't Gina's tirade that finally made her cry, but the fact that her mother, after all this time, had addressed her as Mia.

CHAPTER 24

M IA hung onto the list of her mother's last requests. A wicker coffin – a humanist ceremony run by the celebrant, no prayers no hymns. Two things puzzled her; firstly, the choice of music, 'It's too late baby', by Carole King, followed by the committal tune of 'If you really love me' by Stevie Wonder. She'd expected something by Vivaldi or Bach. It reinforced how little she knew about her mother.

Secondly,

I wish my ashes to be scattered on Mutter's Moor, above Peak Hill, in Sidmouth, Devon.

A bell rung over the door announcing her entrance. She expelled the breath she had been holding. There was no sign of Gina. After the performance in the solicitor's office Mia doubted whether Gina would turn up, but braced herself for round two, just in case.

A woman in a sombre grey suit appeared from behind a curtain and led Mia through to a small room wallpapered in burgundy and cream stripes. Pictures of peonies and poppies adorned the wall over a burgundy couch flanked by matching chairs. Soft music whispered in the background as Mia was led through the formalities. The meeting was hampered by tears, pent-up emotions of the past week, or was it years? Whichever, it left her drained and confused. Mia accepted the offer of a cup of tea from the funeral director while she composed herself. As she waited for the cup of tea to arrive, she re-read her mother's mysterious instructions.

Please place a copy of my obituary in all newspapers covering the East Devonshire coastal area covering Sidmouth. I wish to be cremated and my ashes scattered on the moorland above Peak Hill at a place called Mutter's Moor overlooking the sea in Sidmouth.

It made no sense to Mia. What was in Sidmouth that would pull Constance back there after her death? She frowned, vaguely recalling the mention of a woman, Elizabeth. An aunt or cousin of Constance's perhaps? Had her mother maybe stayed there? Must have been a happy place for her otherwise, why would she want her ashes scattered there?

Mia blew her nose. Naturally, she'd fulfil her mother's wishes. Sidmouth, perhaps Constance holidayed there when she was young, perhaps she grew up there. That had to be the answer – other relatives. *Perhaps I was wrong assuming she was an only child*, Mia wondered. Maybe there were other living relatives apart from her father and Gina, who both appeared to be excluded from the current scenario.

The day had come. Carole King sang softly in the background, as Mia followed her mother's coffin into the chapel at Randall's Crematorium. Outside, there was a mishmash of people dressed in sombre clothing. There seemed to be quite a few, and Mia was unsure if they were leftover mourners from a previous funeral or early arrivals for the next. She raised a hand to the manager of Wycombe Manor and her mother's friends Ivy and Joan. There were other residents she knew by sight who smiled sympathetically at her.

Mia took her seat, skimming the mourners' heads for any sign of Gina, Archie, or their offspring. The tension in her neck began to dissipate with their absence. Flame-red hair stood out against the grey and black as Zannah came into view, Mia's hand went to her heart before she beckoned her forward. Zannah slipped into the empty seat next to her and hugged her.

'It is sweet of you to come.'

'I thought you might need some moral support in case the wicked sister turned up.'

'I don't think she's coming but thanks anyway.'

'What are friends for?' Friends, Zannah couldn't have said anything more comforting.

As the service commenced, Mia sat, silently listening to a stranger try to recount her mother's life with what little information she'd been able to impart.

Next a reading, then a poem by William Wordsworth, *Daffodils*. The room stilled. Stevie Wonder broke the silence, leaving Mia to wonder about the meaning behind Constance's choice of song as the curtain drew around the catafalque. It was done.

The funeral director gently directed the congregation to an exit that led Mia outside to a paved area and a plaque bearing her mother's name. Zannah squeezed her shoulders. 'I'll wait for you in the car and give you a lift back.' Mia watched her go before turning back to the flowers, her eyes brimming with tears.

First was her floral tribute. The fragrance of arum lilies and lily of the valley filled her senses mingling with the heady scent of freesias and rosebuds from Wycombe Manor. Slightly off to one side lay a sheath of yellow and purple iris, almost invisible through the condensation of the cellophane bag, from Tomkins, Timpkins and Mead. A display in the shape of a pillow adorned with pale pink rosebuds embedded in one corner with scarlet cabbage roses, the display was almost the size of her own. Mia bent down to see who it was from. *"Rest in peace and enjoy the heavenly gardens. DQ."* Who was DQ and it did it matter? The last a childlike bunch of wilted forget-me-nots and wild poppies and selling dines. The bunch was tied with green string, Mia picked it up. There was a sadness about the little bunch not just because the flowers would wither and die so soon. It was just their simplicity. There was no card, nothing to indicate who had left them, but she felt whoever had gathered these wildflowers, had done so with affection.

Mia got up and ran an eye over the gathering. The smartly dressed, the well-heeled – soft leather gloves taut over aged-spotted skin despite the warmth of the day. Could she connect the wildflowers with any of them? Surely not. She caught the eye of the funeral director and asked if he knew who they were from. He didn't.

People were making their way towards her. She took her place to one side of the tributes. The mourners filed past, hugged her or shook her hand, offering words of comfort.

Ivy and Joan approached. 'We've organised a little tea,' said Ivy, 'we thought it would be nice for those who couldn't come to a tea in Constance's honour.' 'Will you join us?' Joan asked brightly, 'you'd be most welcome.'

'That's so kind of you but I have a friend waiting.' Though she knew that Zannah wouldn't be offended, the truth was Mia'd had enough for one day. The elderly ladies smiled and began to walk away. 'I don't suppose you know who left the wildflowers do you?' she called after them.

Ivy shook her head. 'No, I'm afraid we don't Mia, but they were all her favourite wildflowers. She talked about how she used to collect them on a hill somewhere in Devon, I think.'

As the last of the mourners passed, Mia's gaze returned to the bunch of wildflowers. It made her smile. Another mystery. *Mother, I look forward to getting to know you better.*

CHAPTER 25

Aᴸᴸ night Mia tossed and kicked at the duvet. Every part of her ached, even though she'd done little to cause it. Affection had never been high on her list; sex yes, but she'd never understood the need for couples to be permanently trapped within each other's limbs. Now, the need to be held swamped her. Hugging her pillow lengthways, she sought a sense of comfort, finding none until eventually, sleep arrived.

The sound of her entry phone buzzer being pressed continuously woke her, she glanced at the clock 3:15 p.m. Kicking back the duvet she padded across the woodblock flooring to the hallway.

'Yes,' she croaked into the speaker.

'Delivery,' a male voice said.

'Just leave it on the step.'

'Sorry, no can do. I need a signature.'

Mia groaned, and running her fingers through her hair, organised her thoughts. 'Take it back to the post office or wherever and leave me one of those card things.'

'Lady, I'm just doing my job. I get paid for delivery, *with* a signature.'

'Okay then for goodness sake.' Grumbling to herself she pressed the release button. Realising she was only wearing a flimsy top, she grabbed a throw from the couch and wrapped it around her shoulders.

The Lycra-clad courier indicated the place to sign before handing over the envelope.

Mia closed the door and shuffled to the couch, careful not to trip on the yards of material draped around her. She flipped the letter onto the worktop. Her stomach rumbled, prompting memories of the elegant breakfast table Teresa used to lay. She blew out her cheeks and, discovering there was no fresh coffee, reluctantly spooned instant into a cup and waited for the kettle to boil.

Opening the fridge, she swore. No milk, with so much going on she hadn't bothered. She picked up the tub of Greek yoghurt, it was still in date. That would have to do. The letter glared at her from the table. What now? What would life throw her way? She opened it. Her eyes widened.

Horton and Cable Solicitors. Gina had carried out her threat and found a solicitor who'd listed her allegations. The letter was cc'd to Mia's own solicitor. She screwed the paper into a ball and hurled it at the bin. Mia hugged herself in a feeble attempt to squeeze out the hollowness inside her. She looked around her apartment but saw only hard edges, cold lines. Nothing was comforting to her. The room was sterile. Everything shone, lacquered, harsh and cold. Durable and impressive, but not a home. It was soulless, without an ounce of personality. The hardwood flooring reminded her of their dormitory at Chartley. She yearned for the welcoming feeling of thick tufted carpet beneath her feet. Even though her floors had been marble and refreshingly cool in both houses she'd shared with Rufus, the only carpets she'd known were in deluxe hotels she'd stayed in. Today she yearned for comfort.

The only colour breaking the taupe and white palette was a dying hand-tied bouquet from Zannah leaning, Pisa-style, to the right, the stems no longer reaching the green water. Wilted petals and a smattering of pollen lingered on the glass counter.

Mia cuffed away a tear with the heel of her hand, deciding that self-pity was not the answer. She slid from the stool and released her mobile phone from its charger. There were four messages and several missed calls, one of which from Zannah. Mia returned the call, but it went to voicemail. She rubbed at her cold feet and padded to her bedroom in search of socks, as she couldn't be arsed to sort out the climate control. Her mother's tapestry bag lay on the floor alongside her black funeral clothes. She closed her eyes to the image, unprepared to probe its contents and turned away; her chilly feet led her into the en suite.

Showered and refreshed, she redialled Zannah.

Zannah's voice was chirpy. 'Hello, stranger. How are you doing?

Mia swallowed away the urge to weep to reply in a quaky voice. 'Yes, fine thanks and you? '

'Hmm, not convincing, Croxley-Smith,' Zannah said in mock sergeant-major tone. 'Is sympathy allowed? Emotional hug. Champagne and dinner?'

Mia struggled to control a juddering breath but failed.

'Ah, I see. How about a bowl of pasta and a good bottle of red wine instead? Always works for me.'

Mia cleared her throat forcing a jaunty laugh. 'Lovely. Sounds good and yes, you guessed it, sympathy's pretty much like a dagger right now. So, none of it, please. I've blubbed so much already. A Champagne dinner, and anywhere classy is out.'

'Mia, for God's sake, it's called grief. You're human you know; just lost your mum. It's allowed. No dressing up, jeans, boots, a sloppy top and sunglasses if you need them. Agreed?'

'Agreed.'

'Even a tracksuit. Mind you, I doubt that you own one.'

Mia's face puckered to a smile; the sensation was warming. How many days had it been since she'd last used those muscles?

'See you at Milano's, seven-thirty. Just wear a smile.'

Well, that had perked her up. Counting Grant, she could boast two friends in England. As she settled into the back of the taxi on her way to meet Zannah, the friends issue raised itself again. Why did she have so few friends?

Because you've been a shallow, heartless bitch — okay, probably a self-preservation mechanism. God listen to me self-analysing. Next thing I'll be sitting crossed-legged on a rug chanting a mantra if I don't pull myself together.

Had she always felt different? Probably. There had never been that anchored sense of belonging, not even at Chartley. Unlike

Grace, Cassie and even Sophie, with their loving families, she'd been dumped and left alone like a stray dog. Without warning, a vision of Miss Viner holding her camera emerged. Mia ran her open palms down her face. Did the other girls have the same awful memories scalded into their minds? Would they talk about it at the school reunion?

By the time Mia reached the restaurant, Milano's, Zannah was already seated. As Mia approached Zannah extended her hand. Mia stared at it. Zannah huffed, grinning.

'Well, I thought a hug was out of the question. Strictly no embarrassing shows of emotion and all that.' She raised a playful eyebrow and Mia held up her hands in surrender.

'That's better, now sit,' Zannah ordered. 'I hope you're up for garlic bread. We've no one to impress tonight and both of us can get away with the calories.'

'Anything. I have no fight left in me.'

They chatted and laughed as they ate. Zannah kept the conversation flowing and Mia discovered that Zannah was somewhat of an art buff. She listened with envy as Zannah mentioned this friend and that.

'So, there she is, no coat, only a wrap over a backless dress and a pair of Louboutins expecting a glorious evening – not a rug and a picnic on Brighton beach in November. Never trust a man who says he's taking you somewhere special. Clarify or freeze to death and ruin a great pair of shoes.'

Mia laughed. 'I'll try and remember that.'

'Good, anyway enough about me. We've known each other for almost a year and you hardly ever talk about yourself.' She interwove her fingers while mimicking a dreadful foreign accent. 'You're like a modern Mata Hari.'

Mia giggled. 'Yeah, I'm the perfect spy, aren't I?' She lifted her coffee cup to her lips desperately thinking of something to say, something to make her sound more interesting. 'There's not a vast amount to tell. I was adopted as a one or two-year-old, I have no idea of my background. My adopted father was in the military, a major—big cheese. He served abroad a lot. I don't think he liked me much, suspect it was to do with the colour of my skin. He was a horrendous racist.' She tugged at her bottom lip. 'Erm, what else? Oh yes, well Gina you know about she was also adopted and was the apple of our father's eye. Most of my childhood was spent at boarding school.'

'Abroad?'

'No Sussex - Chartley.'

Zannah nodded, seemingly impressed.

'I'll see the girls from my dorm later in the year at the school re-union. At the time, we were like a little family looking out for each other, but somehow, with me moving abroad, we all lost touch. Well, at least I did.' Did that make her sound less of a saddo, more normal and not a victim of Miss Viner? A shudder of recollection fizzed up her spine. Had she been unkind to Cassie, she had ordered her around a bit? She had to put that right, all three girls had all managed to help Mia after what happened to Pippa O'Keefe. 'I'm looking forward to it. Grace, Grace Denning -,' she didn't finish her sentence as Zannah jolted forward.

'You don't mean *the* Grace Denning of *What a Thing to Find Out*? Oh, I love her show. Wasn't she married to that TV explorer chappie?'

Mia frowned, pursing her lips. 'I doubt it. Grace was more the proper, safe type, accountant or secretarial. Something... sensible.'

'Well you never know,' Zannah continued enthusiastically, 'Google her name and see if it's her. How exciting. What about the others. What were they like? Who knows, they could all be famous, or indeed, infamous.'

Mia threw her a look of exasperation. 'Unlikely. Cassie was a bit of a doormat. I hate to say it, but I did rather use her at school. She was great at ironing, cleaning shoes, that sort of thing. I probably owe her big-time. I wonder what happened to her. Cassandra – Cassandra... what the hell was her surname?' She should know this. She squinted as she envisaged Cassie, who had the bed opposite her. Cassie who always made the best hospital corners. A photo of her parents and younger sister on her locker. It was Cassie who told the others what Miss Viner had done to her.

Zannah clicked her fingers. 'Hey, where are you, remember me?'

'Sorry, I was just thinking back.'

'Good times?'

'Probably, it's complicated. There are some things we'd all probably rather forget.'

'Hey, what's with the seriousness?'

'I was quite a different person then. In fact, vastly different to eleven months ago when I first came back to England. Sorting out my mother's life has softened me.'

Zannah raised a flat palm. 'Stop right there. Emotion alert. Change of subject required. So, what shall we talk about, oh yes! Grant's charity bash. You are going, I hope? It's always such good fun and I just love Wentworth as a venue. Always looks so romantic, with its little white turrets,' she said, as she reached for the carafe of water and refilled their glasses. 'Last year the money they raised for children's cancer charities was phenomenal – Oh, my goodness! look who's just walked in.'

Mia turned. Two men were requesting a table. One was very tall and dark with fashionable stubble. His shoulders were broad and strong. Well-developed chest muscles nestled under his grey t-shirt. He turned to talk to a waiter. His jeans hugged his taut backside. The other man was slightly shorter, with dirty blond hair and very blue eyes but not as athletic as the first. Zannah wiggled herself out of her seat to greet them, hugging the handsome dark-haired one first.

'Drake! Lovely to see you. It's been ages.'

He gave a crinkly eyed grin. 'Well, you're never at home when I drop by, always at the office. I think she does it on purpose,' he said to the other man, who was waiting, arms outstretched, for his hug.

'That's because she prefers her men with brains, not brawn. Come here you lovely, gorgeous lady.' He pulled her into a bear hug embrace. 'And have a bit of real man.'

'Paul, you're an impossible flirt. How does Cissy put up with you?'

'She doesn't – he's never at home,' said the one she'd called Drake. Perhaps sensing her eyes on him, he looked in Mia's direction, the smile slid from his face. He raised a finger to his chin, rubbing it along the grove, still staring, then looked away.

Mia picked up her coffee cup pretending to drink, even though her cup was empty.

Zannah returned to the table, the men followed. 'Boys, this is my friend Mia Croxley-Smith. Mia, meet Drake and Paul, they are business partners. They run a successful landscape gardening company.'

Mia stood up. Paul pushed forward to shake hands.

'Please to meet you, Mia. Zannah always gets it wrong,' he said sliding an arm around her shoulder.

'What have I got wrong? That *is* what you do.' Zannah objected.

Paul waved his hands around like a conductor. 'Not quite. We are magicians, we create, plan, design, colour coordinate, and build anything from a water feature to a folly, whatever you need or desire. Your space is our fantasy.' He swept a bow in front of Mia.

'Idiot,' Zannah giggled, giving him a playful punch.

Drake didn't join in the banter, and his expression was unreadable. Not wishing to be rude, Mia addressed him smiling. 'And you, Drake, which bit do you do?'

'Me,' he said poking a finger at his chest. 'I'm just a gardener. I mainly fetch and carry.'

'Very hands-on,' Zannah said with a hint of innuendo and a snort of laughter.

Drake's expression and steely gaze conflicted with his previous pleasure at seeing Zannah. He backed away from the table. The action wasn't lost on Mia nor that he hadn't offered his hand in greeting.

'Paul and I have a business to discuss, so if you will excuse us, Zannah, we won't join you.' Paul opened his mouth to say something but a glance from Drake silenced him. Drake dipped and dropped a kiss on Zannah's cheek before moving to an empty table, completely ignoring Mia.

Mia felt wrong-footed by the encounter. Drake made it obvious he'd not wanted to join them purely because of her. He'd looked at her so coldly, but why? She didn't even know him. *What the hell?*

CHAPTER 26

THE niggling memory of her encounter with Drake the night before had put Mia in a bad mood. No matter how hard she tried to convince herself that maybe it was just his manner and nothing at all to do with her, it didn't work.

'Well sod you, Drake, whatever your name is I'll probably never meet you again. See, you're not going to ruin my day.'

Nursing a cup of coffee, she took in her surroundings, a cold, hard space – impersonal, empty like her fridge, and her love life. It lacked anything meaningful. *Well, that's easy to put right. Something I can be in control of.* She wandered from room to room, making a list of what she might buy to make her flat less a hotel and more a home.

Four hours later she struggled home, exhausted but delighted with her purchases. She chose a pallet of turquoise and mint green to lift the nonentity of what surrounded her. The distressed wooden photo frames for her units brought instant colour to the living room, even though she had no idea what she was going to put in them. Perhaps some nice photos of her mother. A pair of watercolours, in muted blues with lacquered silver frames, for the bedroom wall. Another, larger, as a feature for the lounge wall, would be delivered. She'd get the maintenance guy to hang them for her, along with the wall rug for the dining room. The scatter cushions took the edge off the cold leather seating. The artisan pewter bowl looked at home in the middle of the dining table filled with fresh fruit. Mia stood back admiring the transformation.

She had never cooked anything from scratch, her newly acquired spice rack taunted her. She'd never followed a recipe book, so today she impressed herself with a plate of stir-fried vegetables, to which she added prawns and a dash of soy sauce. While she ate her supper, she set up her laptop and typed "Grace Denning" into the search bar. As the page loaded, Mia coughed as the food caught in her throat.

'My God, Grace, it *is* you,' she spluttered. Her eyes widened as she read about Grace's husband Tom's philandering and subsequent siring of multiple children. 'Not the safe husband I predicted, Grace; you married a celebrity!' Mia had heard of the Globetrotter programmes and Tom was regularly featured in magazines she'd read.

There was a link to Grace's programme, *What a Thing to Find Out*. Mia watched mesmerised and slightly proud, as Grace interviewed with both compassion and humour. It was compelling viewing.

'Good for you Grace,' she muttered, impressed at her friend's success. Clearing away her supper things, she returned to her laptop and typed "Cassandra Castle", remembering Cassie's full name but found nothing. Another name from the past was Sophie, but *her* surname still eluded Mia.

Both probably married and changed their names anyway.

She returned to Grace and her rise to fame until a text buzzed into her phone.

Sorry to hear the sad news. Understand if charity night is a no go. G x

She immediately replied.

Thanx Grant, but I've said enough goodbyes – some hellos would be a refreshing change. Looking forward to it.

Well, that sorted out what she was doing tomorrow – buying a dress to wear on Friday. Zannah said she was going solo, a shame Mia thought as she'd have loved to try out the escort agency, but what if who she chose was one of Zannah's favourites – embarrassing. No, she'd leave that for another time.

The emerald green shot-silk dress wrapped perfectly around her slim body. A pair of strappy sandals and a clutch bag topped off her outfit, she'd debated whether to put her hair up but decided against it, deciding that it might be too formal for the occasions.

An hour later the taxi swept up the long drive. Zannah had been right, the building was impressive. Majestically resting at the top of an incline, its castellated walls were standing proud, like a fairy-tale castle.

Her taxi driver joined a queue of Porsches, Mercedes and Bentleys trying to park near the entrance. Mia drew in a sharp breath. Drake was standing close to the entrance, a tall-stemmed glass in his hand, chatting to an older man. Well, that put a damper on the evening for a start, she'd not even considered the possibility of him being here. From his vantage point, he would be able to scrutinise her as she walked up the incline.

She leant forward. 'Can you drive on a bit further and I'll walk back.' The driver pulled the taxi out of the waiting line and drove on past the building.

'This will do fine. Thank you.' She paid him and climbed from the cab, smoothed down her dress and, with a flick of her head, was ready for her entrance. The shoes, she discovered too late, were made for standing, not walking. She teetered her way around to the entrance, dreading she'd walk straight into Drake. Mutterings and laughter led her forward, through the tall oak doors and into a galleried hall awash with people, colour, and noise. She accepted a glass of champagne from a silver tray. Grant spotted her and waved over the heads of his guests as he made his way towards her.

'You're here - great,' he said, kissing her on both cheeks, then cupping her elbow guiding her to the centre of a group. 'Let me introduce you to the rest of the Oakridge team.'

Mia relaxed; Drake was nowhere to be seen. Grant excused himself and his PA, Stella, took charge of introducing Mia to TV celebrities, none of whom she recognised. Not the football heroes from the past nor the ageing pop singer, but it didn't matter. She was out, and meeting people, even talk of the day's golf and banter about rusty putting, had her laughing. She was having a wonderful time, didn't realise how much she'd missed this: flirtatious comments, innuendo, giggling, smiles from strangers, some glamour in her life. Her eyes drifted upwards to the plinths supporting gigantic floral displays. Crystal glassed reflected lights from mammoth chandeliers, as endless flutes of champagne and delicate canapes were passed amongst the guests. Mia supped greedily.

A toastmaster called them to dinner; with everyone else, she shuffled along to the panelled ballroom.

Stella caught up with her. 'Have you seen the table plan, so you know where you're sitting?'

Mia shook her head.

'I think you're on table five.' Stella broke away to check the table planner. Mia waited. 'Yep table five. You'll have a great view of the cabaret. Enjoy.'

The throng of people peeled off to their respective tables. Mia spotted Zannah but couldn't catch her eye so made her way to her table. The four seated guests introduced themselves, others joined them and seated, boy-girl style, including a woman with a dress so pink it hurt Mia's eyes.

The noisier tables to the rear of the room were mostly stag. A James Dashwood sat on her right. He was attentive, continually topping up her glass. Aware of movement to her left she turned. Her smile froze as Drake took his seat beside her. Everyone appeared to know him from the witty exchanges. His smile faltered as their eyes met. She looked away, challenged herself to be nice and make the most of the evening.

The room quietened as the compere took the stage, thanking Oakridge Homes for the excellent day's golf and hospitality, before handing over the mic to Grant.

'Good evening everyone. Thank you for your support of Oakridge Homes 6th annual charity day. Raising funds for Shooting Stars, supporting children with cancer.'

There were cheers and whooping from the back. Drake turned his chair away from her, making conversation unnecessary.

'Last year,' Grant continued, 'we raised forty-six thousand pounds.'

Mia joined in the round of applause and drained her glass.

'We hope to smash that target this year, so I'd like to thank all of you,' he ran a pointed finger across the room, 'for your generous donations so far this evening.' He grinned before adding. 'I would bid on the golfing week in St Lucia, but I think the wife might have something to say about that...' More noise from the rear of the room. 'Now enjoy your evening and empty those wallets.'

Drake started a conversation with the dainty blonde in the candyfloss chiffon. James topped up Mia's glass and made polite chit-chat as she enjoyed her smoked salmon starter.

Apart from Drake, the atmosphere at their table was amiable. Mia joined in the conversations and traditional jokes about golf widows. The table quietened to more intimate conversations as they tucked into their mains.

With the alcohol loosening her tongue, Mia turned in Drake's direction.

'So, Drake - that's an unusual name?'

'Not to me it's not,' he said, slicing through a piece of meat not bothering to make eye contact.

She felt the need to stand her ground. 'It was a question, not a statement.'

He leant towards her, his eyes still focused on his plate.

'Ah, I see. Well, if you want to know if Sir Frances was a distant relation – he wasn't. And no, my parents didn't have a duck fetish either, they just liked the name.'

He tore off a piece of bread to mop up the juices on his plate. Mia's disdain for him mounted as she realised she was on the brink of saying something rude. Her eyes flashed.

'Why don't you just pick up your plate and lick it?'

Christ did I just say that!

He lay down his knife and fork, his face darkened.

'Look, I enjoy my food and I'm sorry if you don't like the way I eat but frankly, I don't care what you think of me. And if it's just an observation, then perhaps you'll allow *me* to make one. The wine on the table is for everyone, not just you, and a drunken woman is not a particularly attractive thing to observe.'

Bristling, she grabbed his arm.

'You obnoxious knob, I'm not drunk, although sitting next to you, I could be forgiven for drinking. And another thing,' she hissed into his ear. 'I'd learnt *not* to judge a book by its cover, but in your case, I'll make the exception.'

Drake picked up his napkin and blotted his mouth, pushed back his chair then lowered his head to speak directly into Mia's ear.

'I don't pretend to be anything I'm not, but I suggest you start on the coffee and leave the wine alone, *Maureen.*'

Her head snapped back. *What did he just say?* Before she could challenge him, he had stridden away from the table. The breath that she had been holding escaped in a puff. Her head spun, not from the effects of the alcohol but shock. Had he just called her Maureen?

A comedian took the stage. There was applause and a song. The jokes came thick and fast, mainly aimed at Grant or the B-list celebrities. Mia didn't laugh. She sat in stunned silence. He *had.* He'd called her Maureen.

CHAPTER 27

THE day started with two paracetamol and a strong black coffee. Mia was unsure as to what extent the alcohol was to blame for her headache or the fact that she hadn't slept well. Her conversation with Drake replayed in her head over and over. How on earth did he know her name? And what else did he know? She became anxious. His knowledge could threaten everything she'd created, her new life, her social standing, her future. He'd rattled her cage all right, maybe it was time she found out more about who he was.

She flipped open her laptop. Damn! Drake who? How could she find out? Zannah would want to know why if she asked her. Grant probably the same. Stella would be easiest.

'Stella, it's Mia Croxley-Smith. I just wanted to thank you for a wonderful evening last night. It must have taken so much work to organise!'

'Glad you enjoyed it. Yes, it's a bit of a headache, we have a two-month gap before we start planning the next one. We're all a bit exhausted today, half the staff aren't in yet.'

'Well I had a lovely evening, please pass on my thanks to Grant, no doubt you'll speak to him before I do,' she paused before continuing. 'Oh, by the way. I was sitting next to Drake somebody, last night. I understand he's a landscape designer. I have a friend who's looking for one. You don't have his details to hand, do you? I seem to have lost his card.'

Stella read out the details. Mia thanked her, before hanging up and hastily tapping "Quaid & Tenielle Landscapes" into her keyboard. *J Quaid Landscape and Design.*

Established in 1954 by Joseph Quaid, originally a nurseryman sup-
plying plants and shrubs to retail outlets. The Landscaping and design
company evolved from there. The two directors, Drake Quaid, and Paul
Tenielle have an impressive portfolio of clients...

'Quaid.' She spoke the name out loud several times, hoping the
more she said it, the more meaning it would have. That wasn't the
case. The aggravation of not knowing stayed with her for most of
the day as she tried frantically to figure out how he knew her as
Maureen. The damn thing was driving her nuts but at least she
had a booking to go to that would take her mind off it. Perhaps, if
she thought less about it, she might remember more.

Mia didn't enjoy her current booking. Thankfully it was only
a four-day holiday cover. The client, Mr Dolby, was flabby and
sweaty, his desk overflowing with papers. It was her job to put
them into order, prepare the data and create spreadsheets for a pre-
sentation he was due to make.

Mr Dolby, who she had nicknamed Mr Blobby, wobbled his
way past her desk. She stifled a giggle at his choice of footwear
– red, crocodile-skin cowboy boots. They were a most unlikely
combination. On top of that, he wore them with a yellow shirt
and creased, grey Farrah trousers.

The work was tedious, and Mr Dolby's desk was directly behind
hers, leaving her unable to check her emails. The day dragged.
The clock suggested another two hours to complete her remit. Mia
toyed with the idea of speeding up and leaving early, but she'd committed to this assignment so had to see it through. Plus, she'd spent
quite a lot recently and whilst her bonus payment remained intact,
it was essential to top the pot up occasionally – losing two hours
pay wasn't going to help.

Lifting her bag from under her desk, she headed for the loo. It
was the only place she could plausibly vanish to without causing
suspicion.

With her mobile switched to silent, Mia scrolled through her
emails. There was one from the undertakers to say that Constance's
ashes were ready for collection and a Save The Date for the Chartley Reunion. She didn't need reminding; it was engraved on her

brain. The only other engagement in her diary was an appointment with her solicitor. Thankfully, Gina's solicitors had forced her to drop her allegations, but even with that problem resolved Mia had delayed the meeting with Mr Mead. Alone thinking about it made her chest feel heavy with apprehension. But it was her duty, after all, to carry out her mother's requests. There might be clues to explain why Constance had chosen Mutter's Moor.

Finally home, Mia unlocked her mailbox and carried her post to the lift; she sifted through them, mostly bills, but one from the crematorium with leaflets on rose bushes, plaques, and entries into books of remembrance. She sighed deeply. No one wanted to be reminded of death. A glass of wine was what she needed. She changed out of her work clothes and placed her shoes on the rack. The peacock bag beckoned her – it had been pushed further into the recesses of the wardrobe because she didn't want to consider that it had been the cause of her mother's fall. You couldn't see it, hidden behind skirts and trousers, but it was there. Waiting, like some ghastly holder of secrets.

'Come on then, let's get this over with.' She reached out to touch the soft leather handle and dragged the bag forward, displacing shoes from racks and dresses from hangers. More mess to tidy up. 'Bag you are a ruddy nuisance.' Her lip began to tremble, this bag had meant so much to Constance - she would never be parted from it. Falling back onto the bed, Mia crushed the precious bag to her – it weighted heavy on her ribcage. She lay still staring at the ceiling. She felt overcome with grief, her thoughts jumped from one to the other as miscellaneous memories came to mind. A shared ice cream. A fluffy cat. Where did that come from? They hadn't ever owned a cat.

Her mobile trilled. She welcomed the distraction, lay the bag beside her and answered it. The number was one she didn't recognise... *Probably a cold call.* She prepared herself for a sickly-sweet voice to ask how her day was going.

A male voice said, 'Is that Mia?'

She hesitated. Did she recognise that voice? It couldn't be, could it?

'Speaking.'

'Mia, It's Drake, Drake Quaid. Zannah gave me your number. I rang to apologise.'

Mia rolled her eyes, the last person she wanted to talk to right now was the obnoxious Drake Quaid. She'd only clapped eyes on him twice and neither time had been agreeable, *and* he'd called her Maureen.

'For what exactly?' she replied, her voice as cold and flat as she could level it. She had no wish to be friendly.

'I was rude to you. In fact, I was *very* rude to you. Zannah told me you just buried your mother. I think, under the circumstances, you deserved a drink.'

What a condescending… 'I beg your pardon what exactly do you mean by that? Do you mean it's okay for me to be a bit tipsy because my mother died? And by the way, she was cremated not buried. Or do you mean you are not normally rude unless, of course, it's me you're talking to?'

'I'm sorry I… That came out all wrong.'

'I think, Mister Quaid, that it has been the case ever since we met. I obviously offended you in some way, but I do not need your apology, or anything else from you, for that matter.'

'Mia, it's not that; it's just…'

'Just what? Zannah pricked your conscience, so you felt obliged to call. Well please be assured, Mister Quaid, I don't need your sympathy.' With great satisfaction, she cut him off – within seconds he rang back. She rejected the call and switched her phone off. That felt good. He'd allowed her to tell him exactly what she thought of him, and this time he'd called her Mia, not Maureen; perhaps she'd misheard the other night.

Mia went to the fridge and poured herself a glass of wine, her hand still trembling from the encounter. She wanted to put Drake Quaid out of her mind and decided to busy herself cooking supper from scratch, from a *show you how* website. Previously, she'd considered it a chore, but now it had almost become a hobby. Her thoughts wandered to Sardinia, to Teresa or the cook they had in the Barcelona Villa, when mouth-watering smells were filtering through the house. Then an earlier memory – a cook at home, pre-boarding school. Her father shouting at a woman wearing a sari who was crying, wiping her eyes on her apron. Green, the apron was green with a big pocket. He was telling her to get out of his house when he'd caught Mia watching from the back door. The cold stare had made her turn and flee to her hiding place. Why had he been so angry? Was it, now she had the benefit of hindsight, because the woman had had a coloured skin? Their normal cook, Mrs Barber, had been a chubby lady with big hands. There was no recollection of the other woman, perhaps Mrs Barber had been sick, and she the replacement – fact or imagination?

CHAPTER 28

M<small>R</small> Mead welcomed her into his office. 'Please take a seat, Miss Croxley-Smith.'

'Please call me Mia. Croxley-Smith is such a mouthful.'

He smiled, 'Thank you, it is rather,' before settling himself at his desk, a blue folder in his hands. 'Now where did we get to? Ah yes. As we discussed at our previous meeting with Mrs Evans, your mother left her estate to you. There was a private income from a family trust that she rarely touched.' He pushed a paper across the desk for her to view.

Mia examined it. 'I don't understand. I dealt with all of the paperwork. I didn't know this account existed.'

'Probably not. As you can see, it's in your mother's maiden name. She, er, wanted it kept that way.'

'Away from my father you mean?'

Mr Mead taped the tips of his fingers together but didn't comment.

Mia read the document shaking her head. 'I can't believe she did this for me and not just recently, which would have made more sense.'

'A nice surprise then?'

'Very much so. I'm renting now and everything is so expensive.' She held the paper to her chest and closed her eyes for a brief moment. 'Oh, Mummy thank you. Thank you.'

When she opened them, Mr Mead was smiling. 'That's the part of my job I enjoy, giving good news. I'll arrange for the transfer to your account.'

'Thank you, and can I give you these for safekeeping?' She handed him the life policies her father had taken for Gina's children.'

'I'll pass them on to your father's solicitor for safekeeping. We still hold some documents in the archive, I'll request them for you.'

'Thank you. I haven't been through her personal belongings yet. I keep putting it off.'

'Of course. A natural reaction I'm sure.' He sat back in his chair tapping a ballpoint pen against the top of an index finger. 'I take it you'll have no problem fulfilling your mother's last requests, vis-a-vis her remains?'

'None at all. I'll drive down to Devon as soon as I have them.' Frowning she got to her feet, 'Funny request, isn't it? I guess the location meant something to her. I haven't discovered what yet. I didn't know my adoptive parents very well.'

Mr Mead cleared his throat, pushed himself to his feet and handed her the file.

'I'll see you out.' He held the door open for her and offered his hand. Mia took it. 'Best of luck, Mia. Don't hesitate to call if you need any help with anything. Anything at all.'

Mia sat on the bench near the bridge on the river Mole, glancing from the blue folder on the bench beside her to the painted ladies flitting from head-to-head a fluffy white cow-parsley, leisurely opening, and closing their wings to the sun. They had had many butterflies in the villa gardens, Rufus was always passing comment. She smiled, savouring the warmth of the sun on her skin as a moorhen guided its chicks to the safety of the wild yellow iris and celandines on the opposite bank.

Celandines, the wildflowers at the crematorium. I'll never know who left them. Someone who cared, like Rufus.

She linked her fingers resting them in her lap; reflecting how appallingly she'd behaved. She tried drafting another letter to Rufus in her head.

Dear Rufus,

I hope you found someone to share your life with, someone less shallow than I was. You're a good man. I'm so sorry I hurt you. It was right that you disowned me. Cast me adrift like that log floating past right now – how far will it drift before it finds a place to stay.

Thing is, you have no idea that having my back against the wall's forced me to become a better person, learn and explore new talents I never knew I had.

And then, the most wonderful thing of all, if I hadn't been here with nowhere to go, I wouldn't have discovered my mother loved me. I'll never understand it all, but I never knew that Gina had been so spiteful and intercepted our letters, letters that showed I've always been loved, that Constance had written back. I hadn't been abandoned. I don't know why I want to tell you this now when I had so much opportunity before. Mummy sent birthday cards too they just never left the house. If only I'd known, I might have been stronger, and Miss Viner might not have spotted a weakness in me. But you never knew about her either. I was too ashamed.

No, it didn't feel right. Not yet. And why did she mention Miss Viner? He wouldn't know what she was talking about. She'd leave it for now and write it another time.

CHAPTER 29

Constance's ashes sat on the cabinet between the two empty picture frames. Mia had got into the habit of talking to the urn, greeting her mum's remains with a cheery good morning and blowing it a kiss at night. She accepted that she couldn't do this forever but was she ready to let her go just yet?

The weather forecast said sunny spells. Mia questioned the suitability of transporting her mother's ashes in the shiny white Prada carrier bag with its snazzy silver handles – leftover from her past. A rucksack would have been a better option, but she didn't own one. So far, her plans to scatter the ashes had been scuppered, both by bad weather and a desire of not wanting to let her go, but now there was no excuse. The thought of the long drive and faf of hiring a car felt overwhelming; Mia convinced herself that Constance would have preferred her last journey to be by train, much better for them both.

Mia settled in her seat, enjoying the ever-changing scenery where the imposing corporate buildings and industrial parks were replaced by green hills and deep valleys with black-faced sheep staring in the direction of the passing train. Tractor trails in cornfields left symbolic swirls and tracks with dead ends. How beautiful was England?

Above her on the luggage rack, her largest suitcase held the peacock-embroidered bag. When she got to Sidmouth, she promised herself that she'd carefully go through it before saying goodbye the Constance.

There were no available taxis at Honiton station, but within minutes a green double-decker arrived. Mia couldn't recall ever riding one before. Sitting on the top deck, she heard the swishing and dragging of summer-heavy boughs across the thin metallic roof. She peered down into cottage gardens and up at hills beyond. The view was exhilarating, and she experienced the pure child-like excitement of butterflies in her stomach.

In the distance, the triangle of sea expanded as the bus drew closer. It became her focus; she couldn't wait to breathe in its salty air, take a stroll and stretch her legs. She hoped there was sand – such a simple thing she'd taken for granted previously.

The plan had been to stay a single night, but the charming regency town had already started her thinking of extending her stay. After all, she'd nothing to rush back for.

The taxi swept eastwards along a smart seafront where Regency hotels and mellow-coloured buildings nestled in the vee below terracotta cliffs topped with an expanse of green in front of trees standing upwards like broccoli stalks against the sky. Mia felt her heart swell, this was just what she needed. The road rose and parted, and Mia could see her hotel on the right, prominently settled on the rise of the hill, with an open-air pool alongside a stone terrace, flanked by stunning gardens.

A nice place to sit and get her bearings, she thought. The taxi pulled in front of the entrance and her eyes took in the original Regency design in redbrick seamlessly merging with modern decor. Glass doors opened up, leading into a small reception. A porter appeared from a side door, a slightly built man with silver hair and a jutting jaw. He showed her to a lift the size of a telephone box.

'Sorry 'bout the size of the lift. Rest of hotels bein done up, this'll be next. I'm Sam, anything you want, just ask. We're a friendly lot in Sidmouth.'

Mia flattened herself against the side as Sam clamped the lift doors and pressed buttons. The lift stopped with a jolt. He pulled back the concertina metal door then pushed open another outer one, then turned left and walked along a short corridor.

'Make sure you close the outer gate,' Sam said in his heavy Devonshire accent. 'Otherwise, ain't nobody else getting' up. This 'n's yours.' He unlocked a door and stood back to let her pass.

Her face registered disappointment.

'Now don't be thinking you ain't getting something nice. We have rooms twice as big and what they call refurbished. Poshed-up I call it but look out that window. Best view of Lyme Bay in Sidmouth.'

Mia stepped towards the window – it had a deep sill, the sort you could sit on or work at. Her chest swelled with pleasure as she leant forward and took in the view.

'Oh, it's beautiful. Stunning.'

The clouds had parted, azure blue punctuated their whiteness. Pretty houses with thatched roofs dotted the cliff edge. Her tiredness evaporated. Renewed energy made her want to freshen up, get out and explore.

'Thank you, it's perfect.'

'Good. Glad you likes it. It's one of me favourites, even if it is the smallest room but we's fully booked you see. Don't know why they always leaves it to last. Can see for miles both ways if you bother to look.'

Mia showered and changed into a strappy cream t-shirt and linen trousers. She removed the urn placing it on the windowsill and stood back to confirm that it sat in the exact middle of the sill.

'See you later, Mummy. Enjoy the view.'

She reached the door and her hand hovered over the door handle. Turning back, she picked up the shiny paper carrier and placed the urn back in the bag. 'On second thought, let's take you on a trip down memory lane.'

Mia walked out into the sunlight and stood for a moment, taking in the rooftops of the town below snuggling into the bay. The tide was out and the sandy beach dotted with people enjoying themselves.

She'd done little research so far but assumed the great hill in front of her to the west of the town was Peak Hill, her mother's final resting place.

A voice from behind made her turn.

'Never get tired of that view,' Sam said, 'makes me think what a lucky chap I is to live here.'

'Very lucky indeed.'

They fell into step and started their descent. 'Follow me - this 'n's a shortcut.' Sam led her across a tarmacked path, passing the swimming pool enclosed by a low shrub hedge.

'Have you lived here long?' Mia enquired.

'Man, and boy. Never found a reason to leave. Went to London once - awful place, all noise and people.'

She nodded a silent agreement.

'No, Sidmouth'll see me out. I have family here as well. The wife passed but I have my son and two granddaughters who keep my pockets empty.'

'Have you always worked in hotels?'

'No. No. Started on the railway. It closed years back now. Silly buggers built it too far out of town. Idea was to keep it posh, discourage day-trippers. Daft idea, but it seems to have saved us from going the way that Seaton and Beer have – all candyfloss, and shops selling rubbish. Mind you, 'avin' a sandy beach helps.'

They were almost on level ground; Sam halted their progress.

'See that hotel that looks like a small castle down there? Union Jack on the flagpole?'

'Oh yes. It's quite pretty. Looks a bit odd stuck between the two larger hotels.'

'Aye but it's a bit special. You ought a look while you're 'ere. Queen Victoria stayed there as a littlun. Almost got killed. The bullet holes marked in the window. You interested in history?'

Mia answered honestly. 'Not really. Well I mean I did it at school, but not local or anything like that.'

'Well, there's plenty here. More blue plaques than you can shake a stick at,' he chuckled. 'Got a nice little museum on Church Street too if you fancy a look. Near the church. We're proud of that too.'

They had reached the bottom of the hill and crossed to the esplanade.

'How long you on holiday for then?'

'No, not a holiday,' Mia hesitated. Sam had been so friendly and engaging that she had the urge to share but out of habit held back, 'I'm only here for the night, have a few things to do. Then back to London.'

Sam grunted disapproval. 'Shame, lovely place. Lots to see,' he scratched his ear whilst checking his watch. 'Right I'm orf for me break, back to work at five. I like to get away, sort of spaces out me day a bit. If it's the shops you want if you go along here till you come to where the big pub, Drake's, is then you come to...'

Mia stopped him. *Drake's*? Just the name made her blood rise. 'Thank you but I'm not here to shop. I'm on my way up there.' She indicated the high cliff ahead of them. 'I'm going to take a walk up Mutter's Moor. Looks steeper than I thought now I'm closer. Glad I have the right shoes.'

They both stared down at her feet snuggling in soft cream pumps. Mia frowned, realising they were far from being the right shoes.

Sam laid a hand on her arm. 'None of my business, but I think you need something with laces. And you say you want to go up Mutter's Moor?'

'Yes, yes that's right.'

'Then you be taking the wrong route,' he gave a sharp jolt of his head. 'That be Salcombe Hill. Mutter's is the way you just come - top 'a Peak Hill.'

Mia looked back the way she'd come. Above her hotel, buildings with dark thatched roofs clung to the cliff's edge. The road wound upwards before vanishing into the greenery. Only a few scattered properties hugged the hillside. The incline didn't look as steep as Salcombe Hill, but it did seem longer, more drawn out. Disappointment clouded her face.

Sam tutted. 'It's not for me to say, lady, but I think it might be good for you to get your bearings before you start making off in the wrong direction. Both are big climbs. Mind you, I used to run up them in my day,' he said, chuckling dryly. 'Now if it were me, I'd walk along the seafront till I gots near the Lifeboat station. From there you can see the tourist office and get a map. They're all free. Well, I'd best go. Have a good day. We got rain coming in later, but it will be gone by morning.' He waved goodbye over his shoulder and left her.

The quaint streets of Sidmouth were a joy to roam, Sam was right, for a seaside town there was a surprising lack of tat. She located a sports shop and bought a pair of trainers; if she were to make it up that hill, she needed the right footwear. En route to the till she spied a display of sturdy rucksacks. On impulse, she selected one and a blue waterproof hooded jacket. A cagoule, the retail assistant had called it. The woman showed surprise when Mia produced the Prada bag, lifted out the urn and placed it snugly into the rucksack. Perfect fit.

'Would you mind putting this in your bin for me please?' she said as she handed over the glossy white carrier bag. The woman gave her a sideways look as she took it from her. Mia shot her a winning smile, 'Thank you so much that is most kind.'

The cagoule turned out to be a godsend. The rain that Sam had promised blew in from the sea. She took refuge in one of the elegant hotels guarding the seafront. The rain thrashed against the windows as blobs of colour passed by, people running to cars or seeking shelter. As she sipped her cappuccino, Mia gave her attention to the maps and leaflets she'd obtained from the Tourist Information Centre. A sensation of happiness warmed her as she tried to imagine her mother carefree and as unbuttoned as she could be – everything she hadn't been when Mia'd known her.

Sidmouth was famous for its annual Folk Festival, she screwed up her eyes. Could she imagine a younger Constance free and happy, laughing, not a care in the world? She opened them again shaking her head. Did her mother dance barefoot? It seemed so unlikely, but then so was the funeral music.

A leaflet advertised this year's event – there were pictures of hundreds of happy dancing smiles and yes, most were barefoot. Suddenly, Sidmouth didn't feel an odd choice. Constance had been happy here. Mia felt as though she'd swallowed a question mark as she tried to balance the two personalities. How had Constance ever come to marry Charles Croxley-Smith? It was such a contradiction.

CHAPTER 30

THE weather, as Sam predicted, cleared overnight and Mia woke to a chalky blue sky with tufts of white meringue dotted across the skyline. She inhaled deeply, feeling joyous at the new day.

'Morning, Mummy, enjoying the view?' Her new trainers were laid out ready, she tied a cotton jumper around her shoulders, just in case the blue skies and shimmering sea were deceptive.

'Just going for a run, Mummy, I'll be back soon.' She bypassed the lift and skipped down the two flights of stairs to reception. It was deserted. She checked her watch; 6.15 a.m. She suspected chefs and waiters toiled behind the scenes somewhere. Stepping through the sliding doors, she sucked in a satisfying gulp of fresh salty air.

'Morning, Miss.'

Mia turned, smiling, to see Sam with a hosepipe. 'Wouldn't have thought you'd have needed that after all that rain.'

Sam exposed bare gums, where his top set should be. 'I know, right kerfuffle this is, but the 'angin' baskets on this side don't get no rain. Roof covers 'em. You off for a walk up the moor then? Lovely day for it.'

'No, not yet maybe later. Thought I'd have a jog around the town while it's quiet. I seem to have got quite fond of the place already. Everyone's so friendly. I've been living abroad for years, so it's been a refreshing change.' There she was again, opening up to a stranger. 'In Esher, everyone goes about their business, rushing down the A3 into London, no one has time to stop and chat, and I'm as guilty as the next.'

Sam chuckled, twisting the hose's nozzle until the flow of water dribbled to a stop.

'You call it friendly, I calls it nosey. Daughter says we're all guilty of that in Sidmouth. Want to know everyone's whys and where's. Well, I'd better get on, or the guests won't have a newspaper to read in bed 'afore breakfast.'

Mia took the path to the steps and down to the road. There were two cottages on the opposite side, both had blue plaques. She crossed the road and read one of them before continuing her journey downhill, speeding up as she remembered she had to vacate her room by eleven and there was still the task of taking the path up Mutter's Moor to scatter her mother's ashes. The thought provoked a feeling of panic that battered beneath her breastbone. It was all happening too quickly. Was she ready to say goodbye?

When Mia returned from her run, Sam was moving suitcases into a cupboard behind reception.

'How did the climb go?'

Mia wrinkled her nose. 'I'm afraid I haven't done it yet.'

His expression showed no surprise. 'Well if there's no rush, I think your room is free till Tuesday.'

Mia shook her head. 'Oh goodness. Another night perhaps, but I have to get back to London.'

Sam pursed his lips. 'I can talk to housekeeping 'bout the room. Think on it over breakfast.'

The charming maître d' seated Mia by the window. The stunning view of Lyme Bay provoked an unexpected sense of belonging. There was no denying she was beginning to fall in love with the town's quaintness; it piqued her interest to know more about the place that was special to Constance.

Reluctantly she left the table, dragging herself away from the vertical view of the esplanade, with its smattering of dog walkers and late joggers, and returned to her room.

Her hands caressed the urn. 'Ok, Mother, let's move you over here and see what stories you have to tell.' She placed the urn to the side of her mother's embroidered bag on the dressing table that doubled as a desk. It would have been easier to upend the bag and tip the contents onto the bed, but she wanted to take her time. If there were surprises, then she wanted to savour them. Her fingers stroked the soft fabric of the tie. She pulled it free of the bag.

'Now, what are you doing in here?' She wrapped the tie twice around the neck of the urn before tying it in a formal knot. 'There you go, Mum, look after that.'

Like a child with a lucky-dip bag, she fished around for the lone photograph of the swarthy smart-suited man with a polka dot tie, took it and propped it up against the kettle at the corner of the desk; she imagined he smiled back at her. The next thing Mia extracted was a bundle of papers held by an elastic band. The outer edges were dog-eared from handling. She released the band and selected the folded paper from the top of the pile of It was a festival programme for a John Kirkpatrick, who sang and danced with a "Morris Rapper." Mia had never heard of such a thing, Morris dancers yes, but rappers? She seriously doubted that Snoop Dog or Ice Cube featured amongst the attendees. Most of them probably weren't even born.

The flyers dated back to July 1967, but the last was from 1973. So, she'd probably been right about her mother holidaying here. Gina being the eldest made her wonder if she'd come along as well or stayed home with Lisa.

A hollow sadness made her close her eyes, as she envisaged Gina holding her mother's hand paddling through the cold surf. She pictured them making sandcastles, buying ice cream. The moistness found its way to her cheeks again. Rising stiffly, Mia slipped into the bathroom and washed her face. Glancing at her watch, it was twelve-fifteen. She should have checked out by now.

The receptionist smiled at her request. 'It's no problem at all,' she said. 'Sam thought you might want to stay longer so he told housekeeping.'

'Oh, that's brilliant,' Mia said brightly, 'but it may only be one more night.'

The receptionist grinned. 'That's what I said when I came here four years ago,' she raised her palms. 'Still here. Anyway, the room's available until Tuesday; and the sun is shining, enjoy.'

'I will,' Mia said, returning the smile, 'There's so much to see. Thanks, and if I'm still here on Wednesday, kick me out.'

Mia took the stairs back to her room, still adjusting to the fact that people were so friendly. Did it have something to do with the fact that she now found herself smiling at most people she met here? Perhaps something about the sea air and relaxed atmosphere was affecting her, she certainly felt different.

The papers lay scattered as she had left them, on her unmade bed. She placed the "*do not disturb*" sign on the door. An unmade bed was no threat; in fact, it was comforting. She roughly pulled the duvet into shape, then seated herself at the dresser-cum-desk and rested her head in cupped hands, examining her face in the mirror.

'Who are you? Mia? Maureen? Who were you before that when you were held by another set of arms? The arms that gave you up.'

It had been a while since she'd thought about where she came from and who her birth parents had been. The reason why they'd put her up for adoption. Were they still alive? Did her birth mother mark the date of her birthday each year? Had Constance known something of her mother's story from the adoption agency? Mia had never been told about the circumstances. Was there anything in the archived papers that might give her a clue?

Her tummy rumbled loudly. The sea air had given her an appetite. She took a notepad and pencil from the drawer and grabbed her bag. A glass of rosé and a salad might focus her thoughts.

She took her seat on the terrace and forked a mouthful of mackerel salad into her mouth, picked up her pen and started making a list:

Who am I? – she scribbled through it. Overdramatic.
Who was Constance - did she adopt me from choice or circumstance?
Who was my birth mother? Does it matter?
Who was my biological father? Do I need to know?
Are there other siblings?
Who is the man in the photo? What about the tie?
Why Sidmouth?
Why Mutter's Moor ? Or Peak Hill?

Lisa Farrant – was with us for years. Was she at the funeral and if so, would I have recognised her? Did she leave the wilting flowers?

'It's about time I looked her up,' Mia said, addressing herself in the mirror, 'I wonder what she knows.'

CHAPTER 31

Was it only four days that she'd been staying in Sidmouth? It seemed longer but then she had fitted so much into each day. Two mornings in a row she'd risen early and joined the joggers on the promenade. They were a friendly lot who stretched and hung around a while after their run was complete. As she said her good-byes, choruses of 'see you soon' made her stand a little taller. The warmth of their company had given her a weird sense of belonging. It was the second time that Sidmouth had felt like an emotional hug. She made her way back to the hotel reluctantly, sad that to-morrow she'd be back in Esher.

The ornate metal gate separating the hotel grounds from the street creaked as she opened it. Sam was on the terrace water-ing the hanging baskets. He lowered the hose and watched her approach.

'Morning Sam, you need a bit of oil or something on those gate hinges.'

He flashed her a gummy smile. 'It's on me list. Good run?'

'Last one.'

'So, you'll be leaving us today then?'

'Fraid so.' Mia turned in the direction of Mutter's Moor.

'Great view from up there,' Sam said following her gaze.

She made an apologetic shrug swallowing it back with a strand of guilt.

'I'm afraid I still haven't been up there. I seem to keep putting it off. But it does give me a reason to come back.'

'Make it a longer stay next time.'

'I'll try, Sam.' She held out her hand. Sam looked at it, crewed up one side of his face, rubbed his palm on his trouser leg and took hers.

'Be nice to see you back here any time.'

'Sorry Mummy, I did mean take you up the hill *and* read your secrets, but I don't want to say goodbye just yet. I promise we'll be back.' Reverently she lifted her mother's ashes, placing them in the rucksack, the spotty tie still knotted around the neck. She tucked in the ends before zipping it shut. Her train wasn't until 12.30, plenty of time to have breakfast before catching the bus to the station. Smiling to herself, she approached the dining room mischievously toying with the idea of asking for a table for two, as she'd bought Constance with her. The head waiter greeted her, she followed him to a table by the window. Usually she faced downhill, but today she set the rucksack there instead.

'There you go, Mummy, make the most of the view.'

The waitress looked at her oddly as she placed tea and toast on the table.

'Sorry, talking to myself again.'

The girl smiled, exposing a grid of wires. 'My mum does the same. I never know if she expects an answer.'

Through the window, she could see, a family posing and taking photographs of each other. How happy they looked. If only she could do the same, but the moment a camera pointed her way she wanted to run. Denying the memory, she forced it down with her tea.

How's the view Mummy? I wish you'd have asked me to bring you here when you were alive. You could have told me your story instead of making me snoop and spy through your things.

The train was relatively empty until Salisbury; from there, Mia had to clear some space on the table for other commuters. Handling the journal she'd purchased from the quaint blue-and-white gift shop along with some postcards to remind her of her stay, she couldn't help but think about the chatty jolly lady who'd served her.

They'd talked about nothing in particular, but she'd taken the time to be friendly. Mia opened the journal and wrote, *Be nice!*

So much was slopping about in her head. *I'd better get more organised.* Forming the words on paper felt cathartic. Unravelling *the mystery of Constance.* It sounded like the title of a novel. Like a fresh exercise book at school, she recorded threads of thoughts and unanswered questions, neatly and precisely, as her mother had been. Constance, she no longer thought of her as a lonely old woman seated by the window in that awful, smelly house. She'd made herself a better life, and her secrets played in Mia's head just like a game of hide-and-seek, with Mia being *it.*

CHAPTER 32

MIA had arranged to meet Lisa Farrant in a coffee shop in Richmond. She assumed she'd recognise Lisa, even though there were little stored memories to assist; more like snapshots, snippets of being pushed on a swing, sitting in a paddling pool, and being buttoned into an itchy school uniform.

Lisa arrived a few moments later, not as tall as Mia remembered, now maybe in her late 50s or early 60s.

Mia watched Lisa make her way from the counter glancing around her. She didn't stand out, her clothes were functional: a conservative pale-blue blouse with pearl buttons, the blue lifting her pale skin. Hitched across her chest was a brown no-nonsense satchel-type bag. Mia stood and waved; she noticed the threads of grey in Lisa's once coal-black hair as she drew nearer.

Mia smiled a warm welcome and although Lisa returned the greeting, there was an edginess to it. She dismissed it as nerves. After all, she'd been quite cagey about her reason for their meeting.

'Maureen, how are you? What a surprise. It's nice to see you again.' Lisa's hand was unsteady as she set her coffee cup down on the table. She squeezed into the seat opposite, lifted the strap of the bag over her head and placed in her lap. 'I was sorry to hear about Constance. So sad, such a lovely lady.' The words felt rushed, guarded. Mia searched her face for a clue. *What was her worry?* 'Sorry I can't stay long, but as I said –.' There was plumpness to her face, an age-softened jaw, deep-set eyes, and downy olive skin. Lisa's high cheekbones suggested she'd once been a beauty. Had she? Mia couldn't recall. Lisa's eyes looked everywhere except directly at her. 'It was kind of Constance to mention me in her will.' Was that it - did she think Mia was unhappy about that?

'Not at all. You looked after us well. I—'

'Well as I said. I can't stay long. I have another appointment.'

'It's kind of you to come.' Mia attempted to level her thoughts; she'd said in her note they'd meet at Lisa's convenience, so why set a time that wasn't? She'd expected more. This didn't sit right. Lisa had seemed fine when they'd spoken on the phone and Mia had said she wanted to pick her brains about a few things.

'So how have you been?' Mia asked with an open smile. Hoping that would make Lisa feel more comfortable.

'Good, yes thank you. but I don't know what you want to know. As I explained, it was a long time ago and I've worked in many households, they all become a bit jumbled in my mind.'

Mia couldn't hide her disappointment. 'I was hoping you were one of those people who kept a diary, notes on the family, that sort of thing.'

Lisa drew her teeth across her bottom lip, her eyes shifting left to right – table to coffee and back again.

'Not really. I did have a memory box. It's in the loft, I think. Or it could be under the stairs. I haven't seen it in years. It was where I travelled to with the families, holidays, and the like. What exactly is it you want from me?'

Strange way of putting it, why didn't she just say how can I help?

Mia unclipped her handbag and pushed the photograph across the table.

'I've been trying to solve a mystery. Do you know who this is?'

Lisa bent her head and briefly glanced at it, then shook her head.

'Sorry. No. Never seen him before.' She placed a finger on the image and slid it back across the table. 'There weren't that many callers in those days and Constance didn't have many friends.'

She's lying.

'Please. You can tell me anything, you don't need to pretty it up ...' She pushed the photo back across the table.

Lisa barely gave it a glance. 'I said, I don't know him.' Mia waited as she picked up her coffee cup, raised it to her lips then put it down without drinking. 'Your father was a bit…'

'I think the word you're looking for is bastard – not to mention a racist bully. Listen, let's not beat around the bush. He wasn't a nice man. I just need the truth. This is about my mother, not him. I thought Constance was an open book, but she keeps surprising me.'

Lisa nodded for longer than was necessary.

'She put up with a lot. I think it had something to do with him serving in India. He just didn't seem to like anyone with darker skin. I remember they had a formal dinner once, your mother had agency staff. One was foreign – Indian. The Major went ballistic —' she pressed her lips together as if she'd said more than she'd planned. 'I can't remember any more. It was a long time ago.'

'I remember that. The woman wore a green apron and he was shouting at her. He saw me watching and I ran to hide.'

'By the shed.' Lisa said softly.

Mia smiled, pleased she'd remembered but Lisa wasn't smiling back.

'What was she like my mother – I believe you were her confidante, weren't you?'

Lisa shrugged, her gaze falling above Mia's left shoulder while considering the question.

'I felt deeply sorry for her. She tried hard to get things right. I kept my nose well out of it, just saw that we kept you out of his way.'

'Because I'm mixed race?'

Again, that furtive look, she knows more.

'I'm sorry you lost your mother; Constance was a dear gentle soul. She still wrote to me.'

'You kept in touch?'

'Occasionally. I know she was happy in the retirement home. She called it "a new lease of life".' A smile tweaked the corners of her mouth. 'I hadn't heard her sound so happy in years. She told me she'd been to the Opera. *Tosca*, I think it was. I'm so glad she had some good times. Hers wasn't an easy life.'

Unexpectedly, a memory surfaced. Her father red-faced and shouting. Her mother standing quietly, eyes fixed on the floor as he picked plates from the draining board and hurled them at the wall, Constance flinching, as each missile barely missed her.

'I have to ask, did he hit her?'

Lisa shook her head frantically. 'I never saw it, but she often had bruises, a sore wrist but it was more than that. Today we'd call it psychological abuse, verbally wearing her down. Undermining her in front of you and Georgina.' She glanced at her watch. 'Sorry, I have to go.'

A family with a pushchair approached and Mia was forced to lean forward to allow them to squeeze past.

There was so much she wanted to know, was Lisa hiding something from her, maybe to protect her?

Mia spoke quickly as Lisa prepared to leave.

'Please Lisa. Did she have any close friends, family, anyone you can think of that she saw regularly?'

Lisa pursed her lips. 'Not really. A few women used to come and play bridge. They took it in turns to host – they were mainly army wives.'

'What about relatives?'

'None that I recall.' She fussed with the leather strap of her bag and appeared to be drawing saliva into her mouth.

'Not even an aunt, uncle or cousin? Someone who lived in Devon?'

Lisa ducked the question. 'Loved her garden, did Constance. Used to spend hours out there pottering about. She always wore a straw hat to keep the sun off her face.'

Mia straightened on the hard seat. 'You must have known where she went? Do you have a contact address?'

'Mm of course. Devon. Sorry, there have been so many other families since then.'

'Did you ever go with her?'

'No.'

'Not to a place called Sidmouth?'

'Never. I'm sorry. I can't remember.' Lisa tilted her wrist to check the time, as a raspberry pink splash flooded her cheeks.

'Did she ever take us with her? Me and Gina I mean.'

Lisa pursed her lips at the question. 'Sorry, I can't recall.'

'Perhaps I hadn't been adopted yet? How old was I when I came to the house?'

Lisa tugged at the sleeves of her blouse. 'Around a year, 18 months. I don't recall exactly.'

Look at me, you liar. Lisa raised her cup and took a few gulps. 'I'm sorry Maureen, I really do have to go.'

Lisa sidestepped the table and hugged her awkwardly. Mia caught the fragrance of sandalwood soap, triggering a memory of Lisa reading her a bedtime story as they were lying side by side on her bed. The scene complexly at odds to how she acted now but there was no point pushing, Lisa wasn't going to tell her anything useful.

'Thank you for coming, you have my number if anything springs to mind.'

'Yes. Yes, of course, so lovely to see you again after all these years. Constance said you'd changed your name. Sorry I called you Maureen. Mia suits you and you look like life was kind to you, after all.' For a second, Mia felt Lisa had dropped her guard and been herself. She watched her walk away. Disappointment growing with each step and hardly any the wiser about her mother's life than she had been twenty minutes before.

CHAPTER 33

ZANNAH was coming to supper. Although apprehensive as this was the first time Mia would try out her newly acquired culinary skills on anyone else, she was confident that her Thai green curry would be acceptable, after all, she'd cooked it twice following a video cookery tutorial.

The intercom buzzed announcing Zannah's arrival. Like a whirlwind, she swept through the door, her auburn hair swinging loosely around her shoulders. As usual, Zannah looked stunning, dressed in a pale-grey silk shift dress that skimmed her slender figure. Mia opened her arms in greeting. As they hugged, she caught the scent of Chanel's Chance wafting from Zannah's skin.

'You look bloody gorgeous, how the hell do you do it?'

Zannah raised an eyebrow. Sweeping her gaze across Mia's black and orange pant-suit.

'Bloody gorgeous yourself,' Zannah said with a waggle of her head. 'Now, a cheeky glass of wine, a tour of this fabulous apartment, then feed me. I'm ravenous and judging by the smell, it's going to be yummy.'

Mia had started on the alcohol before Zannah arrived, had already downed a large gin and tonic before dinner. Now, after having eaten the curry, which Zannah devoured, they enjoyed an after-dinner wine. Mia's shoulders were loose as she relaxed back into her chair rolling the stem of her wineglass between her forefingers and resting her head rest against the chairback. The word tipsy slipped through her mind, conjuring up memories of her last encounter with Drake.

'So, Drake whatshisname, what's his problem?' Mia said lazily.

'From where I stand, he doesn't have any, but that's because I class him as eye candy.' Zannah raised her arms above her shoulders and stretched lazily.

Mia was curious. 'Did you ever?'

'No. Definitely not. Never mix business with pleasure. A golden rule.' Zannah swished her wine around her glass eyeing Mia over the rim. 'So, he called you, right? I gave him your number.'

Mia wrinkled her nose. 'Yes, he called twice to apologise,' she shrugged. 'Honestly Zannah, he was so objectionable that night. He doesn't do much for me – thinks he's God's gift.'

Zannah stifled a yawn.

'Methinks you doth protest a wee bit too much. He's a catch and was mortified when he found out you'd just been bereaved. He was very fond of Constance.'

Mia rocked forward with such force that she spilt wine over the back of her hand.

'What did you just say? He knew my mother?'

'Of course, and your sister.'

Mia's lungs squeezed, dizziness swamped her vision. How could this be? She felt small and vulnerable. That's why he'd called her Maureen. But how could he know her family?

'I don't understand.'

Zannah was studying her, enjoying the moment.

'No great mystery. His uncle and aunt lived opposite. He keeps a few private clients thankfully, me being one. He used to see your mother in the garden, they'd talk flowers and stuff. Sometimes your sister made him coffee. She mentioned you.'

'I bet she did,' Mia said, angry at being caught out by the man, she now realised, she'd summoned from a tree to carry her bags. No wonder he'd been sarcastic, Gina had fed him her poison and he'd swallowed it. It explained his behaviour, his preconceived opinion of her; she lived up to her reputation or Gina's version, ordering him about. She cringed remembering his dismissal when she offered him a tip. Small wonder he'd taken umbrage.

'Don't look so crestfallen. You can put him right.'

Mia shook her head. 'Why would I want to? If he's stupid enough to believe anything that Gina told him, he's an idiot.'

Zannah's grin widened. 'So, you don't care what Drake thinks of you?'

'Too right. Self-centred -'

'Of course he is.'

'Don't humour me. He was so obnoxious.' Mia said, flipping her palms. 'And please stop grinning.' She didn't. 'Okay I give up, I suppose I sounded a bit of a bitch, but still no excuse for his behaviour. He should have at least wanted to decide for himself.'

'Based on what?'

Mia narrowed her eyes. 'He told you, didn't he?'

'That you got him to carry your bags?'

Mia buried her face in her hands and groaned.

'You'll soon see the funny side once you get to know him.' This time, Zannah didn't attempt to conceal her yawn. 'Time to call a cab. Work in the morning,' she grimaced. 'Oh God, I've got a whole week of staff appraisals to look forward to, never the happiest of times. Still hey-ho – onward and upward.'

Mia got Zannah's coat and held it out for her.

'You know you have got Drake all wrong. He's warm, funny– '

'Kind to animals, loves his mother. Sounds like we're talking about two different people.'

Zannah gave her a measured look. 'I think one day you'll change your mind.'

'I wouldn't bet on it.'

With Zannah dispatched in a taxi, Mia loaded the dishwasher, distracted by thoughts of Drake Quaid and Gina gossiping about her. Though, admittedly, she hadn't exactly made a good first impression. Her hoity-toity manner could only have confirmed what he'd been told. As she cleaned her teeth, she realised the DQ floral tribute to Constance stood for Drake Quaid.

That night's sleep was fretful, she fought with her bedsheets, holding imaginary conversations with Drake as she pleaded her case and he, in turn, laughed in her face.

Although keen to pursue her mother's past and return to Sidmouth, Ella had tempted Mia with a booking in Copenhagen, at an international conference. Her job was to oversee everything, from seating and food service to timings of speeches, and assure the delegates enjoyed a seamless experience.

As the delegates filed past at the meet-and-greet part of the event, Mia smiled. Everything seemed to be going well. In the past, she would have enjoyed the attention, but this was her job and she kept it professional: it was germane that she did it well. The venue buzzed with activity as the suited and the powerful were efficiently seated.

Mia spotted the outline of his head before his face appeared. She gulped as their eyes met – his widening in surprise. Stepping forward, she pasted on her best smile.

'Mr Stone. It's genuinely nice to see you again. I hope you have a pleasant conference.'

His lips parted then closed and it was the first time Mia had ever seen Rufus Stone lost for words.

For the rest of the evening and the following two days, she managed to avoid him. As the conference ended, their paths crossed. Rufus lowered his head in the hint of a bow. It was a nice gesture, was it a gesture of appreciation or recognition for old-time's sake? Either way, it pleased her he'd witnessed her doing a respectable job, considering the way their relationship had ended.

The following morning leaving the hotel, she spotted Rufus, he wasn't alone, his hand rested on the small of a woman's back. They were too far away to see if she recognised her. The chauffeur blocked Mia's view as the woman climbed in followed by Rufus. Mia briskly stepped back into the foyer before the car passed, God forbid he caught her spying on him.

It was nice to be home, Mia thought as she unpacked her suitcase and slipped on a pair of joggers and a tee-shirt. Rufus remained in her thoughts. Whoever the mystery woman was, she hoped she'd love him for himself, not his money. Would it hurt to Google him and see if there was any mention of who she might be? Of course, she shouldn't, it wasn't her business. A ping on her phone reminded her that tonight was the last in the series of Grace Denning's TV shows.

It was unbelievable to see the woman she'd become. It was Grace who calmly instigated the end of Miss Viner's antics. Grace had never been summoned, unlike herself and poor Pippa. Grace organised and planned roping in Sophie and Cassie to help. Viner hadn't shown any sign of remorse, not even at Pippa's memorial service. That had sickened them all.

CHAPTER 34

MIA woke with a sore throat and a temperature and groaned. She was due to start a new booking that day and hated letting Ella down but just didn't feel well enough. Having called the agency to apologise she climbed back into bed, dosing fitfully. Several times she was disturbed by her phone – she ignored it. The entry buzzer got the same treatment – whoever it was could go away.

The next day she felt marginally better, hungry even, but the fridge held nothing to tempt her. Her hair was lank and greasy as she dragged it back into a band, barefaced but who cared, she was only going to be a few minutes. Pulling on a crumpled T-shirt and jogging pants, purse in hand she headed out. The mirrored lift magnified the angry red spot on her chin, she ignored it, apart from the security man no one knew her, and the local supermarket was only a few hundred yards away.

Roaming the aisles, she selected grapes, fresh mango, strawberries, yoghurt, a pot of honey, and some milk. Turning into the bakery aisle she almost dropped her shopping. There, in the checkout queue was Drake Quaid. Panicked, she pressed herself against the chilled sandwiches, before slowly making her way back down the aisle and retreating out of the sliding exit doors. A firm hand grasped her arm.

'What the—?' She turned to confront whoever it was to see a uniformed security guard.

'Excuse me, Madam. I don't believe you've paid for those items. Would you care to accompany me back into the shop?'

Before she could explain herself, he half-escorted, half-pushed her back inside the store.

'Will you take your hands off me, please? This is all a mistake. I was just…just trying to avoid someone.'

'The person on the till was it?' he said sarcastically.

'No — No. Oh God.'

Mia coloured as faces turned in her direction, Drake's included. His expression read surprise followed by a look of mild amusement.

He stepped forward. She swallowed, shutting her eyes. This couldn't be happening.

'She's quite right,' he said, pointing to himself. 'She was trying to avoid me.' He wagged his head slowly in mock sadness. 'You've got to stop doing this and accept that we're going to bump into each other from time to time. It's over. You have to understand and stop stalking me.'

Mia's pulse quickened. 'What you— You're enjoying this, aren't you?' Her cheeks burned with humiliation. People were staring, hovering, enjoying the drama. 'Don't be ridiculous, I'm not stalking you.'

The store detective loosened his grip. 'So, you know this woman, Sir?'

Drake nodded over-zealously. 'Yes. I do. This is Maureen Croxley-Smith. Isn't it, darling?'

'If you were a foot closer, Drake, I'd, I'd…'

'Right let's just pay for the shopping and get out of here.' He turned to the security man. 'Can we go now?'

The guard glanced from Mia to Drake and back again. 'All right. But in future, Miss, don't take unpaid goods out of the store. No matter who you're avoiding.'

Mia pushed past him and made for the till, Drake behind her. Frantically she scanned and paid for her shopping. She left the store but, feeling his presence behind her, spun around.

'Go away.'

He smiled broadly. His eyes sparkled; he was enjoying himself at her expense. 'Calm down, you'll give yourself a heart attack.'

Home was less than fifty paces away, she speeded up, anger flipping to vulnerability.

Oh God, please don't let me cry in front of him. Desperately she tapped her pockets for her entry key. *Did I pick it up? Oh please, this can't be happening.*

The security guard-cum-concierge was nowhere to be seen. She pressed the call button and waited. A tear rolled down her cheek. She cuffed it away, exhausted and humiliated.

Drakes hand reached out to take the carrier-bag from her.

'I'm sorry,' he said, 'the last thing I intended was to upset you. I tried to make a joke about the situation. I guess it wasn't that funny?'

She looked away. 'You called me Maureen. I hate it, and it's not my name. Not anymore.'

'I'm sorry. I won't do it again. I promise.'

She sucked in a tremulous breath. 'What are you doing here anyway?'

'Actually, I was coming to see you. I wanted to apologise for my behaviour at the charity event dinner. I had no idea that you'd just lost your mother.'

'You already said that when you rang.' She shifted her body out of the sun's glare, straining to look up at him, too drained to argue.

'Mia, I'm sorry I was horrible to you. I liked Constance very much, she was a lovely lady. I enjoyed our chats and would have attended the funeral, but I was in Newcastle so I sent flowers instead. '

'DQ. Yes, I guessed.'

Drake lowered the shopping to the ground forking his fingers through his hair.

'I tried to call you back, but you hung up. I've tried several times since. Then Zannah told me you'd phoned in sick. I thought if I came with flowers, you might throw them at me. So, I got you this instead.' He reached down and opened his carrier bag, 'Grapes, fresh mango, strawberries. Lots of vitamin C oh and yoghurt, honey, and some milk too. I hope you'll accept them as a peace offering. I feel awfully bad about everything.'

Mia managed a weak smile.

'I bought two wholemeal rolls as well but wasn't sure if you did carbs or not. I can take them away if you want?'

His words were soothing, she found herself staring at the way his Adam's apple moved up and down. The down was the one that was affecting her.

Drake shrugged. 'Still, you could always feed them to the ducks.'

'I've never fed ducks in my life.'

He feigned shock, comically raising both brows.

'What? Not even as a kid?'

The mention of her childhood broke the moment. 'Not even as a kid.' Behind her, the door slid open. The concierge appeared, his eyes magnified behind thick lenses, his mouth down-turned. There were crumbs on his navy jumper.

'No fob again?' He tutted. 'Put a note on the back of your door so you read it before you go out. I was on my lunch break.' He shuffled away, his trousers sagging on his shapeless bottom.

Drake followed her to the lift. 'Well, I'll be off then,' he said, handing her both bags. 'I really am sorry Mia. Perhaps you'll let me take you out to dinner sometime so that we can get off to a fresh start?'

Mia pressed the button for her floor, starting to grin. He deserved a bit of slack. She stepped into the lift.

'And I need to apologise too, it wasn't the best start ordering you down ladders to haul my suitcases. It seems we both got it wrong and thanks for the shopping. I —' The lift doors closed, ending the conversation. As she rode to her floor, she wondered how long it would take her to eat two jars of honey, the yoghurt, fresh mango, grapes, and strawberries. The ducks would go hungry though – she hadn't made it as far as the bakery aisle to get her rolls. Was the double shopping a sign or just a coincidence?

CHAPTER 35

MIA decided she needed to keep her mind off Drake. It had been a week since the supermarket incident and she had begun to warm to him, realising that perhaps Zannah was right after all, maybe he was one of the good guys. She'd been avoiding exploring the contents of Constance's bag, but diving back into the mysteries it contained would certainly keep her occupied.

The bag sat on the cabinet by the urn, like a mini altar. Feeling like a child with a lucky dip full of prizes she didn't understand, Mia wiggled her hand inside the heavy fabric to retrieve a notebook with items pressed between its pages. She ran her fingers over the embossed butterfly catching against the desiccated rubber fastening that snapped before she could slip it free. The loose contents flitted to the table. She picked up a handmade card, Happy Mother's Day – a drawing of a purple skinny cat. A tingling entered her fingertips as she recalled making it, trying not to crayon outside of the lines. Three large X's were scrawled at the bottom in a shaky line. A lump caught in Mia's throat. Another sign that her mother had loved her, why else would she have kept it? Under the card was a cream-coloured Basildon Bond envelope with her mother's address written in what was Mia's handwriting. Inside, two letters she'd written from Chartley. So, her father or Gina hadn't managed to intercept all of their mail. She was careful not to damage the pages that looked like they'd been folded and unfolded so many times.

September 2nd, 1988
Dear Mummy,
We all had to write a letter home but don't have long to write it,
so I will keep it short and write more later. The girls in my dorm are
nice. They are called Cassandra, who we call Cassie, Grace, and Sophie.
Sophie talks too much and gets on my nerves and Cassie is dreadfully
untidy, but Grace is nice. I hope I'll get picked for the hockey team and
I've almost grown out of my pyjamas and don't be surprised if you hear
I've died from cabbage poisoning, it's disgusting.
Love Maureen x
—

April 1989
Dear Mummy
I don't understand why I can't come home for Easter. I know you said
you have lots of guests, so Daddy thought it best. I would stay in my
room and be very quiet if only you'd let me come home. It's horrid here
when everyone's gone for the holidays and Matron's a bit creepy. Will
you please ask Daddy again? I promise to be good.
Love Maureen x

The pleading words she'd written in desperate loneliness hung
in the air. The memory was a painful one. She clutched the letter
to her chest and thought her heart would break. Standing, she
reached for the urn.

'I'm so sorry. I thought you didn't want or care about me. I felt
so worthless but now I see that you couldn't help me. I'm sad for
both of us.' She dropped a kiss on the silver top of the urn, then
settled it beside the letters on the table. 'Let's do this together.'

'Oh, look Mummy, a birthday card.' The writing was loopy and
flowing. "Happy Birthday, Constance, we think of you every day.
Love Elizabeth and Memmi."

'Memmi? Not a name I've heard of, who was she, Mummy,
friend or neighbour?

Perhaps Memmi was short for something and Elizabeth, well
you keep popping up, don't you?'

Her gaze swept across the array of things she'd already cata-
logued. She picked up the intricate mother-of-pearl fan, wafting

it gently. The gold bangles looked tiny but slipped easily onto her wrist, playing a tune as they jangled against each other. The ornate turquoise and gold earrings were so unlike the plain pearl studs Constance favoured. They were certainly weighty, and it was hard to imagine Constance wearing them, they'd have dragged on her lobes.

'Were they a gift, Mummy, never worn but kept out of sentiment like the bag you kept them in?' One of the folk festival flyers had slipped to the floor, she picked it up. 'Is this where you danced barefoot?'

Pulling her laptop towards her, she keyed in *John Kirkpatrick, folk music.* A Wikipedia page took her through his career with Steeleye Span. YouTube clips engrossed her as she scoured the faces in the crowds. Was her mother, Constance one of them? Her ringing phone distracted her.

Reluctantly, she answered the call.

'Is this Miss Croxley-Smith?'

'Speaking.'

'This is Ashmead Military Home.'

A flash of something, was it guilt, made her blood chill. She had only visited the once. off.

'It's not good news I'm afraid.'

Mia tried to focus.

'It's your father, Major Croxley-Smith, he died this morning. It was very peaceful. I'm sorry to be the bearer of bad news.'

No words came. She concentrated on her breathing. The news was like a slap to the face. It wasn't that she'd forgotten him, how could she? It was just that she thought Gina would have changed the next of kin details to her own as his beneficiary.

'Have you called my sister, Mrs Evans?'

'We did try, but her phone number's unobtainable.'

'I see. And did Mrs Evans give you instructions for any funeral arrangements?'

'I'm afraid not. We haven't had any contact with her since your father came here. Will you be coming to see him? Someone will need to handle his personal affairs and effects...'

Mia closed her eyes, trying to avoid the imagery of the bulk of her father swinging from a hoist, his eyes popping from his head as he screeched the jumble of hatred.

'Yes of course. It will take me a few hours at least to get there.'

'There's no rush. Take your time. Again, my condolences for your loss.'

The phone slid through her fingers. She sat back in the chair, the papers from her mother's past spread out in front of her, conflicting emotions flooding her thoughts.

'This isn't right, Mummy. Once again you take back seat for him, I'm sorry.' It felt disloyal to her mother's memory to pack away her things and go to him, but someone had to.

The tea was still hot even though she'd been sitting by the body of her father for some time, balancing the cup and saucer on her knee. She'd never been in her father's proximity long enough to study him. His head was large and square. He no longer had the military moustache and the wayward eyebrows had been trimmed into an orderly fashion. The whiteness of his bedsheets echoed his death-mask pallor.

Her voice came out in a croak, devoid of sadness in contrast to the grief of losing Constance.

'Why? Why were you so hateful? What made you like that? Were you ever kind to anyone other than Gina? Christ, you never even knew me,' she took a sip of tea. 'Bit of a joke isn't it, that I'm the only one here to say goodbye. That would have enraged you. Well no more, Daddy – Daddy, what a silly word that is when it's pinned to you.' She blew out a breath. 'I'll see you get a good send-off, but it looks like your darling Gina may be a no-show. I hear she didn't visit, tsk, the irony makes me want to cheer, but my conscience is clear. At least I saw to it that Mummy ended her days happily and I did the best for you.'

There was nothing more to say, the tea had grown cold as she'd sat reflecting. Cold – just like her father.

She got to her feet taking one last look at him as the faint smell of lavender slipped into her senses. 'Bye Daddy, I hope it's as hot as hell where you're going. You certainly won't be seeing Mummy there. Turns out Mother had her secrets, and I'm going to find out what they were. Did you hear that? She wasn't who you thought she was. And thank God for that.'

The nursing home organised everything. A bugler from her father's regiment, plus a couple of residents who'd served with him stood, ramrod straight, medal-chested; they saluted as the *Last Post* was played and her father's coffin vanished behind the purple curtain.

Gina had been informed of arrangements via her solicitor but as expected, she didn't turn up. Well, that was her problem. Mia smiled as she wondered if the *Heir Hunters* would track Gina down as they did on the television, to pay out the insurance left to her children. Mia wasn't going to worry; her duties were complete.

Two weeks had passed since the funeral, it was time to conclude her mission for Constance. Although procrastination had given Mia some respite, it was time for closure. She had just sent an email to Mr Mead requesting the archived documents to be forwarded when an email arrived from Zannah. She read:

Impromptu BBQ – weather permitting this Saturday 2.00 until whenever. NO heels please – for my lawn's sake. There was a smiley face emoji.

'Great, just what I need, something to look forward to.' She whizzed back an acceptance, flashed through her outlook calendar, and added it. Her fingers tapped the keyboard adding Sidmouth and a question mark to the following weekend.

CHAPTER 36

Mia was certain the hands on the office clock were glued to its face as she willed time to pass.

Hamish & Sons were based in Hammersmith on the tenth floor of an enclosed oblong of concrete pillars and tinted glass. Desperate to escape the cloying atmosphere, she was relieved when lunch break beckoned.

Outside the air felt good on her skin, it was still warm in the daytime, but summer was almost done. She headed through the back streets towards the park and found a bench to enjoy her deli-bought sandwich.

The flower-lined pathways were busy with people enjoying the weather. Others sat in groups on the yellowing grass chatting happily.

A clang and a yell to stop made her turn. The area was marked off with orange plastic bollards. Workmen in hard-hats and yellow jackets were gathered around a large stone monument that swung from a hoist attached to a lorry. The lorry made a screeching noise as it steadily lowered its clanking chains – one man directed the operator while the others manhandled the monument into position.

'Glad to see you're keeping an eye on things for me.'

Although startled by the intrusion, she didn't need to turn to recognise Drake's voice – she'd know it anywhere. Chewing fiercely, she tried to force down the mouthful, but it went down the wrong way sending her into a coughing fit.

'Here.' He handed her an open bottle of water. She took it gratefully, sipping until the coughing ceased. 'I'm sorry, I didn't mean to startle you.'

He filled the space on the bench beside her, their thighs almost touching. She couldn't see his eyes through his sunglasses but knew they were a rich caramel although, she remembered from the charity event, at night they turned into almost the brownie orange of marmalade. She fidgeted more distance between them and returned his bottle, watching as he raised it to his lips and took a swig. She blinked and looked away. It felt intimate, his mouth where hers had been.

'Don't apologise. I was miles away,' she said, batting away the image.

'Ogling my men, I see.'

She laughed. 'I'm not ogling, just watching. Are they your men?'

'Yes, and the gardening team over there.' He pointed to a team of gardeners planting what appeared to be an intricate coat of arms. She nodded and turned her attention back to the lorry.

'That's a huge stone to manipulate. I didn't know you did things like this, I thought —'

'I just climbed ladders.'

'Touché, so we both got it wrong. Can we call a truce? I don't want to argue with you anymore.'

'I think I can manage that,' he held out his hand. 'Drake Quaid, landscape gardener and creator of all things rural.'

'Nutcase,' she said as she rested her sandwich on her lap and made a show of wiping her hand on her skirt before she accepted and shook it.

'Mia', she emphasised. 'Croxley-Smith – temporary can-do person at Hamish & Sons. Well, this week anyway.'

'Sounds a bit…'

'Boring? It is.' She released his hand. Had she been holding it all this time?

He draped his arm along the top of the bench crossing his legs. She breathed in the manly smell of fresh sweat and cologne. Intimate thoughts made her breath hitch, she looked at her watch for distraction.

'Sorry Drake, lovely as this is, I only have a half-hour break.' She got to her feet and he followed.

'I'll walk with you to the gate. I'm glad I've bumped into you. I've been meaning to call to arrange a dinner date, but things have been so hectic. I hear you're going to Zannah's tomorrow so perhaps we can set a date then?'

She pondered the meddling hand of Zannah.

He misread her silence. 'I'm sorry, perhaps you're not ready, she told me about the Major. I'm sorry.'

She shook her head furiously. 'Please don't be, I know that this sounds harsh, but he never liked me, and it was mutual. Gina and I were both adopted, Gina was his golden girl.'

'You're right. That was harsh, but I understand he wasn't an easy man.' They fell into step. 'Gardeners are often invisible, but we hear a lot. My aunt lived opposite for many years and knew him before the stroke. Difficult to live with, that's what she said.'

'True but I haven't fared too badly. Except for being a class A bitch, but I'm working to rectify that.'

'Is it coming easily?' he nudged her jokingly.

She flashed a smile. 'I think so. I'm beginning to discover more about myself daily.' She felt the need to clarify. 'I know Constance loved me, shame I only found out *after* she died.'

'Ouch! How sad, but better than never to have known I suppose.' He shoved his hand in his jeans pocket. 'That gives us something in common – I lost my father too.'

Mia looked away. 'Not quite an orphan like me though.'

'Guess you win on points.' he said, kicking a stone away to the side.

'Who's counting?'

They had reached the gate. 'Do you know, you really can be quite charming when you try.' She gave him a cheeky wink.

'I deserved that one,' the tip of his tongue slid along his lower lip. She couldn't help staring. 'See you at Zannah's tomorrow then.'

'Yes. Weather looks good, or permitting, as they say.'

'Do you need a lift? I could swing by.'

She had a flirty comment in mind but swallowed it back. Tempting as it was, she wanted to be in control as she began to realise being around Mr Quaid, that wasn't always possible.

'Thanks anyway, but I'm not sure what my plans are earlier in the day.' It was a fib, but it did the job.

'Okay fair enough, I'll see you at the barbecue then, Miss Independent, or perhaps you're bringing a plus one?' Before she could reply he turned in towards her. 'Right, Miss *Mia* Croxley Smith, I will bid you a good day. I look forward to learning more about you, now that we are formally introduced, and brandishing our clean slates.'

He touched his temple in mock salute, swivelled on his heels and walked away. She had to force herself to move, the temptation to watch him take his long strides was hypnotic. His triangular shape and toned body reminded her of just how long it had been since she'd felt a man's body against her own.

The afternoon seemed to pass at normal speed especially after she found herself Googling Drake's website and clicking on the "meet the team" pictures so that she could examine his photograph; feeling like a teenager, she quickly closed the page. It wasn't stalking exactly, more like the sort of thing a fourteen-year-old would do, but that's how he made her feel, young, vulnerable, and giggly. How could they have got each other so wrong? It would be enjoyable showing him her real self and, in return, discovering him. But there was one burning question. Why was he still single?

CHAPTER 37

Dresses, skirts trousers and tops lay discarded on the bed like a jumble sale.

'Damn, why did I sell everything from Sardinia? What the hell can I wear?' Mia slumped to a clothes-free spot on the bed. 'What would Zannah wear? A barbecue yes, but think classy, think yacht, not the shorts and tee-shirts variety. Think elegant.'

A few items remained on hangers at the back of her wardrobe. From under a black jacket, she spied a glimpse of turquoise. It was a simple silk dress, an impulsively purchased bargain from a backstreet boutique. She slipped it over her head and shimmied it over her body. It settled just above the knee.

'Ah, that could do it. What do you think, Constance?' She dropped to her knees and began rummaging in the closet. 'Sandals, sandals, where are you?'

The buzzer on the entry phone announced the arrival of her taxi. Sandals located, she slipped them on fastening the delicate ankle straps. En route to the door, she turned to her mother's urn and whoever's tie.

'See you later, Mum.' Closing the door behind her, she hesitated and reopened it. Her hand searched inside the tapestry bag and rested on the box of jewellery. The turquoise earrings were a perfect match. She gathered her hair in a simple knot securing it with pins.

'Thanks, Mum, good to go.' The gold bracelets jangled together on her slim wrists as she climbed into the back of the taxi, smiling happily at her new look.

She had expected the house to be large and was not disappointed. The taxi drove through pillared gates. The driveway mimicked a glitzy showroom full of top-end cars.

The front door was open, Mia stepped into an oval entrance hall with a semi-circle of marbled stairs leading to a galleried landing. Exactly the sort of home she imagined Zannah living in.

'Everyone's in the garden,' announced a fresh-faced teenager who seemed to appear from nowhere. He held out a hand.

'Sorry, we haven't met. I'm James.'

Ah! Zannah's son. 'I'm Mia. Nice to meet you.' He had Zannah's eyes, though his sun-bleached hair was a warm strawberry blonde.

'Would you like me to walk you out there? Mum knows some scary people,' he said, his eyes twinkling with mischief.

'Really! Then thank you,' Mia smiled, 'I hate the bit where everyone stares.'

James led her through the house and outside to an extensive patio. The sweet smell of roses wafting from the borders mingled with mouth-watering smells from a canopied area.

'Mia!' Zannah called, extending her arms as she approached. Heads turned and looked her way, she felt self-conscious.

'See what I mean?' Mia whispered to a nodding James.

'So, you've met my son and heir? James, darling, can you find Mia a glass of something pink with bubbles please?' She beamed at Mia. 'Acceptable?'

'Perfectly.'

'Right, let me introduce you to a few people. Ah, Helen—'

Before Mia could take a single step forward, she felt a hand on the small of her back.

'Don't move, step backwards and into the kitchen.'

Mia tilted her head and her eyes met Drake's.

'Trust me you'll thank me for it.'

She attempted to turn to face him, but he held her shoulders firm.

'Don't turn just step back.'

She obeyed, but he'd annoyed her. 'What are you playing at? Zannah's waiting to introduce me to someone.'

His hand hovered over the knife block on the counter, settling on the scissors.

'What the—?'

'Turn around please.'

She obeyed and felt a tug and a snip of the scissors. Drake dangled a set of labels over her shoulder.

'New dress I take it? Just wanted to save you any embarrassment.'

Mia groaned. 'Thank you.' She glared at the two-inch-long label he'd removed. *Reduced, half price.* She wanted to sink through the marble floor.

Zannah appeared at the door.

'Drake Quaid, I might have guessed. You can't keep her all to yourself. I want to introduce her to a few of our friends.' She took Mia by the hand and pulled her away. 'Come on. You can talk to him anytime.'

As Zannah led her back outside, the flush of colour melted from Mia's cheeks.

For the rest of the evening, Drake kept his distance. Instead, he made faces at her across the heads of others. At one point he blew a kiss, at another he childishly poked out his tongue. It took an effort to halt a cascade of giggles and hold a sensible conversation because of his playful manner. She'd never imagined him so humorous. It was so refreshing. He'd certainly raised the bar. Amused and, more alarmingly, aroused, visions of bedroom games sneaked in – with neither taking the other seriously. Mia shifted position to give Grant's wife her full attention.

'Stunning earrings,' Helen said. 'So unusual. Did you buy them in India?'

Mia raised her hand, feeling the cool of the turquoise stone against her skin.

'I'm not really sure. They were my mother's. I found them in a treasure-trove of her belongings.'

Helen touched her arm lightly. 'Grant told me you'd lost your mother. I'm so sorry.'

'Closely followed by my father.' Mia was horrified to feel her eyes moisten.

Helen was mortified. 'I'm sorry I didn't know, how dreadful, losing both parents and so close together. I expect they were devoted to each other.'

Mia swallowed, imprisoning her words as a tray of hors d'oeuvres passed in front of her. Grateful for the interruption, she accepted something dainty and mushroomy.

'I hear you have two girls, Helen?'

'Yes, our two little monkeys, although they're growing up so fast, I won't be able to say that for much longer.' She dropped her weight to one hip. 'Do you have children? Sorry, Grant talks so much about his clients that I forget who has what.'

'That's understandable, he seems to know a lot of people.'

They both caught Drake in their vision. This time Helen laughed.

'Look at him. What is he like?'

Drake walked past a group, bending his knees, and dipping down as if walking down a set of stairs then climbing up again. 'It's nice to see him laughing again.'

'Too much bubbly I think.' Mia said, grinning.

Helen shook her head. 'No never that, he's a one-glass man. I wish Grant were the same. It's a taxi for us tonight and a hangover for him in the morning. He works hard but plays even harder. Look at him flirting with Zannah. He's incorrigible but harmless.'

Mia grabbed the opportunity. 'So what's Drake's story? I'm seeing a whole new side to him. And why the drinking rule? I'm fascinated. I had him as a bit of a rugger-bugger.'

'Oh no. You couldn't be more wrong.' Helen's smile faded and she became serious. She raised her glass level with her mouth to mask her words. 'He doesn't like to talk about it, but he went through a pretty rough period. It's good to see him more of his old self again.'

Mia was intrigued. 'Why? Sorry, I'm *so* nosey at times.'

Helen leaned in, furtively, running her tongue across her top lip, her eyes deciding something.

'Please don't mention it to him. That's a stupid thing to say, of course, you wouldn't. Drake and Laura, his fiancée, were on holiday in Italy. Laura was driving. They'd been partying most of the day. There were no taxis available. Drake got into the back seat. That's what saved his life. He was asleep when it happened.' She leaned in closer. 'Laura took a bend too fast. A woman was crossing. They think Laura only saw her last minute, swerved and hit a parked lorry. She died instantly and the woman she hit was paralysed. Drake blamed himself.'

Mia opened her mouth to speak but an attractive blonde woman was approaching them, and she smiled a greeting instead.

Helen finished hurriedly. 'He was in a bad way for a long time. Oh, Joanna lovely to see you!'

Mia excused herself and went in search of a bathroom, pleased to have a moment to digest the knowledge. *It all makes sense. That's why he made such a fuss about me drinking at the charity do. It was as much about him as me.*

Until now she'd never really thought about how complicated relationships were. Sustained baggage, yes, but life-changing tragedy? How did you ever resolve that?

CHAPTER 38

THE party mood had deserted her. Having phoned for a taxi, she sought out Zannah, feigning a migraine, and slipped out quietly avoiding Drake. Helen's revelation had given her further thought – time to reassess her feelings. She really liked him, and far more than she'd admit, but until she knew who she was and what skeletons hung in her closet, she didn't dare entering or even thinking about a relationship.

August bank holiday kept its promise of being rain-free. While families planned trips and get-togethers, Mia planed a second visit to Sidmouth. Two hours later she was on the train, Constance's ashes in their usual mode of transportation. As the first-class compartment was reasonably empty, Mia dug her hand into her mother's bag, removing the now-familiar notebook, and unfolded the newspaper clippings.

Highlights of our 35 years of dancing have included three firsts: First ladies Morris side ever to appear at Sidmouth International Folk Festival; First ladies' side to be officially invited to perform in the arena (1978); And, first ladies Morris side to appear on television (Pebble Mill at One). We have toured overseas, performing in Sweden, Guernsey, and Finland, as well as becoming a permanent fixture at many of the major UK Folk Festivals. The Morland Morris dancers are named after the historic brand of matches manufactured in Gloucester for about 100 years by the Morland family.

Why had Constance kept this, what was the significance? Am I related to the Morland family? Or am I looking for clues in the wrong place?

She made a note on her pad before replacing the cutting. The next was even more intriguing.

The most wonderful thing has happened, in my whole life.

The newspaper clipping read:

Sidmouth Herald February 25th, 1978.

Snow buried Sidmouth High Street under a three-foot layer. Snow ploughs and mechanical diggers worked 24 hours a day in a three-pronged attack from Sidbury, Ottery St Mary and Honiton to clear the newly opened Sidmouth to Honiton road. The effort was hampered by abandoned vehicles in snowdrifts of up to 14 feet high. Twenty-one people were stranded for several days at the Hare and Hounds pub, their cars buried up to their roofs. Locals remarked that the town had "become like the Marie Celeste."

The best day of her life? How odd, the dates don't tally. Surely that would have been the day she got Gina? God this is all so confusing. If only Constance were here to ask. 'Odd,' she said out loud, 'my birthday's 9th November 1978. Unless.' She worked it out on her fingers, nine months back would have been February. *Had Constance met the woman who, newly pregnant, had agreed to give Constance her baby? It was possible, but something must have gone wrong because when I asked Lisa how old I was when Constance brought me home, she was vague. I need to see the adoption papers. Why hadn't I made that a priority?*

As the train drew nearer to her destination there was a sense of coming home. Letting her imagination run away with her she wondered if she'd passed her birth mother or father on the streets, in a shop, walking on the seafront? Were they still alive? Who had handed her over to Constance for safekeeping? Questions swirled in her head like a whirlpool. Nothing else mattered, the future would have to wait, it's the past that gave her hope. Was her real mother still out there?

Mia slept through her first alarm. And her second. But the third dragged her awake to stare at her phone.

'Shit.' She'd overslept.

The dining room was empty. *Bugger.* She'd have to go to reception to order. As she turned to leave, the girl with braces on her teeth came out of the kitchen.

'Am I too late?' Mia asked, smiling hopefully.

The girl dithered, undecided about what to do with the tray of glasses in her hands.

'Er, I'll check, but chef's on a break.' She found a clear flat surface for the tray and scurried off.

Mia took her place in her favourite seat by the window, gazing across the pristine lawns and down the hill to the promenade, busy with people going about their daily routine. Affection for the town swelled in her chest. Deep inside she felt content.

The girl returned. 'Kitchen porter says breakfast's over, but he can do you boiled eggs?'

'Lovely, thank you that will be great – and coffee?'

'I can do that.' A short time later she reappeared with two boiled eggs, toast and a cafetière. 'Can I get you anything else? Juice, fruit?'

'No that's perfect thanks.'

Mia poured herself a coffee and tapped at the first egg with a teaspoon, flipping off its little shell hat.

'Oh no.' The egg was almost raw, the white had only just started to opaque, she couldn't send it back. They'd been so sweet. Mia stared at her toast, her appetite diminished. Glancing over her shoulder to check that she was alone, she gathered a pile of paper napkins, opened them flat and poured the contents of the eggshell into the middle, forming a small parcel. Quickly, she made her way to the cloakroom where she flushed the oozing mess down the toilet.

It was a déjà vu moment.

CHAPTER 39

1996 – Chartley

'*Christ, not boiled eggs again!*' *Cassie moaned. 'I think the bursar's got shares in a hatchery.*'

'*You mean a poultry farm,*' *Maureen said in a superior tone.*

'*No. I meant egg farm; just how often do we have chicken? I could kill for one of my mum's Sunday roasts.*'

'*In your dreams,*' *Grace said pulling a sucked lemon face at her undercooked egg.*

Maureen pushed hers away.

'*Do you want mine?*' *Cassie offered. 'It looks okay to me.*'

Maureen took the egg cup from her. 'How come you got the only good one?' *She wrinkled her nose. 'Have you been eating this?*'

'*I only had a bit,*' *Cassie muttered apologetically. 'You can use a clean spoon.*'

'*Disgusting.*' *Maureen dragged the large metal teapot towards her and, lifting the lid, tossed in the egg. The uncooked white floated like jetsam to the top.*

Cassie huffed. 'Gross, that's awful. Maw, you're asking for trouble.'

'*Not today. Viner's day off.*'

In an instant, the atmosphere in the dining room changed. The chatter died, eyes lowered as the door from the staff room opened and Miss Viner appeared walking in measured strides, as if on stepping stones – the rubber on her sensible shoes squeaking on the polished floor. Her hands clasped behind her back. Heads raised briefly, she looked frowningly at Mrs Reed, who, until that point, had been on duty. Mrs Reed nodded and slunk out of the dining room...

'Oh, God. I thought she had the weekend off,' Grace murmured *tersely.*

The appearance of Viner brought a chill to the room. There wasn't a pupil amongst them not terrified of her for one reason or another. Miss Viner was a woman, squat with cold grey eyes and wispy fine hair, her teeth protruding like marble slabs. The silence suffocated. Pupils chewed in quietude as she circulated the room. As each table finished eating, the designated table leaders cleared to the serving hatch. Cassie lifted their stacked plates unaware of Viner's approach.

'Just a moment, Castle.' Maureen watched Cassie freeze as Miss Viner peered at the tray.

'Four egg-cups but only three shells? Have you taken to eating shells, Castle?'

'No Miss.'

'Then where is it?' She stepped around Cassie to Maureen's side. 'I'm waiting.' Cassie stared the teapot. Viner followed her eyeline.

Sophie sprang to her feet stuttering, 'It was mum-ma- mine Miss. It was undercooked and —'

'And?'

Sophie lowered her head, desperate to hide the crimson flush making its way above the collar of her school blouse. Grace kicked Maureen under the table, who flinched then gave a defeated nod accepting the blame.

'It was my fault, Miss. I told her to put it in the teapot, you know. To cook it a bit longer.'

Someone on the next table tittered.

Viner narrowed her eyes. She smirked satisfaction. 'On your feet, Smith. Castle, Cogan — sit.'

Maureen stood straight-backed, her eyes closed, her breath caught somewhere inside, afraid to venture out. Viner came closer, her coffee-breath to enveloped Maureen's airways as she spoke into her ear.

'You again? Miss High and Mighty. Do you think it's right to waste good food?'

'No Miss.'

'And do you think it's acceptable for the kitchen staff to have to deal with—' she lifted the lid on the teapot. The eggy mess was floating in the half-empty pot. 'And clean up this disgusting mess?'

Maureen closed her eyes waiting. 'No Miss.'

'Would your parents allow you to do this at home?'

Her father never needed an excuse to lock her in the cupboard, but she wasn't about to reveal that. She tilted her head ever so slightly and made eye contact. She was done for. When would she learn?

Viner's' voice came in a low jubilant rumble.

'You dare to stare me out, Croxley-Smith? Silent insolence,' she announced to the room, 'will not be tolerated.' Her attention switched back to Maureen. 'You think you're above discipline, and good manners,' she said in a chilling voice. 'And do you think I'll let you get away with it?'

'Yes, Miss.'

It took a moment for the deputy's head to realise what was wrong with the answer. The atmosphere was charged, cups hovered below mouths, chewing ceased. The whole school was focusing on the event, and somehow, the rest of the teaching staff had filtered in, they were spread out, like a choir ready to set the scene to music.

'What did you say, Smith?'

'I meant no Miss.' What she wanted was to slap Viner's ugly face, to scream out who the teacher was and what she made them do.

Viner turned on Maureen, her jaw clicking from side to side. Cassie looked on, stupefied with fear, her hand clasped over her mouth.

'How dare you? Go to my office and sit there until I tell you otherwise. There will be no school dance and no shopping trip to Chichester as punishment. I'll teach you some manners. Now clean up your mess.'

Someone sniggered – a freckled-faced girl sitting next to Pippa O'Keefe. Like an animal homing in on its prey, Viner raised an arm and pointed a finger, not at the culprit, but Pippa.

'Find it amusing, O'Keefe?'

Tears were already forming in Pippa's eyes. 'It wasn't me Miss.'

'Liar, you will take the same punishment as Croxley-Smith,' she turned back to Maureen smiling, 'together.'

###

At first, it had been a whisper then a constant buzz and stutter of gossip. Pippa hadn't slept in her bed, Pippa couldn't be found. One of the gardeners, the one who always waved when they passed, discovered Pippa hanging from a tree by lower field. Depression, homesickness, failing grades were blamed as the cause. Matron gave a talk about always "being there" if anyone of us wanted to talk. Fruitcake and scones were served for afternoon tea instead of bread and preserves. Did they think a slice of fruitcake could wipe out the memory of a dead girl?

Only Maureen knew the truth. Viner had chosen them both for their lack of a loving family. Like her, Pippa didn't get letters or expensive birthday presents. There was no one to clap for her at prize-giving or to cheer her on at sports day. Viner was safe in the knowledge that they wouldn't tell.

How many eggs had it taken to recall why Pippa O'Keefe committed suicide? The shock, the tears. That memorable morning assembly, where their weak stuttering headmaster asked the whole school to pray for Pippa's family.

The four friends returned to their dormitory, angry, tearful and frustrated after the memorial service, each venting their anger – making inane suggestions what they'd like to befall their perverted teacher.

'I know she's weird; I mean why would a teacher watch us shower after games. Pervert, weirdo. It's all her fault, poor Pippa. You won't do that will you, Maureen promise please?' Tears rolled down Grace's cheeks.

Sophie's blonde ponytail swung up and down as she nodded in agreement.

'She picked on Pippa, all the time. She drove her to it.'

Maureen had provided the vodka, purchased from a corner shop on a trip into Chichester. The more she drank the more maudlin she became. None of them had ever known Maureen to cry, but now it seemed she couldn't stop as she confided what Viner had been doing to Pippa and her.

They huddled around her bed, Grace pulled her to her, softly whispering, 'It will be alright. You should have told us.'

'How could I.' Maureen sobbed, her body shaking against Grace as she held her.

'It's hardly your fault. We could have tried to do something,' Cassie said, tears spilling down her face.

Eventually, the crying subsided, and the group fell silent. Sophie slid from Maureen's bed to her own. She was the smallest of the four and normally had plenty to say, but the events today had shocked them all.

'Can't we just tell someone,' Cassie said hopefully, leaning across and helping herself to some of Sophie's tissues.

Maureen pulled away from Grace and made her way to the sink in the corner of the room splashing water to her swollen eyes.

Sophie sat cross-legged on her bed. 'No one would believe us. They'd say we made it up.'

'There must be something we can do. Supposing she finds another victim. No, this

has to stop,' Grace said, returning to her bed. They all looked at Maureen who was doing her best to repair her dishevelled appearance. She faced them tapping her hairbrush against her palm. 'You can't tell anyone. Ever. Pact.'

'Pact.' They mumbled - bar Sophie.

'So, she said if you ever told anyone, she'll put them on the internet, right?'

Maureen nodded. 'Can we change the subject please.'

'No, listen I was thinking. The photos were all taken in her flat right?'

'Yes.'

'Then Maur, don't you see if she did they could probably— well if someone wanted to, find outright. Check out the background, the curtains, shoes. There'd be something – and what about Pippa? She's responsible for her, well you know… We have to get the photos back.'

Maureen shrugged. 'Impossible.'

Grace pushed herself up on her elbows. 'No Soph's right, Maur. If we could get into her flat and steal them what could she do? She could hardly go to the police, could she? Right here is what will do…'

Cassie watched Miss Viner's Ford Escort disappear down the drive and ran back to the dorm.

'She's gone.'

'Are we really going to do this?' Maureen was nervous. 'What if she hasn't left a window open?'

'She has, I checked,' Cassie said.

Within minutes they'd cut through the rhododendrons flanking the deputy-head's flat. Sophie tucked the roll of bin liners stolen from the cleaners' trolly down her waistband.

Cassie kept watch as Maureen and Grace lifted Sophie, who was the lightest – onto the ledge, supporting her weight until she was able to balance on the sill and reach through the smaller window to open the side one. She giggled as she vanished inside.

Maureen began to shiver with fear as she listened to the sound of Sophie banging around inside.

'Good job Viner's accommodations are away from the rest of the staff quarters,' Grace said.

'What if she can't find them?' Maureen said in a voice that wobbled.

Grace threw her a smile. 'Relax, she'll find them.'

A second later, there was a thump as a plastic bag landed at their feet. A few moments later another, followed by rolls of film, uncurling across the lawn.

'One more.' Sophie shouted from inside. Maureen stared at the ground where one of the bags had split on landing and let out a whimper. Grace rushed forward, pushing the images back inside the bag and out of Maureen's view. As the last bag flew through the air Grace caught it.

Sophie closed the big window, they waited for her to reappear from the other side of the building via the front door as planned.

'Bloody hell, 'Sophie said, picking up a bag. 'There were hundreds and hundreds. I couldn't believe it. Girls who've left ages ago. She must have been doing it for years. All those damaged people.'

Grace threw her a silencing glare.

'Never mind about that, let's get going before we get caught. We need to make it to breakfast, so everything looks normal.' Grace tugged at Maureen's arm, 'Come on, hurry up. It's done, you're free of her.'

They half-ran half-dragged Maureen to where Cassie was waiting and made for the props store, hiding the bags behind pieces of scenery where they would stay until the janitor was off-site and they could safely dispose of them. That evening, the girls swore an oath never to discuss anything they knew about what had happened to "Viner's Victims" as Sophie said, it was better not to name names.

Maureen dreaded the following day, the girls marched into breakfast in unison.

'Christ it's eggs.' Cassie hissed.

'Well I don't care what they're like, I'll eat them,' Maureen said. As they ate, Maureen thought her heart would stop as Viner stood rocking on her heels.

The woman circled the table. Hovering at Maureen's side, she hissed in her ear, 'Think

you're clever, do you? Well, he doesn't scare *me*.'

Maureen had no idea what or who she was talking about and shrugged the comment off as Viner walked away. Later, as she made her way up the hill, she vowed she'd never go to Viner's flat – ever again.

Cassie rushed into the dorm. 'Girls, you'll never guess.' She glanced toward Maureen's empty bed. 'Where is she?'

'Up her hill, as usual,' Sophie said, examining her teeth in a hand mirror.

Grace looked up from her book. 'Cas, I was enjoying the peace and quiet.'

Cassie looked crestfallen. She'd wanted to deliver her news in a way that would give the most impact. She threw herself down on her bed.

'So?' said Grace impatiently.

Cassie sat up sulkily. 'Two things. I went to check on the … the stuff from Miss Viner's flat.' She looked at both of them. 'It's gone!'

Grace removed her reading glasses. 'Gone? Are you sure?'

'Positive.' Cassie gave a serious nod.

'Christ, do you think Viner found them?'

'No, I don't, Sophie. Why would she even look in there?' Grace said.

'Then who?' Sophie's eyes widened.

Grace furrowed her brow. 'You said there were two things.'

Cassie hitched to the edge of the bed. 'Viner was having a row with one of the gardeners – the one who often waves at us. I couldn't hear what he was saying but she looked scared. She was backing away and nearly fell over a bush. He was waving his arms about and—'

'But why?' Sophie cut in, abandoning her mirror.

'I don't know. All I saw was he was really angry, and she looked like this.' Cassie clutched her throat and went cross-eyed.

'And that's it?' Sophie lips drooped in disappointment.

Grace jolted to her feet. 'Was he the one who found Pippa?'

Cassie shrugged. 'I think so. Why?'

'Well, if he came across the photos and saw Pippa and Maureen —'

'But he wouldn't have had any proof it was Vinner that took them,' Sophie interrupted.

'I don't know. Perhaps he saw things – called her bluff.'

Cassie had picked up her sketchpad and was busy tracing Sophie's outline.

'So, what do we do now?' Sophie said. 'Maureen will be—'

Grace raised a silencing palm.

'We don't tell her. We say *we* got rid of them if she asks. This could tip her over the edge. We have to keep it to ourselves and hope they've been destroyed. It's important we stick to this. Pact?' Both girls nodded.

'Forever?' Cassie asked, her eyes fierce as they alighted first on Grace, then Sophie.

'Forever!' they chorused.

As Grace went back to her book she hoped they were doing the right thing, but for now Maureen's welfare was more important. Only time would tell if they'd stopped Viner, and perhaps by then they'd find out the photographs had been destroyed.

CHAPTER 40

B ACK in her hotel room, Mia stared at the remaining items from the bag. She'd read all of the letters, cards, and clippings. The battered copy of selected poems by Leonard Cohen was held fast with yet another crusty band that disintegrated on contact. She fanned the pages, discovering pressed flowers preserved in tissue paper the edges browned with time, along with scribbled jottings in an unknown hand:

"It's impossible," said pride.
"It's risky," said experience.
"It's pointless," said reason.
"Give it a try," said the heart.

The poem stirred inexpressible emotions. Reverently, she placed it back inside the book.

Two distinct piles now lay in front of her, her mother's history. She put the pile she'd gone through back in the bag, leaving the smaller "mystery" pile on the table and re-read her notes.

Who was the man in the photo with the tie? Vikash?

The man's appearance and the name seemed to fit together. Constance was delirious when she called his name, so perhaps it was nothing at all. She'd also referred to the girl. Her? Gina? Lisa?

· *Who gave Constance the jewellery?*

Perhaps she bought it herself – unlikely though.

· *What was significant about the Folk Festival flyers and newspaper cuttings?*

Just memories? A reminder of happier times?

· *Ditto – the tapestry bag*

· *Elizabeth – a cousin?*

So far, no surname to trace her locally.

· *Why did Constance want her ashes scattered on Mutter's Moor? What happened there – a lover?*

After the poems I've just read that seems likely.

· *Who left the wildflowers at the funeral?*

· *The death announcement – who did she want to be informed in Sidmouth?*

'Well, Mother you certainly have a lot of secrets. I just wish you'd given me a few clues; I'm floundering a bit here. Yet I have a feeling you want me to know everything.'

Sighing, she gazed out of the hotel window. The sun was dancing its diamond toes on the sea. Further down the hill, a group of walkers with heavy backpacks were leaving the crescent bay that protected the town behind, for the long hike up Peak Hill. She glanced back at the urn.

'I'll get you up there, I promise. I just wish I knew why.'

She wrote in her notebook.

· *WHO AM I?*

· *Who was my birth mother? Friend or stranger?*

· *Did she live in Sidmouth? Does she live in Sidmouth?*

'Right let's have a look at what you have to say.' She selected the tick brown package sent by Mr Mead and shook out the contents.

A book fell to the bed, square with a strangely spongy, padded leather cover. *A photo album?* Cautiously, unsure of what to expect, Mia gingerly lifted the front. A postcard-sized photo, blurry and colourful. A small, dark-skinned girl on a swing. Mia's heart began to thud against her ribcage. She turned the page. The same, dark-skinned child feeding ducks, the stranger holding her reins a shadow on the riverbank. With clammy hands, she turned another plastic-covered page and sucked in a breath. Her vision blurred with the realisation – she was that child. Scooping her hands through her hair she forced back the tears, but the images wouldn't fade, they swam behind her eyelids. Slowly, she rubbed her index finger between her brows until the intense feeling went away and she was able to look down and turn to the next page. A baby with masses of thick black hair in a Babygro. Tiny knees pulled up to its chest, arms splayed above its head, its mouth a circle of a yawn. The next page the same shot, but a windy smile on the baby's face – no. Her face. Surely, she was that baby. She smiled as she stroked the image with her forefinger. This was her; she was sure of it. On the next page, she was propped up by cushions, a rattle, tiny fingers clasped awkwardly around it. Eyes almost crossed in concentration. Next a coach-built pram, a fringed sun-canopy, she squinted, was that Salcombe hill in the background? It certainly looked like it. She peered closer, to see the stream that ran past the Lifeboat at the end of the promenade.

This was way too much. She ran her fingers through her hair knotting and twisting. Swamped by conflicting emotions, happy and sad, a weird tenderness. A sense of identity and a glimpse into her past. A baby loved and cherished before her adoption.

Proof.

She should have felt elated, thankful, but her first thoughts were who to share her joy with? No one would understand the enormity of what this meant. Not Gina, not Zannah, not Drake, even phoning Inika in Sardinia would give her little joy.

She helped herself to a can of Coke from the minibar, her mouth dry, sipping directly from the can. Her fingers flipped through meaningless papers held for no purpose or interest as far as she could see; halting her fingers, she selected a long slim envelope. Its size and shape intrigued her and as she turned it over, she mewed a cry: *Birth Certificate*. She hesitated; this was the moment.

'This is it. This is who you are.' Her fingertips tingled with excitement.

Father: Vikash Kumar. Aged 35. Railway Porter.

Mother. 'No, it's not possible! It can't be.'

CHAPTER 41

MOTHER: Lisa *Maureen* Farrant. Spinster...
A weird sound escaped her lips. The sensation of being kicked in the guts forced the air from Mia's lungs.

'Lisa Farrant, the nanny?'

Mia fell back on the bed. Anger burned, she gulped and flapped in its wake, bubbles of snot, tears of rage, salty and sticky ran down her face. *Lisa was her mother?* God, it stung.

No wonder she acted so awkward and was uncomfortable when we met, she lied through her teeth about Sidmouth when all the time she'd given birth to me right here.

The document slipped from her hand to the floor. A numbness overtook her. Everything was out of focus; the world was upside down.

How could she have sat casually no, callously, in front of me, keeping up the pretence? Hardnosed. Like me. Is that where I get it from?

Mia swung her feet from the bed and picked up the document. She refolded it and put it back in the envelope, gathering everything else from the bedcovers, she shoved it all into the peacock back.

Even with it out of view, her stomach clenched. Bile, bitter and acidic accompanied light-headedness. Dropping her head into the palms of her hands, she tried to absorb the knowledge.

The mother in her head had always been faceless, an unknown. But Lisa! Lisa had cared for her and Gina, lived in the same house until Mia had been sent to boarding school. Was that to separate them? Had there been conflict between Constance and Lisa?

She shook her head, not from the way Lisa talked, they'd been friends, had still corresponded, even recently. She'd even known about Constance going to see Tosca and Mia's change of name. But it was true, the coal-black hair, the dark brown eyes: Lisa's pale skin mixed with Vikash's Indian. Coffee and cream. Tea with milk. This was her heritage, her mixed race, Lisa and Vikash – 'Oh God.'

She sipped her drink. It was clear now, why the major hadn't liked her, she recalled those words, 'A touch of the tar brush.' Racist. But surely, he must have known. Agreed to it. Constance too. Or had Constance and Lisa planned it all without his knowledge?

So much information to process. Vikash Kumar was her father, the name her mother called out at the hospital, something had made her think of him in her delirious state.

The walls of the small room seemed to shrink and expand as if breathing. It was too much. She needed fresh air. She left the hotel, this time turning right and taking the incline up Peak Hill. *There must always be a hill.* Her breathing was heavy by the time she reached Connaught Gardens, but she kept going. On her right, the land fell away widening into meadow and scrubland. The higher she climbed, the more the red cliffs reappeared like closed quote marks to Salcombe Hill's open one. Her path continued upward in a straight line. Gasping for breath, she turned off the path and sank onto the warm grass, springy beneath her touch. Ahead of her was nothing but the azure blue of Lyme Bay, the vast expanse of sea that grew wider and then faded to the horizon. Above her, the ridge met the sky and, out of sight, Mutter's Moor, the place where Constance would rest. The air was so clean, so fresh. Mia lay back resting on her elbows gazing back the way she'd come.

Someone down there knows something more.

The only sound was the breeze disturbing the tall grass and poppy heads. Even the seabirds were avoiding her today.

Vikash? Lisa and Maureen, Maureen? The awful name handed down from my mother. Only she doesn't feel like my mother. She's Lisa the nanny. No wonder she couldn't wait to get away.

Trailing her hand though the warm grass, she pulled at a Sea Pink, its bloom browning at the outer petals. Just out of reach a clump of Sheep's-bit waved, like tiny pale blue cornflowers. How did she know their names? Someone had taught her.

Above, the clouds parted as the sunlight forced its way through. A shadow crossed its path. Behind her. A man, an old man. She raised her hand to shield the sun from her eyes but couldn't see his face. He mumbled a *good day* and carried on up the hill, his shooting stick swinging on his arm. She watched his progress. He halted where a thin line of trees bent in an arthritic arc against the wind.

The shooting stick jogged a memory. Rufus used one at the races and when he went grouse shooting in Scotland. Rolling on her side she examined the ground, tiny blooms flattened against the breeze. She watched a passing butterfly unable to make up its mind where to settle. Settle, would she ever settle? Well, at least she knew how she'd ended up being called Maureen.

Once, in an English lesson, they'd had to research and write about the meaning of their name. Maureen: Star of the sea – Bitter – Little beloved one, and the French version; Dark skinned. Well that was true, but it was also an Irish name, perhaps she had been named after some ancestor of Lisa's. She muttered to the wind in frustration.

Did it bloody matter? Her feelings squirmed and jostled against each other. Anger, but what or who at? Was it because she wanted Constance to be her mother, not Lisa? Did it matter? At least she knew now.

Mia got to her feet, brushing grass from her trousers. The old man was still in the same spot gazing at something. He looks as fit as a flee, the climb had made her quite breathless but he hadn't seemed affected when he'd passed.

It was almost lunchtime when she got back to the hotel, she brushed her hair then ran a veneer of coral lipstick across her mouth before going down again.

Sam was out on the terrace putting up sun umbrellas over the patio furniture.

'Ah, nice to see you, Miss. Come out for some fresh air then? Beautiful today.' He rested his knuckles on his hips stretching backwards. 'Really beautiful.'

She nodded agreement, filtering the sea air into her lungs.

'It's so lovely here. You're incredibly lucky to live somewhere so beautiful.'

'Aye, the misses used to say that, 'till the sea mist came in in winter and she couldn't dry the washin'.'

'Sam?'

He turned to her; brows raised in askance.

'I've just discovered I was born here.'

'Well, well. Fancy that.' His weather-beaten face wrinkled in a grin.

'Do you know the name Farrant? Lisa Farrant?'

He scratched his thinning hair leaving a single tuft standing. Mia resisted the urge to flatten it.

'Can't say as I do. Farrant, you say. Hmm. Now was its Farrant that had the post office – no that was Forrest. My memories not what it was. I'll ask next door; Doris knows everyone she does. Now, what about a spot of lunch. Chef has some good fresh crab in today, lovely with a bit of salad.' He held a chair out for her, and she slid into the seat.

'I'll get a menu, shall I?'

'No don't bother, the crab sounds lovely – actually, I've never eaten it, a bit like lobster, is it?'

'No not really, stronger flavour. You has two-colours of meat, the brown and the white, delicious with fresh bread and butter. I'll get Danielle to bring it out, that's if I can find her. Always sneaking off that one.'

Sam was right about the crab. It was delicious and she couldn't understand why she'd never tried it before. Sated, she pushed her chair away from the table lifting the glass of wine to her lips as she ran her eye in a full arc from the rooftops and promenade be-low, over the thatched houses ahead of her and up past the turret building and Connaught gardens. Children's voices came on the wind, and a motor scooter winding up the driveway to the hotel next door. A stooped figure made its way down the last patch of grass, it would vanish behind a building any second.

Was it the old man with the shooting stick? It was too far away to see. She had planned to visit the museum but, as she climbed the stairs to her room, she began to sweat and feel unwell. She peeled off her clothes and got into her nightshirt before sleep fell like a blackout curtain.

Cold. Goosebumps, wet. Am I in the shower? I blink, her face is close to mine. Hands on hips – another squirt of ice water to my breasts.

Click, click, click.

Sit. Spread your legs. Wider.

Click, click, click.

The other in the background sits watching, licking his lips. How can this be happening under everyone's nose?

Click, click, click.

I'm taking myself out of my body to the top of the hill. I'm plotting as I go, but on every tree on the way to the top is Pippa. Poor dead Pippa swinging on a rope, head slumped, face blue. Which hill? Which one is it? The one where Mummy wants to be or the hill above Chartley? No, the villa. But Grace and Cassie are running up the hill towards me both naked, crying. Grace holds out her arms to me – but I fall and turn. Miss Viner's there close with her camera in hand click, click, click. I push as hard as I can. Her eyes bulge with surprise as she falls – I can't hear her scream. Did she?

Pain, my shoulder a raspberry-coloured scratch across my bicep. I'm wedged between the wall and the bed. My heart steadies in my chest. My eyes focus, accustomed to the half-light. Sidmouth. I'm in Sidmouth – just a night terror, the horror, it's not real. Real is here and now, Mum's bag on the dressing table, ashes on the windowsill. I crawl back onto the bed sheets damp from my body, not water from a spray. I'm safe.

Within minutes the room is spinning. I get off the bed unbalanced, bumping into the bathroom doorframe. The skin on my face feels taught, stretched, my lips are engorged and tingling. I drop to my knees on the bathroom floor and am violently sick. The stomach cramps come next.

I'm not dreaming. More punishment for breaking Miss Viner's neck. Did I or was it a wish?

I clean myself up. I don't have the strength to get in the shower, I splash cold water on my face. The reflection in the mirror is unfamiliar, shocking. My lips balloon at me like puffy cushions. My eyes goggle on storks I'm starting to feel itchy all over. My chest is squeezing, tightening. This is no dream. It's something bad. I need help.

'You've had a bad reaction, probably to the crab,' the doctor said.

'But I eat all sorts of shellfish, this has never happened before,' she protested, wanting him to be certain of his diagnosis.

'And my wife loves liver but is sick as a dog if there's even a hint of it or kidney in a pie.'

'Sam said it was fresh.'

'I'm sure it was. It's just your body that doesn't like crab,' he removed his stethoscope from around his neck and placed in his bag. 'The injection I've given you will make you a bit drowsy. Sleep and lots of fluids will have you up and about in no time. I've left you some antihistamine, they'll bring the swelling down. You'll feel fine in a day or so.'

Mia felt the need to apologise for the untidiness of her room, not to mention the funeral urn wearing a tie. But she didn't have the energy.

'The staff here are excellent, they'll check in on you or call anyone you want, family et cetera.'

Family? I probably have a host of relatives living just down the hill. That I don't have a clue about.

The doctor left her, and Mia slipped back into the deep hallucinatory dreams that disturbed her, and she woke herself at one point crying out. It was dark outside now and silent. She drank some water, washed her face, changed into a fresh T-shirt, and went back to bed. There was a light tapping at the door that roused her. stiff from lying in the same position. She stretched, easing out her joints. Then went to see who was outside.

A young boy, the collar of his shirt too big for him, held out a tray.

'Chef says he thought you might fancy something, but not to worry if you don't.' Mia took the tray from him. The smell of warm toast made her tummy grumble.

'Tea and toast, thank you. Just the thing.' The peacock bag was on the dressing table, she balanced the tray moving the bag to the windowsill and sat to pour her tea. Her reflection in the dressing table mirror suggested the swelling was abating, the antihistamine was doing its job. Her skin was looser, her lips dry and cracked. She reached for her makeup bag locating a tin of lip balm. The toast tasted wonderful, comforting, the tea a welcome respite from plain water. She yawned, her energy zapped and she climbed back into bed to fall into a deep restful sleep until the sound of the phone woke her. She reached out to answer it.

'Hello, Miss, it's Sam ere. How you feelin?'

She swallowed, her throat tight, her tongue dry from sleep.

'Much better, thank you, Sam.'

'I'm sorry Miss, 'bout the crab and all.'

'Not to worry Sam, no real harm done.' She was touched by his kindness and concern.

'Anyways – as long as you is okay. Chef says he can send up some 'addock, with a poached egg or praps some soup.'

'Thanks, that's sweet of him but I'm not really hungry right now, but if I could have some more water, and perhaps a ginger tea?'

'I'll get the lass to sort it. You rest then.'

She didn't. Instead, she moved from her bed to the window. It was another glorious day. Not a dab of cloud marred the forget-me-not blue of the sky. A figure moving slowly up the hill caught her eye. Was it the man she'd seen yesterday? Too far away to tell.

'Well Mummy, I still think of you as my mother, even if you were a contradiction. How on earth did you settle for beige and boring after so much wildness and colour? I can't see you swaying to the sounds of a flute, drums, a harmonica perhaps, but I wish I could have seen that version of you, happy laughing, even singing. Who cares if you had your secret life. I don't have the stomach for it now I know about Lisa and Vikash, that's it. Well for now anyway.'

Her mobile rested on its charger. She switched it on, there were three text messages, a reminder for a dental appointment, her mobile provider offering an upgrade and Ella from Zannah's agency, asking if she might be free for a booking. Although curious, Mia just didn't have the energy to think about work right now to do much at all, but she would listen to the two voice mails. The first was from the concierge at her apartment, asking what she wanted doing with a delivery of flowers. She deleted it and moved to the next.

Drake. *'Hi, it's me. You slipped away from the barbecue a bit sharpish. Didn't even say goodbye.'* His tone was playful. Then became serious. *'If it's the flowers – Lisianthus and stocks, not your cup of tea? I thought roses a bit too kitsch. Hey, what the hell. I hope I've tempted you to call me. No big deal, but I do have a delicate ego.'* A chuckled laugh. A sense that he was reluctant to end the call. *'Bye-e.'*

Her face creased to a smile. He hadn't been the person she'd thought at all, and she could hardly blame him for his initial opinion of her. She'd appeared a horrid person, neglecting her mother and disabled father. And poor Gina, exhausted with their care, her children and hospital duties. Yeah, right. But then when they first met, she'd behaved like a princess. She cringed.

If only he knew the whole story. Would she ever tell him, lower her defences, and let him in? She thought of Drake, his strong arms, broad chest, the cleft below his Adam's apple. The smell of him, leather, and lemon. Even in her weakened state, the vision turned her insides molten. Was it time to let him get close? Could she risk it?

CHAPTER 42

B REAKFAST of scrambled eggs on a toasted muffin had removed the hollow feeling in her stomach, but the spaced-out sensation remained, probably the antihistamine tablets, Mia decided.

Leaving the restaurant, she carried her coffee to the lounge, selected a newspaper from the centre table next to the piano and made herself comfy in a Buddha-like armchair.

When had she last read a daily paper? Glossy gossipy mags had been her choice before she came to England. Shallow, that's what she'd been. Self-interested, self-obsessed... god how she despised what she'd once been. She was far happier now making her way through life, earning a living.

There was an interesting article on how a shortage of bricks was contributing to the housing shortage and a less interesting article on a footballer denying an affair with a model. She folded the paper and placed it on the table. Outside, a flat, grey sky met the horizon with only the barest hint of white. The palm trees on the lawns swayed from offshore winds. Not a day for her to attempt the walk to Sidmouth Museum. She watched a couple braving the chill. His arm affectionately draped around her shoulders. Hers across the small of his back. Lovers. With a sigh of regret, she returned to her room.

She'd stopped using the "Hello Mum. I'm back" greeting. It seemed wrong, somehow inappropriate. And she'd lost interest in the peacock bag, for now, anyway. It somehow seemed redundant now that she knew her provenance.

Her phone beeped, a message distracting her from her thoughts.

Is it something I said? and a smiley face emoji from Drake.

Feeling guilty, she called his number. Voice mail.

'Hello, Drake. Sorry, I haven't called, I'm away in Devon. Some family stuff. I'm afraid you wasted good money on the flowers. I'm not there to see them, sorry. Er...' She was rambling. 'I was only supposed to be here a day or so, but I got poisoned by a crab.' That sounded wrong. 'I mean, I had an allergic reaction to a crab salad. Anyway, catch you when I'm back. Thank you.'

Why the hell did I mention the crab? Bugger, he'll think I'm nuts.

She hung up yesterday's clothes and tidied the mess on her dressing table, returned Constance to the windowsill and opened her laptop.

What about you then, Dad?

Entering the address, a row of cottages appeared on the screen. They seemed familiar, perhaps she'd walked past them? She jotted down the address. It was a start, but before she could do more her phone rang. Drake. Her tummy hitched.

'Hello?'

'Hi. How are you feeling after your crab attack?' Loud banging squashed his voice. 'Hang on a sec. Rod, take a tea break or something, will you? I'm on the phone.' The banging ceased. 'Ah, that's better.'

'I thought you were a gardener, not a builder.'

'Even summer houses need a hammer and nails.'

'True. Anyway, thank you for the flowers.'

'Are you back at home then, surely they're dead by now?'

'Stop winding me up. You know what I mean.' She pulled a pillow up against the headboard of the bed and wiggled to get comfortable. 'No, I'm still in Sidmouth, and I will never eat crab again, *ever.*'

'Don't blame you. I'm the same with strawberries – not nice. So, what's the attraction with Sidmouth? Business or pleasure?'

God that's a tough one.

'Erm neither really. Family stuff.'

'You have relatives there?'

'Not exactly.'

'You're a strange one to figure out, Mia. A woman of mystery. Okay so when are you coming back?'

'Not sure, maybe Friday?'

'Tomorrow Friday?'

'Gosh, what happened to the week?' Her eyes settled on Constance's ashes. She must at least fulfil her duty. 'No that's probably too early. It depends on the weather. Probably Tuesday, to be on the safe side.'

'Are you sailing?'

'No.'

'Sunbathing?'

'Stop it,' she said, laughing. 'It's something I have to do in good weather, well not a howling gale, or a thunderstorm.'

'Sounds intriguing. Anyway, what about dinner tomorrow night – promise to eat nothing that walks sideways.'

'I can't. I just said. I won't be home.'

'I'll come to you. I could do with some sea air and a change of scenery.'

'What! No, you can't.'

'Why not? Tell me what hotel you're in, and I promise to book elsewhere,' he let the thought grow. 'Mia, I am a gentleman.'

'I wasn't saying you weren't.' A little fizz of excitement was starting to gain momentum. 'Do you want the bother? It's a long drive.'

'Hour or two at the most. Call it doing me a favour. Apparently, I work too hard.'

She felt suddenly coy and flushed, remembering sweaty one-night stands where she couldn't remember their names. This was different, a fresh start, courtship. *Why not?* 'Another hotel, you promise?'

'Scout's honour.'

She let out a puff of breath. 'All right. It's a deal. I'm at the Old West Cliff. Do you want me to book a restaurant?'

'Nope leave it all to me. I'll text you.'

'Drake, you're completely mad!' The fizzing feeling was turning into tiny popping fireworks. 'Okay, I'll look forward to it.'

'Me too. Till tomorrow. Bye.'

The line disconnected before she could respond. She twisted to address the urn.

'Well, Constance. What do you think of that? Drake Quade, coming all the way here to take me to dinner!' She plonked down onto the bed rocking her legs, grinning broadly. 'I can't believe I'm so excited. He makes me feel like a silly teenager, but don't worry, I won't bring him home to meet the parents. Not on the first date anyway.'

CHAPTER 43

WHAT could she wear? She'd nothing suitable for a date with Drake. She'd thrown together a suitcase with no expectation of fine dining, let alone with a man. And not just any man. She had a feeling he was going to turn out to be special or was that just wishful thinking, either way, she must look her best, but she hadn't even got a lipstick with her.

That fizzy feeling revisited, poking once again at her sternum, like some weird addiction. She was beginning to like it.

There was nothing for it, she needed something new. Her only hope was the one department store in the town.

Its pale primrose and white Regency facade hadn't even attempted to disrupt from its grandeur with modern window dressing. But once through its doors, the maze of rooms boasted an unashamedly well-stocked Aladdin's cave that could give John Lewis a run for its money. She was delighted the cosmetics department stocked her usual brand; at least she could put on some slap even if she couldn't find anything to wear. But she was wrong there too. She carried the unpretentious floral silk wrap-over dress to the till.

'What a lovely dress,' the assistant said, taking it from her. 'I missed that when I was looking for something for my daughter, she's about your age.' Deftly, she folded the dress between tissue and placed it with care in a shiny carrier bag. 'Gosh, bargain too.'

Mia grinned as she found herself joining in.

'I know, unbelievable price. I used to live in Sardinia, the same dress would have had another zero on the price tag.'

'Sardinia, how lovely. I've never been.'

'You should, it's beautiful, but then so's Sidmouth.'

The assistant held out the bag, Mia thanked her and took it, her eyes roaming around the store.

'Shoes, is it?' The woman said smiling.

'Mind reader. Yes. I only brought some flatties and a pair of trainers.'

'Just through there, you'll see the sign. We have a new Italian range just in. I think you'll find what you want.'

Mia did indeed, purchasing a pair of cork-soled mules that would withstand a hike up and down the hill but wouldn't detract from the dress.

The hours ticked by without any sign of the promised text from Drake. By five-thirty, disappointed, she'd given up on him and ventured to the bar. She nursed the crushing sense of disappointment by ordering a gin and tonic. She was on her second when her phone beeped.

Meet u at the btm of the hill by sea wall at 7.00. Then a happy face emoji.

'Shit.' Her watch said six-fifteen. She took the lift to her room, showered, washed her hair, dried it, wet it again. Her makeup was all wrong, her eyeliner wiggled in the middle. She cleaned it off and started again. This was ridiculous. She'd never got in a state like this just going out to dinner with a man. *Get it together, Mia! It's just dinner*, she admonished herself. *Yes, but he's special. Well, he could be.*

Oh, the pressure!

Making her way downhill, she felt exposed, thinking he was probably already down there watching her make the descent. She pretended to look nonchalant, stopping to look at a shrub and smelling a rose.

'Hello. Dead on time. I'm impressed.'

He made her jump. She squealed, slapping her hand against her chest in surprise.

'I didn't expect you to suddenly appear out of nowhere. You said the bottom of the hill. Not the hotel next door.'

'It had parking, so that's in its favour. It's a bit grand for me. Flouncy. I'd be happier in a Premier Inn.'

Her eyes widened, he looked gorgeous and smelled it too.

'Come on then, let's get going.' Mia said, conscious that she'd been staring. She started to move away, and he fell into line beside her. They jangled out of step, bumping sides where the path narrowed where Drake did a sort of skip to mirror her pace.

'Well, this is a find,' he said, 'what a lovely place. I haven't had much chance to look around but it's very...'

'Quaint?'

'I was going to say sea-sidey.'

'Is there such a word?' She picked up on his discomfort; he was as nervous as she was. 'I know what you mean though. Old fashioned. Charming, unspoilt. I love it, no tacky arcades, kiss-me-quick hats or candyfloss.'

'Exactly and they have a croquet lawn. I saw it as I drove in. Grown-ups playing a serious game.'

They came to a road junction and he cupped her elbow as they crossed, she liked the gesture, another gentlemanly act. She was beginning to relax, and she hoped that wasn't just the effect of two gin and tonics, but his company. They halted while he got his bearings.

'Ah, we have to go down here. I'm relying on Trip Advisor and the hotel receptionist so let's hope they're both right.'

The place was perfect, small but not so small that you were sitting in the next diner's lap. It was dimly lit, mainly by pillared candles placed inside rustic iron holders. Andrea Bocelli sang through the warm atmosphere as aromas of rosemary and garlic wafted on the air.

'You look lovely by the way,' he said, his eyes twinkling in the candlelight.

Before she could thank him, a dark-haired waiter approached and welcomed them warmly. Once seated, he handed them each a menu then passed the wine list to Drake.

'White, red, rosé?' Drake said, his eyes still focused on the wine list.

'Actually, I'll just have water please.'

Drake raised a questioning brow. 'Still not a hundred per cent?'

'I thought I'd keep the detox going for a while.'

He scrutinised her. 'You're not abstaining because of me, are you?'

Mia realised she had missed an opportunity to ask what he meant by that, but it would open up a conversation they should probably have another time. If there were another time.

'I really would prefer water.' The waiter hovered. 'Still water, please.' He dipped his head and backed away from the table.

They sat in comfortable silence studying the menu.

Drake was first to slap his shut. 'So, what's your poison – sorry couldn't resist that one.'

She grimaced. 'Careful. I can reach your shins under the table, and I'm pretty accurate.'

He held up his hands in surrender, smiling. 'It's not a bad menu, is it? Something for everyone, and not a crab in sight! Sorry, last crab reference, I promise.'

The waiter returned with a basket of warm bread and a bowl of olive oil and balsamic vinegar for them to dip it in.

'Ready to order?'

Drake nodded for her to go first. 'Seabream please.'

'Calves liver for me.' Any awkwardness between them quickly dispelled and she had to plead with him not to make her laugh anymore.

The waiter delivered their food and the conversation lulled as they ate. The opportunity to study him was as delicious as the food. Pangs of something she didn't understand made her spirits zing. She liked the way his smile commenced at one corner of his lips and rippled across to the other. The golden flecks in his eyes were more prominently reflected by the flickering candle. The thickness of his hair, a thread of silver raw against the rest, molasses dark. She excused herself, afraid he could read her thoughts as a sudden urge to run her fingers through it made her blush. By the time she returned he'd already paid the bill.

It was warm for a September evening. The beach was deserted, except for the sandpipers and wagtails wading in the ripples of the incoming tide, and still early enough for the seagulls to screech at each other. Their path led them onto the sand. Drake kicked off his loafers.

'Come on, I dare you.'

'No way. It'll be freezing.'

'Only one way to find out.' He jogged to the water's edge and hitched up his trousers and waded in. She looked down at her feet, *why the hell not*, stepped out of her shoes and followed him.

'It's freezing you madman,' she said, inching her way towards him.

'Rubbish. It's just a little chilly. Shame really, we could have skinny-dipped.'

She threw him a haughty look. 'Er, I don't think so. I'm sure the good people of Sidmouth have seen it all before, but I have no intention of spending a night in Sidmouth nick. That's if they have one.'

He was studying her; she could feel the intensity of his eyes burning into her. She looked away.

'C'mon, my toes are turning blue.'

He waded to her side. 'Spoilsport.'

They strolled up the beach, kicking off the damp sand and laughing. When had she last enjoyed herself so much doing something as simple as paddling in a chilly September sea, or had she ever?

They reached the promenade and he guided her to a bench. She perched on the edge of the seat to knock the sand from her feet.

'Here,' he said, removing a handkerchief from his pocket and stooping to one knee. Gently he dusted the sand from between her toes. 'Don't want you rubbing up blisters do we.' He took her shoes from her and lined them up by her feet before sitting to dry his own. She was still grinning.

'What's so amusing?'

'Nothing really. I was just thinking, "If they could see me now".'

'Who's they?'

'Oh, just; well it was probably more me – in my head. Thought I was above it. Stupid really.'

'You talk as if you were someone else.'

'I was. Gina wasn't entirely wrong.' She laughed, 'You bring out the honesty in me. I'm not selling myself in a particularly good light, am I?'

'You don't need to try to be anyone you're not. Not with me anyway.'

Mia didn't think his comment warranted a reply. It felt nice – comfortable.

They strolled up the hill. She slowed as they reached the driveway to his hotel.

'Thank you, it's been a lovely evening.'

Drake kept walking.

'Hey, this is your stop!' she called out.

He spun around shaking his head, walking backwards.

'I'm walking you to your door.'

'Don't be silly, it's only a few hundred yards.'

He stopped to let her catch him up.

'And for those few hundred yards, I will accompany you. I insist.'

'Ah! a true gentleman.'

'Well, we are in a Regency town.'

She made him stop at the curve of the hill and look back. 'It's so beautiful here, even in the darkness.'

He took her hand; she didn't pull away. It felt good, warm and strong, and she liked the way his fingers laced through hers.

At the hotel entrance, he turned towards her. Her heart pumped with the expectation of a kiss. He released her hand.

'Goodnight, Mia.'

'What, no coffee? There's a nice lounge,' she said, wanting him to stay.

'Tomorrow. I'll pick you up at ten. I'm whacked now and you're still recovering. Tomorrow you can show me around the delights of Sidmouth. Deal?'

'Deal.'

He stepped forward and kissed her on both cheeks, turned and walked away. The desire to follow him and drag him up to her room was incredibly strong, but not as strong as the feeling of being treated with respect. Was he courting her? It certainly felt like it.

CHAPTER 44

DRAKE sat near the piano in the lounge, reading the paper, looking fresh in a pale blue long-sleeved shirt and taupe-coloured chinos. She blushed at the memory of her dream of them together bound by entangled sheets. It was made worse by the sight of his hair still damp from the shower, drying in soft waves. Waves that she had the urge to sink her fingers through.

He smiled and stood up when he saw her approach, folded his newspaper, adding it to the pile on the nearby table.

'Morning.' He stepped forward to greet her, giving the traditional two-cheek kiss. His fresh lemony aftershave with a hint of spice stayed on her face. The scent lingered after he pulled back from her, reminding her of the dream of their bodies tangled up in bedsheets.

'So, is it up or down?'

'What?'

'Up the hill for a walk, or down to the town. The town might be a better bet, according to that man.' He nodded towards Sam, who was moving a floral display. 'Says it's a "bit dark over Will's mum's."'

'Who's Will?'

He laughed. 'It's a local saying apparently, but I've heard it before, in Gloucestershire. Just refers to storm clouds. I'll look up its origin sometime. Looks like it's downhill then.' He glanced at her feet and the laced-up trainers.

'At least you're not one of those silly girls that can't pick the right shoes for walking.'

'Well, you said you wanted to explore the town, and I came here with a limited wardrobe and limited options.'

The town was bustling with Saturday shoppers, and people stopping to chat with each other. There were lots of shampoo-and-set ladies walking small dogs. They passed two girls wearing wet suits, their dad lagging, a surfboard tucked under each arm. Now they had left the town centre and wandered past the church to a small park, Drake steered her towards a bench in a quiet corner.

'Charming little spot. This place is full of surprises, isn't it? And you haven't said yet what brings you here.'

She gave the matter some thought before replying. Was she ready to share her thoughts with anyone? The discovery of Lisa being her mother still stung. But perhaps talking it through would give it some structure.

'It's a complicated story but basically, I came here to find out who I am.' He reached for her hand, his thumb stroking her skin. 'It's okay, I'm not going to burst into tears or anything. It's just facts really.' Did she believe that? 'You see, Gina, and I were both adopted and well, home life for me was a bit of a horror.' She paused. He'd know most of this from his aunt. 'The Major hated me, and I think I've finally worked out why. Anyway, I got sent away to boarding school, while Gina got to play the loving daughter and stayed at home. It never made sense until now. When I was eighteen, I went to live abroad. That was until eleven months ago when Gina tricked me into coming home.'

'Tricked you. How?'

She paused before answering. Not wishing to sound mean or needy. Or mention Rufus.

'She let me believe Daddy wanted to make amends – deathbed forgiveness and all that. Said he wanted to apologise for how I'd been treated. It was a complete lie, of course. He went berserk when he saw me. Gina said she would be away for the weekend, another lie, she went to Australia. Anyway, that's by the by, she did me a favour.'

'How come?'

'Well, I got to see a different side of my mother. I don't think I considered what fear she lived under, although the memories came back as soon as I entered the house. I realised she couldn't have helped me as she was a victim herself and I even got to... well, love her.' She swung her feet backwards and forwards under the bench. 'I'd never been allowed to spend so much time with her before. Turns out it was reciprocal. So, I made sure she had a bit of fun before she died and it sort of brought out another person, she was alive again. It was terrible living in a big smelly house, stuck indoors all day, him making awful noises in the room next door. Strangely, he got better than he deserved. I owed him nothing but accepted his life must be torturous, locked up in his own body. Hanging from that sling thing, hours and hours of nothingness to occupy himself with.'

Drake drew his shoe through the dusty ground, forming a groove.

'What did you do with him, sorry that came out wrong.'

'It's okay, I know what you meant. With a bit of research, I found several places who could take him and provide a bit more stimulation than he was getting stuck inside that room.' A saddened breeze blew her hair across her face, she caught it and tucked it behind her ear. 'The best was a military retirement home in Windsor. They offered all sorts to benefit him: hydrotherapy, and social stimulation. I may have detested the man but I'm not cruel, he seemed to thrive in the time he was there. I went to see him after he was settled and for once he didn't seem so infuriated by my presence. Anyway, that's another story, it's not why I'm here.' He didn't break into her thoughts, waiting for her to arrange them in order. 'I came here to solve a mystery but got more than expected.'

He ran his hand over his chin. 'And?'

'Mum – let's call her Constance, less confusing. Well, she had this tapestry bag, embroidered with peacocks. It went everywhere with her. I never knew what was in it until she died.'

He nodded, 'I remember it. Go on.'

'Well, it was filled with unbelievable memories. Lots of things. I'm still going through it. Loads of newspaper cuttings, flyers on the folk festival they have here, notes, scribblings. Unlikely jewellery. A photograph of a man, dark and foreign. Asian. I believe his name is Vikash Kumar, and I think he was my real father, that's what it says on my birth certificate.' Her words tapered out to a sigh. She stopped as a ball, yellow with red stars, bounced against her foot. A girl, a toddler, in a dress with stars matching the ball, ran towards the bench. She stopped a few feet from Drake and Mia and smiled shyly. Drake reached down, touched the ball and rolled it towards her.

The little girl's mother walked towards them. 'Say thank you, Millie.' The child mumbled something and toddled away.

'Where was I?'

'You were saying about what was in the bag, the jewellery, papers, but that wasn't all.'

She heaved a sigh. 'When she died, Constance wanted her ashes scattered on Mutter's Moor.'

'The hill up past the hotel?'

She looked at him, frowning, 'You got your bearings quickly.'

He shrugged. 'Not really. I got talking to the gardener chap, Sam. Mutter's Moor - odd name.'

'Named after Abraham Mutter, some ancient landowner and part-time smuggler, according to Sam. Anyway, the last resting place of my mother and all that. Can we go and get a coffee or something? All this talking's making me thirsty.'

The town had emptied. They found a coffee shop with cluttered tables, frantically being cleared before the next wave of customers invaded. They ordered coffee and Drake resumed the conversation.

'You said she wants you to scatter her ashes up the hill?'

'Yes,' she said, sipping her coffee.

'You haven't done it yet?'

'No.'

'What? Where is she now?'

'In my room, enjoying the view from the windowsill. I keep putting off saying goodbye.'

He chuckled. 'Ah, that's why you said about the weather not being blowy. I understand. So, if Vic – what's his name?'

'Vikash.'

'Vikash was your father, and your mother?'

'Lisa Farrant – our nanny.'

'What? Weird.' He rocked back in his chair. She could feel his eyes boring into her.

She folded her napkin, flattening it back into its creases.

'Even odder was she looked after me until I went to boarding school. Constance must have – well, she did – known Lisa was my birth mother. In her things was a photograph album of me as a little one, Lisa holding me and with two other women. Scribbled on the back in pencil it said Memmi and Elizabeth.'

He raised a finger. 'Ah, she was your – no Constance's cousin. Elizabeth.' It was Mia's turn to be surprised. 'She told me once she had a cousin, lived in a big house in Devon. Talked about the lovely holidays they had. Memmi doesn't ring a bell though, perhaps it's a nickname or means nanny or grandmother, I'm only guessing of course.'

'Really? She told you about Elizabeth?'

'Yup. She often told me the same things when I did jobs for her, that's how it stuck in my mind. So, your nanny was your birth mother? A bit strange though, to give her a job looking after you.'

'Even stranger. I met Lisa for coffee a while back, to ask her about the man in the photo and the connection with Sidmouth. She couldn't look me in the eye. Denied knowing the place, or who he was when all the time they'd been lovers.' She picked up her spoon scooping the last remnants of foam from her coffee cup. 'The birth certificate says he worked here on the railway.'

'Didn't even know they had one.'

'The station closed in 1967. Honiton's the nearest now. I came down by train. It's an easy journey.' The waitress cleared their table, Mia waited till she'd finished.

'Oh, and that's where the name Maureen came from, Lisa *Maureen* Farrant. Again, don't you think that a bit sick? Constance employs my mother and gives me her name, then carries around a photograph of my father and keeps his tie. It doesn't make sense.

Like the funeral flowers and the notice in the paper. It's all weird. I feel I've made headway but now I find myself backed into a corner.'

A huddle of people crowded the doorway waiting for an empty table.

Drake pushed back his chair and stood up. 'Time to go. I think they want their table.'

As soon as they were on the street, he took her hand again.

'God, what a mess. You poor thing. I thought I had a tragedy in my life. Yours was worse.'

'I wouldn't exactly call it a tragedy, but I wish I'd known somebody had given a shit.' She looked away surprised to find tears pooling her eyes. Thankfully, he didn't push her, and they ambled back to the beach.

'Fancy another paddle?' Playfully he tugged her arm towards the sands.

'Er. You go ahead. I'll watch.'

'Chicken.'

She smiled up at him, raised an elbow and made a clucking noise.

When they had both stopped laughing, he said, 'So where shall we go for lunch?'

'We just had coffee.'

Drake glanced at his watch. 'I know but it's half twelve and my stomach says lunch, must be the sea air.'

'Isn't it about time you made your way back home?'

He took her other hand and turned her to face him. 'Are you trying to get rid of me, Croxley Smith?'

She was lost in his warm brown eyes. He held her gaze, teasing. She struggled for something witty to say, but nothing came and without warning, he leant forward and dropped a kiss on the tip of her nose. Light, gentle, without threat, just surprise. She felt coy, an alien sensation and probably the wrong word but he made her feel like that, there was no other to word to explain it.

He was smiling now, breaking the circle of their arms, pulling her along at a lazy pace. Two people in no rush to be anywhere.

'Ah, a pub.' He tugged her sideways into the pub's garden to a table out of the wind.

'Back in a mo. I'll get some menus.' She found herself staring at the door he'd vanished into, hating the sense of separation. When he reappeared, he had a glass of white wine in one hand and a beer in the other.

Mia feigned surprise. 'I thought you didn't drink?'

'Non-alcoholic.' He gave her a sideways look. 'Who told you?'

'Helen.'

'I'm glad. It will make it easy for me to tell you my story. Listen to me "my story".' He looked lost for a moment, fiddling with the menus.

It was her turn to reach out and take his hand in support.

'You don't have to tell me now. Tomorrow is soon enough. And only if you want to.'

'You don't mind if I stay a bit longer? I better be honest, I booked until Tuesday.' A deep comforting feeling like melted chocolate settled inside her.

'That would be lovely, and you can tell me "your story" tomorrow. No more secrets for today. Tomorrow...'

CHAPTER 45

THEY kept their promises, talking about anything apart from secrets or past lovers. Mia shared selective tales from Chartley and told Drake about the upcoming reunion and how disappointed she'd been when it had been put off until later in the year due to unexpected building works.

He, in turn, told her about his family in Kent, how his mother was into every charity event going. His sister Trudi was a singer with a rock band. He joked that every time he visited; his mother drowned him in hints about becoming a grandmother before she "dropped off the perch" as his sister wasn't exactly the maternal type. Lunch stretched over two more glasses of wine and lively conversation. Before they knew it, it was gone six. They left the pub and strolled through the maze of lanes threading through the town. Much to her disgust, they had yet another meal before heading back.

They reached the entrance to her hotel.

'Nightcap in the bar?' she asked. His reply came in the form of a stifled yawn. 'I'll take that as a no then.' Standing on her tiptoes, she kissed him softly on the cheek. He, in turn, surprised her by enveloping her in a hug. She savoured the smell and feel of him and wondered if this was what *safe* felt like.

'See you in the morning then,' he said, releasing her from the warmth of his arms. 'In fact, why don't you join me for breakfast? And we can take up where we left off.'

'Okay. Nine thirty? Though I'm not sure about the left off a bit. I think I've done enough soul-bearing, it's your turn.'

'I was thinking we might take advantage of the day and drive along to Exmouth or even Budleigh Salterton. I'll let you choose.' He was walking away from her backwards, it was beginning to be a habit. Leaving her wanting more.

'So, bring what you need for the day.' He shouted backwards, waving.

She slept well, woke feeling refreshed. Then, as she drew back the curtains, she noticed a lone figure was making its way up the path; it was too far away for her to decide who it was. The person was followed by two other shapes. Perhaps they were in a group, hikers maybe, she thought as she turned from the window to get ready for her breakfast date.

'Looks a bit grey over Will's mum's,' she said aloud. She liked that expression, it was something new to ponder on. Who was Will? In fact, who was she? She picked up the urn.

'Well Constance, I'm Maureen Farrant, or is it Kumar-Farrant? We could double-barrel it. In truth, I don't feel like either.' She put Constance back on the windowsill – suddenly angry, she plucked her mobile from her pocket and pressed the green button by Lisa Farrant's name. 'Let's get this out in the open. I'm wasting my life on this.'

The call went straight to voicemail. Fuming, she threw the phone on the bed.

It was a chilly walk down to the Victoria and Mia was glad she'd brought a warm jumper. The hotel was a massive affair, set back off the road at the end of a long drive. On one side, sweeping beds of late summer flowers still offered a colourful show. Mia entered the foyer; the formal reception desk was unmanned.

American voices floated on the air, a man and woman - matching red baseball caps, they threw a "Good Mornin to ya," as they passed. Other guests, older, shuffled or strode past her, all in the same direction. *Breakfast* she thought but stayed put to wait for Drake. She selected a flyer from the display reading of the hotel's Edwardian history.

'Morning,' he said, his distinctive scent – familiar and enticing floating into her senses. She treated herself to another in-breath of him trying not to stare at the way Drake's hair formed soft waves still damp from his shower. She dragged herself from the distraction.

'This place is a bit…'

'Old School?'

'Yes, makes me want to whisper.'

'REALLY,' he said in a very loud voice.

She folded her lips over each other so as not to burst out laughing, play-punching his biceps.

'THEN WE WILL DO THE OPPOSITE,' he bellowed, laughing, as they made their way through rooms with over-fussy drapes. Mia kept her head down, not wishing to see the faces peering above broadsheets and tutting. The place reminded her of a stately home she had visited on a school trip. It was the smell, a mix of furniture polish, lilies, and food.

After breakfast, they climbed into the car and drove along to Budleigh Salterton, a pretty place with its bluff of trees even more sedate than its next-door neighbour. They wandered, hands brushing occasionally, through the small town. Everything seemed perfect but she still had one thing more to tell him. No more secrets, they'd said, but she still had one.

After she'd told him about what happened to her at Chartley he held her close against him for a long while. She closed her eyes, feeling his heartbeat against her pounding one until she calmed. One day, one day soon, maybe she could forgive herself and start to heal.

He kissed her forehead gently. 'Thank you for trusting me with your secret. We will never speak of it again.' She slid her arms around his neck, relief at telling him and his reaction lifting a burden from her soul.

'Let's get a drink and warm you up,' Drake said, you're shivering.'

They drank coffee, watching the sky darken, and witnessed the sheet of rain coming in from the sea, forcing them to rush back to Drake's car. The downpour reached them before they made it, drenching them in seconds.

Drake turned the key in the ignition of his Audi, then immediately switched it off again as his mobile rang. He mouthed the
word *sorry* to her.

Shaking the rain from her hair, she dabbed at her streaking mas-
cara with a damp tissue until the one-sided conversation alerted
her.

Colour drained from his face. 'How many are injured? – serious?
Lifting gear. Oh my God. Had he been drinking? The machine
– counterbalanced – it shouldn't have happened. Yes. Yes. Of
course. Tell them I'll get there as soon as – I know. Thanks, Cissy.
Try not to worry. Be strong, don't cry. He'll be fine.'

Mia shivered, not just from the cold and wet but from the change
in Drake. He didn't speak, his eyes were darting from his phone
to the steering wheel. He appeared older, smaller. She rested her
hand on his knee, waiting. His head fell back onto the headrest
whilst his hand thumped the steering wheel.

'Sorry,' he said again as if he'd almost forgotten she was there.
He rocked forward rubbing his palms up and down his cheeks.
'There's been an accident. Paul's been hurt. One of the diggers
rolled back down an embankment. They shouldn't have even been
there today. Fuck. Sorry, sorry.'

'God how awful. Look don't worry about me. Do you want me
to drive while you make phone calls or something?'

He shook his head and let out a heavy sigh. 'Great lummox.
What was he doing there? His job is in the office. Some things
are best left to me.' He shook his head slowly staring into his lap.
'Apparently, there were loads of kids on skateboards, only one got
hurt jumping out of the way. I've got to get back.'

'Of course.'

They drove with only the flip-flop-flip-flop sound of the windscreen wipers to break the thickening silence. A grey mist hung
across the hedgerows as the rain was sucked out by a sharpening
wind. Without warning, Drake pulled off the road.

'Sorry I have to make a call.' He got out of the car, pacing back
and forth on the wet grass verge. She looked away as Drake ges-
ticulated, his face taught. Feeling like she was eavesdropping, she
switched on the car radio.

Low pressure and squally weather forecast until Friday.

The car was misting up. She turned down the fan and rubbed at the glass. Drake was leaning against a farm gate, phone to his ear. He appeared calmer but unaware of the torrential rain lashing down on him for a second time.

It was an easy decision to go back with him. If the weather was going to be like this, there was no point in staying, no doubt she could pick up some temp work. She'd just finished sending a text to say when she'd be available when the car door opened, and Drake climbed in. He reached over to the back seat to retrieve a sweatshirt.

He offered it to her. 'Here, dry yourself with this.'

'No way, you're twice as wet as I am.' She pulled down the visor angling it towards him. 'Look at you.'

He nodded and rubbed his hair with the garment.

'Is there any more news?'

'They didn't tell Cissy, but I think Paul had a cardiac arrest in the ambulance,' he said, his voice hitched with emotion. 'He shouldn't have even been there. Christ Mia, they've got two lovely kids... God, what a mess.'

She thought of platitudes, *I'm sure he'll be fine, he's in good hands*, none were fitting.

'It may not be as bad as you imagine.' He didn't comment, blowing on his hands to warm them instead. 'I thought I'd hitch a lift back with you if you don't mind? It's not the weather for scattering ashes. If you don't mind of course?'

Her words clicked him out of it. 'Thank you. I'd appreciate the company.'

Back in Sidmouth, she warmed up in the shower before packing her bags in minutes. Constance was once again returned to the confines of her rucksack. She left the room and went to the foyer to wait for Drake.

Sam appeared from a doorway marked staff.

'You off again then Missy?'

'Yes, Sam. Looks like I ran out of good weather.'

He nodded, removed his cap and scratched his head. 'Reckon it's going to take you another visit if you ever going to get up on the moor.'

'Another reason to come back.'

'Weather will be good in the autumn. October's a good month.'

Drake appeared at the entrance wearing a pale blue sweater and jeans.

'Your chariot awaits, madam.'

Mia breathed a sigh of relief at the lift in his mood. Sam picked up her bags and followed them outside to the car. The rain had softened to a drizzle. Drake looked impatient as Sam offered him advice on shortcuts and better routes. She could tell he wasn't taking it in.

Once they were underway, she ventured, 'Any news?'

'Yep. Cissy called from the hospital. Paul had more of a panic attack than a heart attack. His leg's pretty messed up, and he's not brilliant with blood. He'll be out of action for a bit, but it's not as bad as we feared, thank God. It turned out Jimmy, one of the machine drivers, was showing off a bit in front of the skateboarding kids, putting the digger through its paces. Stupid sod. Paul was trying to get his attention to bawl him out when the cab tipped. He was too close. Could have been worse. Doesn't bear thinking about.'

'Oh, great news that he's okay though. Still a good idea to get back and see for yourself.'

'Mia, it's sweet of you to come back with me. I feel bad about you cutting your trip short.'

'I think Constance quite likes the commute now, she's done it a few times. I'll come back after I finish the booking I've just accepted in London and do the deed.'

The evening was drawing in. Drake put the car headlights lights on. The journey felt companionable, talking quietly to each other in the dark.

'Will you go and see her? Lisa?'

'I don't know. Probably. I need the full story and she is the only person who can tell me.' She lapsed into thought.

But do I want to? What have I got to gain? It won't change who I am, knowing some sordid little story about a silly girl and a man called Vikash. But then there's still the mystery of Constance's wishes. Bugger. I'll sleep on it and give it some consideration. It does feel like unfinished business.

CHAPTER 46

IT was good to be home after the long drive back in what had felt like a conveyor-belt of rain. Unlocking the door to her apartment, her nostrils were affronted by an unrecognisable stench. It took a few moments to suss out the culprit – decomposing bananas in the fruit bowl. They had festered into a runny slime and minuscule fruit flies hovered around the bowl.

'Well Constance,' she said as she removed her from the rucksack and placed her back on the side. 'As you can see, I still haven't got this domesticity thing right. Otherwise, I would have thrown these out *before* I went away.' She scooped up the rotting gunge with kitchen roll and put the bowl to soak, then lit a scented candle to freshen up the place.

Kicking off her shoes, Mia made herself a gin and tonic. It had been a long day with much to think about. There were two messages on her house phone: one from the agency with her booking confirmation the other from the concierge saying he'd tried to deliver her flowers but had given them to his mother and hoped she didn't mind.

'Well, at least they didn't go to waste.'

Her thoughts, unbidden, wandered back to Lisa and Vikash. She had his address from her birth certificate – would he still live there after all these years, should she try writing a letter? But if she got no reply she wouldn't know if he'd received it or ignored it. What if he was dead? Something had stopped her from just going to the house, not just Paul's accident. Being with Drake felt like moving forward, not wading through a mire of questions and mistakes made over thirty odd years ago, by Lisa and Vikash. She'd love to just put it all behind her but the presence of the urn wouldn't let her be.

'Why couldn't you have just told me? I'm a big girl, I would have understood. We could have got together, the three of us. I could have shared your reminiscing. God this is all so exhausting, and I know I have to let you go but something keeps stopping me.'

Exhausted from the day's events, she rested her head back into the soft leather and closed her eyes. Nothing fitted together or made any sense.

Her headspace grazed across the years, trying to remember when Lisa had vanished from her life, surely it was when she went to Chartley, but why had she given her up for adoption and then continued to look after her? *I keep asking myself the same question. What I want are answers.* No, actually I have a *right* to answers, and Lisa held them all. Would she ever answer her phone? Mia guessed Lisa was avoiding her.

One last try and if she doesn't answer then I go to her house.

'Lisa, it's Mia. Please can you call me when you have a moment? I need to talk to you urgently. We both know what it's about. My number is…'

Right, Lisa, you've got until Friday to call me back or I'm turning up on your doorstep.

A text arrived a few minutes later to say Lisa was unable to respond as she was abroad. No mention of where or when she'd return. Mia wasn't convinced but had no choice but to wait and see.

CHAPTER 47

Mia hated the daily commute but to take a cab or drive a car with the stress of traffic and costs of the congestion charge and parking, it wasn't worth the hassle.

As she moved to take her place on the escalator, a voice that reminded her of Rufus's carried on the air. When she thought of him now, her memories were guilt-ridden. The need to apologise was as strong as the urge to see Lisa. She made up her mind to send him that letter. The one she'd drafted so many times but never sent. If she handwrote it, even Monica, his trusty PA, wouldn't dare open it.

Normally she'd have walked across the park, but few people were taking that route and a woman had been attacked the week before. The main road was longer but busier and therefore safer.

The church clock said eight-fifteen. It had been a long day with a demanding client, but the upside was he expected her to accompany him on business lunches, take notes and instructions. Consequently, she had eaten extremely well in the last week and not needed to cook when she got home. She planned a long bath and another call to Lisa then an early night.

Rounding the corner, a shadowy figure appeared from the lane by the side of her building, seemingly heading her way. She slowed her pace and glanced around. The street was deserted. Should she run back the way she'd come?

'Mia. Thank goodness. I thought you were never coming home. I lost my phone so couldn't call.'

The adrenalin spike faded as Drake came into view.

'Christ, Drake, you scared me.'

'Sorry. I didn't mean to.'

'What are you doing here? I wasn't expecting you.'

His smile slipped. 'I just wanted to see you.' They stood awkwardly looking at each other. 'Look I should have rung first only —'

'You lost your phone. Look, I'm sorry. It's lovely to see you. Let's get indoors. It's freezing and my feet are killing me.'

He looked down at her heeled court shoes, scrunching up his face in disapproval. 'Haven't got into the commuter fashion then.'

'God no. Trainers are for running in. Come on, let's get into the warmth.'

They took the lift and Mia began to relax. The unexpectedness of Drake's appearance brought that fizzy feeling back to her stomach. Standing so close to him in the lift made her insides do a little dance.

'You look frozen,' he said, removing his coat once they were inside her flat.

'I am,' she was rubbing the tops of her arms.

'Go and take a shower and warm up. I'll fix us some drinks.'

'You know, you are incredibly bossy.'

He grinned, and she had to look away, knowing she was staring at his mouth.

'Okay. Tea and coffee in the kitchen, juice in the fridge and there may be a diet coke in there as well.'

'Great, now go,' he said, waving her out of the room.

The warm water made her skin tingle. Was it that or the thought he might appear naked through the steam, and join her? She turned the dial to cold, then off.

Mia. Behave yourself. She towelled her hair, then slipped into a pair of lounging trousers and a soft wool top.

He was standing with his back to her as she entered the lounge. He turned, acknowledging her.

'Ah, here she is now.' He had a mischievous twinkle in his eye. 'I was just introducing myself to Constance. She's been telling me how you were a handful as a child and scared of frogs. I told her I don't believe a word of it.'

Mia grinned from ear-to-ear. 'You're nuts, you know?' stepping towards him, she gave him a gentle shove into a chair. 'Mind you, I talk to her all the time. Annoyingly, she doesn't tell me what I want to hear. Anyway, enough of that, how's Paul?' she asked as she settled into the corner of the sofa and curled her legs beneath her. She didn't trust herself to be too close to him.

'He's on the mend, but still in hospital for a few more days at least. They're worried about his leg. It's not healing so well and he's so ruddy obstinate – keeps talking about discharging himself, but Cissy talked him out of it. Believe me, she can be a force to be reckoned with.' He shifted forward in his chair, resting one hand on his knee, and gestured to the side table. 'I made you a gin and tonic, you looked like you needed one.'

'Thanks, but I would have been happy with juice.'

A flicker of annoyance crossed his face.

'Mia, can we get this straight – I'm not an alcoholic. It's not that I can't drink. I just choose not to. So please stop trying to play the AA buddy, will you? Deal?'

She raised her glass. 'Deal. So, lovely as it is to see you and enjoy your riveting wit, was there a reason for the visit?'

'Not really. I just wanted to see you, that's all. I was enjoying myself in Sidmouth and it all ended so abruptly. I was wondering if you had any thoughts on going back. If so, I'd like to come with you. If that's okay with you?'

Mia rubbed her temple. 'I haven't had much chance to think about it. This job I'm doing is pretty full-on. If he had his way, I'd work till midnight.' She sipped her gin, 'I got a call from one of Zannah's girls, asking if I was looking for a permanent job. She laid it on thick – lots of travel, surprisingly good package.'

'And are you considering it?'

'God no. My life wouldn't be my own. Travel doesn't enthuse me the way it used to. I'm quite happy here.'

He nodded, his forehead flattening, and the conversation took a beat.

'I've been thinking about this Lisa Farrant.' He glanced in the direction of the urn still adorned with the spotty tie. 'I could help you do a bit of digging about him – your father. Railway records, local paper archives, electoral rolls.'

'That's sweet of you. I've left Lisa a message to call me.'

'No reply?'

'Yes, a text to say she's currently abroad.'

'Convenient.'

'Just what I thought. She must know I've discovered the truth by now.'

'And you still need to know more?'

'Yes, I do. I want answers. I somehow feel there's more to this.'

'Will you let me help you?'

He looked like a little boy keen to get a "yes" to a request for sweets.

'Yes, I'd like that.'

He glanced at his watch. 'Fantastic. Time to go I think and let you get to bed. I'll get a new phone; I need your number again. It will be the first I add,' he said as she reached for a pad and scribbled her mobile number. They both stood up at the same time. She led the way to the door, wondering if he would make the first move.

They turned their heads simultaneously, bumping noses awkwardly. She leant back, kissing him lightly on the lips, then pulled away.

'Call me at the weekend. If you have a phone by then.'

'I will.'

She watched him make his way to the lift, desperately wanting to call him back, but he'd said he was a gentleman, so she must play the lady. A role she was not familiar with.

'I know, Mother, patience is a virtue, and everything comes to those who wait. Ruddy clichés. How about I want to tear off your clothes. I know, unbecoming of a lady. Sod the clichés, look where they've got me.'

CHAPTER 48

Her current boss, a Mr Matsoukata, a squat, ugly man with a bulbous nose, was used to getting what he wanted, and he'd not taken kindly to Mia's refusal of a permanent job. Zannah phoned her personally to plead with her to accept an extension to the booking, which now included a formal dinner at the Savoy.

'It's only two days more Mia and the money's good. He is one of my top clients.'

'Is he?'

'No, but his contacts are. Thought I'd try a guilt trip.'

'Huh. You do realise he's repulsive. Do you know I carry around a can of deodorant for him and do you know what for?'

'Sweaty pits?'

'No, he takes his shoes off and sprays his feet. Puts them up on his desk. It's gross and he farts, just lifts his cheek like a schoolkid.'

Zannah exploded with laughter.

'And he flosses his teeth at the dining table. Can't someone else do it? Please?'

'Sorry, it won't wash. He only wants you. It's a big fee for the agency… I'll even throw in supper at *Zuma* next week. Please for me.'

'Damn you. Okay, but I want an armed guard outside my room in case old Moussaka thinks he might get lucky. And, I'm not sure I have anything suitable to wear.'

'Hire something and put it on expenses.'

'I had a hot date for this weekend.'

'Don't fib. Drake said nothing was fixed. Anyway, he'll under-stand.'

'Is nothing a secret around here?'

'No. And I'm watching you closely. I may even consider opening another agency – a dating agency.'

'Good luck with that, this romance is moving at a snail's pace.'

'Problem?'

'No actually – a refreshing change.'

'I might have a little news on that front.'

'You mean Drake?'

'No, you're not the only one with something to tell.'

'Zannah!' she squealed. 'Tell me.'

'Only if you go to the ball with Mister Moussaka.'

'You'd resort to blackmail?'

'Yup. See you Tuesday. I'll book for 6.30.'

So Zannah has a man. About time! She's far too lovely to be on her own. Roll on Tuesday.

No matter how hard she looked there was nothing suitable for a black-tie dinner. This was the second time she'd wished she hadn't sold all her evening dresses. As if by magic, her phone pinged. She grinned. Zannah had sent her a list of exclusive dress hire agencies.

'Ruddy blackmail.'

Zannah's cryptic message of having someone in her life made Mia desperate to speak to Drake, she'd saved his new number when he'd texted it through. The phone rang, then went to voicemail, she'd have to leave a message.

'Hi, it's me. Do you fancy a trip to Sidmouth? The week after next, the twentieth. I've not heard a thing from Lisa, but it's time I lived up to my obligations. Call me when you can. I hope Paul's doing well. Bye.'

Mia booked two rooms at the Savoy, careful not to choose a room with adjoining doors; hers was two floors below his and half the price. There was time for a luxurious bath and a manicure be-fore she had to collect him from his room for the reception.

The gown she had chosen was a rich emerald green crepe, with a one-shoulder fastening of gold and green stones. It fell in simple folds below the bust and she had teamed it with emerald shoes and bag. Her hair was swept upwards and held in place with an emerald and gold clasp. Unfortunately, Mister Matsoukata had chosen to finish off his outfit with a broad red cummerbund, thus resembling an Easter egg.

Sneaking a glance at herself in the mirrored lift she was pleased with the result. Though she wasn't looking forward to the endless speeches and stilted conversations, it was nice to be at such a prestigious venue.

She'd memorised the seating plan and knew she had the Greek ambassador on her left and old Moussaka on her right. Thank God, she only had another forty-eight-hour with him – but it was getting harder not to address him as a pasta dish.

The evening passed reasonably quickly, the highlight being an after-dinner appearance by Il Divo – spoiled marginally by the two Greeks talking across her through most of the performance. The evening ended and she managed to excuse herself as the men retired to one of the bars for more brandy. An attractive blonde, who'd been sitting opposite and who'd hardly spoken a word all evening, caught Mia's eye, she smiled, inclined her head slightly toward the man next to her and went cross-eyed. Mia tried not to laugh and copied the head movement toward Moussaka and raised her eyes to heaven. She caught up with her on the way out of the ballroom.

'God what a boring evening, my guy spoke so little English. Still nice to say I've been here. How about you, are you working?'

The woman had spoken earlier, Mia noted the upper-class diction, now her accent was more Roehampton than Roedean.

'Yes, but only until tomorrow morning.'

The girl pulled a face. 'Rather you than me. I just stick to the escorting. No extras.'

Mia stopped abruptly, digesting the words.

'What! No. No, you got it wrong. I am working but as a temp PA. Thankfully, tomorrow is my last day. We're interviewing for my replacement.'

'Oh, I'm sorry, I just thought pretty girl-ugly man. I'm always putting my foot in it. I didn't think I'd come across you before. A PA? Lucky old you. One of these days I'll get lucky and my date will be like Richard Gere. Love that film. I've watched it at least six times. Hey, fancy one for the road, Jilly and Chloe are here as well. Looks like I got the short straw, Jilly got a yank and Chloe a Frenchman. In fairness, she is fluent, but I got Mister-no-speaky-English. It's a bugger staying sober all night.'

Mia was about to accept when a group of suited men crossed the foyer. She stepped back as Rufus walked past, deep in conversation with his friend Sandy Calder. Luckily, both were oblivious to her being only steps away.

Her heart thumped in her chest. She didn't want to be seen here on her own, worse still with Mister Moussaka. If Rufus was staying here and if the blonde had thought she was an escort, might he?

'Sorry, long day and even longer tomorrow. I need to stay sharp.'

'Nice meeting yer.'

'Yes, you too. Goodnight.' Mia made swiftly for the lifts.

In her room, she unpinned her hair and stepped out of her gown as she looked out of the window. The Thames, black and silent, stirred below, only the flickering of lights across its surface broke its menace. She wrapped her arms across her body and hugged herself. Strange, how something so majestic by day appeared so daunting at night. Who would have known fate would put Rufus in her path twice?

Of all the gin joints in all the world... how true. Everything was for a reason.

Her thoughts yo-yoed between the good times she'd had with Rufus and how disloyal she'd been. Shame made her coil into a ball on the vast bed. How would she have felt if the roles were reversed? Tonight, had been a bit of a shock. Imagine if they'd been at the same function – the same table. She wanted him to think well of her. It was particularly important, as was the apology she owed him. Sat up, knowing sleep wouldn't come until she'd drafted a letter. The first draft she'd written previously was nowhere near acceptable. This letter would take many edits to get it right but get it right she would. It was part of who she was now. A person with ethics and morals.

CHAPTER 49

Zuma was heaving with men in expensive suits and well-dressed women. All freshly decanted from high-rise offices. Spotting Zannah at the bar, Mia edged her way through. Two men stood in her way, their backs to Zannah and a man she was chatting to.

No, it can't be, ruddy hell. Surely not him.

Zannah caught her eye and beckoned her forward, the two men parted to let her through. Zannah slid from her stool and the two women hugged.

'Bloody hell, you didn't say it was him,' Mia hissed in Zannah's ear.

'No, you idiot, I'm no cougar. Let me introduce you —'

Mia stood awkwardly. 'No need. Who doesn't know who he is?'

He leaned forward and took her hand planting a kiss on her cheek.

'Delighted to meet you, sadly it's brief as I have another engagement.' He kissed Zannah goodbye and vanished between his two bodyguards, a crush of bodies parting to let him pass.

'Your face is a picture.'

'Well, what do you expect. You tell me you have a love interest and I walk in and find you with a royal.'

'An old friend, from when I was married to Royston. As a Right Hon, we moved in illustrious circles. Come on let's go to our table, this could be a power-gossip, but you first.'

As they sat down, a barman approached, and replenished Zannah's glass then poured one for Mia.

'I haven't got much to tell. Drake came down for the weekend, he was lovely, kind funny —'

'You forgot handsome, sexy and available.'

'Will you get that twinkle out of your eye. I'm being cautious.'

'You don't need to be, he can't stop talking about you. Awful business with Paul. Cut the visit short, I hear.' Zannah strained to look over Mia's head as a large party pushed their way into the restaurant. 'Quick, let's order before they do, I'm starving.'

Mia knew Zannah's chilled demeanour was a front. She was enjoying the intrigue of building up to the big reveal and Mia wasn't going to spoil her moment.

Zannah sighed. 'Well, I suppose I'd better give you my news,' she said, extending her left hand to show off the biggest champagne diamond Mia had ever seen.

'Oh my God, Zannah.' Mia cupped her friend's fingertips with her own, leaning in to examine it. 'It's stunning.'

Zannah beamed. 'I know I just love it. I can't believe it, I feel like a schoolgirl, all coy and excited. Oh, he's so wonderful.'

'Where did you meet him?'

'Zurich. I was at a conference; he was over for some high-power meeting. It's all been a bit of a whirlwind. I've only known him a few months, but it seems right. He makes me feel cared for, special. A little bit girlie. It's wonderful. I was beginning to tire of being a "sharp-suited businesswoman." There's more to life than employment law, temps and staff who can't get along with each other.' She scrunched up her shoulders and raised a curled fist to her mouth. 'I want to scream his name from the rooftops. Oh, Mia, it's amazing I never knew what love was until I met him. We even finish each other's sentences. Spooky.'

'I'm just so happy for you. There's hope for me yet. So, when am I going to meet him?'

Zannah drained her glass and tapped her mouth with her napkin as the waiter topped up her glass.

'Sadly, you just missed him, he's been in London all week, but flew out to Abu Dhabi yesterday. I'm joining him next week – I can't wait for a bit of sun after this weather. Then on to Australia to meet some of his family. I'm gaining two stepdaughters, Sophia, and Jazmine – Jazz for short. I hope they like me. Jack's looking forward to it, he's flying out as soon as Uni breaks up, he's very keen to meet his new stepsisters, says he's been an only child for too long.'

'As least he's onside, that's a bonus. And why wouldn't they like you? There's nothing not to like. Anyway, tell me more – what's he like, apart from being the love of your life?' She shifted back in her seat, watching as Zannah pursed her lips thoughtfully, her eyes shining with happiness.

'Well, he's tallish and broad. Not traditionally handsome, no chiselled jaw. A little scar on his chin from a riding accident, erm, what else? Hates opera, thank God, and kippers.'

'Kippers?' Mia laughed, 'Bit random.'

'I know. We played the twenty things you don't know about me game, hilarious.'

'And does he have a name?'

'Haven't I said? Alexander Calder. He prefers Alex, but most people call him Sandy. He's in steel…'

Mia felt the smile slide from her face. For a second, she zoned out of the conversation, her mouth suddenly dry, a burning heat rising in her chest. It was a good job she was sitting. Her legs felt peculiar and a cold sweat had formed along the ridge of her lip.

She felt sick, dizzy, panicked, she wanted to scream out No-No-No. *The lies I told Zannah about Sardinia when we first met, all that waffle about my work experience, trying to sound respectable, capable. She'll know how I treated Rufus, how I hurt him. I don't want her to know that person. It's too sordid. God, how long have I known Sandy? Years, he and Rufus are best friends. Sandy a frequent guest at the villa. Oh God, this can't be happening. Rufus would no doubt have explained my departure in unfavourable terms. I know he's a gentleman, but he must have been upset. He would have confided in Sandy. If Drake learns about this and thinks I'm the unfaithful type, he'll back off. I've enough baggage he already knows about but affairs with tennis coaches and chauffeurs sound so sordid. It's not who I am now. Getting close to Drake has made me happy, optimistic. A few words could forfeit the respect and friendship of those who matter. I couldn't bear to see the disgust in their eyes. No more hiding. I must stop this now, tell the truth, better hearing it first-hand.*

'Zannah. I'm sorry to interrupt, but there's something I have to tell you.'

CHAPTER 50

THE soft fluffy duvet rested across her shoulders; she was in the warm happy place before waking. Fingers curled around the edges she tugged it closer to her chin. Outside a cacophony of birdsong teased her senses. Something wasn't right. With effort, she opened one eye. This wasn't her bed. A groan escaped her lips at the memory of the night before. They were at Zuma and she remembered starting to tell Zannah about Alex and Rufus. Zannah had stopped her, sensing the need for privacy. They had come to Zannah's house.

If she could just stay here forever, she was warm and comfortable, she didn't want to climb out of this bed and face what? What Zannah thought of her. The life she'd made for herself like inky blotting paper, spoiled. She rolled onto her back staring at the ceiling, recalling the conversation and too many glasses of wine. Downstairs, the odd noise alerted her, Zannah was up and about.

Mia stretched and kicked back the covers, she felt groggy and dehydrated, hungover. There was no choice other than to face the music.

Zannah was grilling bacon. Her beautiful chestnut locks were tied loosely back with a lilac chiffon scarf, exactly matching the silk top she was wearing. In the background, Robbie Williams sang Angels with Zannah joining in on the chorus. Everything seemed normal.

Mia breathed in the smell of bacon, warm toast, and fresh coffee, suddenly feeling ravenous. It was nice to enter a room with such a homely feel.

'Morning,' she croaked in a gravelly voice, before clearing her throat.

'Morning, my lovely. Now sit, no argument, you are not leaving until you have a full stomach and a clear head.'

'The latter might not be so easy,' Mia said, taking a seat at the table, while Zannah beat eggs in a metal dish. 'I presume this one's mine.' The place setting had a box of paracetamol beside the cutlery.

'Thought I'd cover for all eventualities,' Zannah said, smiling. 'Can't say I feel too bad myself, but then I didn't finish off the last bottle.'

Mia raised a hand. 'No post-mortems please, I'm embarrassed enough as it is.' She popped two tablets in her mouth and washed them down with juice. 'How things can change so much in twenty-four hours.'

'Hm,' was all Zannah said as she carried two plates of scrambled eggs and bacon to the table.

Mia didn't pick up her cutlery immediately. 'Look, I'm sorry. We were having such a lovely evening and I'm so happy for you, then I went and ruined it all.'

'Rubbish.' Zannah mumbled, forking fluffy yellow egg into her mouth and chewing. 'Firstly, no one can make me stop smiling or take the shine off my forthcoming nuptials.' She giggled. 'I've always wanted to say "forthcoming nuptials." Anyway, I don't know what the problem is. So what if you embellished your past, who doesn't? I've been in recruitment for so many years I can spot a pretender in a nanosecond.'

'Really? You knew I was lying about Sardinia?'

'Not lying, embellishing is a better word.'

'But you gave me work.'

Zannah nodded. 'Eat,' she ordered.

Mia picked up her cutlery and obeyed.

'Yes, I did but I have a nose for a bluffer. Sometimes, it's not about the qualifications, it's the soft skills and a bit of balls thrown in for good measure. And I was right, you delivered. I liked you. I sensed you were in some sort of desperate place but would fight your way out of anything dished at you. You didn't disappoint. I suppose I saw a bit of me in you.'

Mia's forkful of egg hovered between the plate and her mouth. 'I wish.'

'No, it's true. So what if you slept with a few men while you were with Rufus? With him away so much who's to say he didn't seek entertainment elsewhere. How do you think I came by all of this? I married a wealthy man. Royston was a back-bencher when I met him, with the drive to get into the shadow cabinet. But he was a letch, couldn't keep his hands to himself. I'm not saying that about Rufus. Alex speaks highly of him. He does sound like a lovely man.'

'He is. I saw him, you know, Rufus. Twice. Once in Copenhagen and at the weekend at the Savoy when he was with Sandy, but thankfully they didn't see me. You are right about Rufus; he is one of the good guys. I was the wrongdoer. He was only ever kind to me, even asked me to marry him once, but I was busy looking for the next best thing.'

'Or love?'

Mia's head jerked up at the comment.

'You see, we're not that different.' Her face broke into a wide smile. 'I was lucky I got Jack out of the Royston scenario, and the agency of course. I worked my butt off to become successful. Stop with the self-flagellation. I mean, what have you done that's so awful? Grown up? You're not the same person who wandered in off the street and didn't know she needed a passport.'

Mia reached for the coffeepot. 'The thing is in throwing me out he gave me a chance to change.' She sipped her coffee. 'I think I'm beginning to understand why the Major – my stepfather – hated me. It must have been a shock getting a coffee-coloured child. I bet he gave Constance hell. I'm surprised he didn't send me back. He was such a racist. Gina, well who knows what went on in her head, but she's another one who unwittingly changed my life and the upside is that I got to know Constance. I know I made her last year a happy one. Leaving Sardinia made me think on my feet and be more tolerant and less selfish.'

'Thank goodness,' Zannah gave mock applause. 'Now let's forget it and move forward, I have a wedding on the horizon, and you need to help me plan it.'

Mia's smile faded quickly.

'But what about Drake?'

'What about him? You said you'd touched on what you were like in the past. End of. He doesn't know that person, nor does he need to. Don't throw away a good thing by making it complicated.'

Mia's eyes felt hot. It wasn't the over-imbibing of alcohol making her feel vulnerable, it was knowing someone had her back.

'You're such a good friend, Zannah, I don't know what I'd have done without you.'

'Oh no, you don't, young lady. No tears. Go home and get on with your life in that order.'

Through blurry vision, Mia raised her hand in mock salute, 'Yes boss.'

CHAPTER 51

2^{3rd} October 2013
Dear Rufus,

You will no doubt be surprised to get this letter, but it's one I feel compelled to write. I can make no excuses for my behaviour. It was wrong, I was cruel and undeserving of your affection. You offered me a wonderful life and I abused your trust. For that, I apologise.

I'm not the same person now. The one who shared your life has gone and I'm not proud of her. This only makes me more aware I did you the greatest disservice. They say leopards don't change their spots, but I truly am reformed and have you to thank for that.

Since coming to the UK, I have made a lot of discoveries about myself. I have learned a great deal about my upbringing, well-kept secrets I was never meant to uncover. The couple who adopted me (my parents) have since died, but I am a better person for having spent time with Constance, my mother. She left me a bag full of secrets. I have been able to trace my birth parents. Where that will lead, I don't know, but I must follow the clues she gave me and find out.

When I saw you in Copenhagen, I was working for a recruitment agency. I still am. The work is varied and interesting and it seems I'm quite good at organisation. Yes, that from a woman who couldn't pack a suitcase!

I extend this apology not only to you but to Teresa, Monica, and anyone else in your employ who put up with my tongue lashings and bad behaviour. I had thought, wrongly, I was better than they were because of my situation. Truth be known, their lives were probably richer than mine in so many ways.

I have made a life for myself here in England. I have a nice apart-ment, live within my means, and have true friends. I despise the person I once was and ask for your forgiveness. I'm sorry Rufus, you were only ever kind to me. If our paths should ever cross again, I would like it to be as friends. I hope you will find someone who will make you happy. You deserve it.

Mia

It was her fifth attempt since her original draft. She approved the mix of formal and emotional. It was from the heart. Sooner or later they would meet up, not least on Zannah and Sandy's wed-ding day, where she prayed there'd be no animosity to mar Zan-nah's happiness. The letter was the best she could make it, every word she'd written was from the heart.

CHAPTER 52

News of Zannah's engagement had reached Drake's ears. Mia was grateful he had decided to phone and not make a personal call, as the anticipation of losing herself to those alluring eyes made her stomach do the strangest choreography.

The gaps between them speaking, instead of cooling things down, had cantered ahead. Was it news of Zannah's forthcoming wedding spurring him on? She dared not set too much store by her optimism. Drake spoke as if it were already a given they would be invited as a couple. So, was that how he saw them? Neither were teenagers, she was thirty-six for goodness sake. The temptation to jump in with both feet was great but not until her own house was in order.

'Any news from Lisa?' The richness of his voice made her eyelids heavy.

'No nothing, she may still be away, of course. I'll give it the week then go to her home and see if I can catch her.'

'Do you think she's avoiding you?'

'Probably. I think she's hoping to avoid a conversation, imperative to me as is painful for her. But I have to give her the benefit of the doubt.'

'I didn't ask – did she marry? Have other children?'

'Not that I know of, but she could have. God, that would be weird actually, having blood siblings.'

'Don't get your hopes up. I don't want my girl getting upset.'

There was a pause before they both talked over one another. She felt flustered, her heart had picked up a beat and her breath stalled at the unexpected phrase. He'd called her *his* girl. Thank goodness he couldn't see her face.

'Sorry. I was going to say…'

'Yes?'

'Er, nothing really, oh yes. Did you hear? Michael Schumacher – poor guy, Skiing accident. They say the damage could be permanent.'

Should she let him off? It was a rubbish answer. She moved away from her laptop to the sofa feeling bold.

'Was that really what you were going to say?'

She heard a phhht sound. Then a small cough. 'Damn it, Mia. You make me feel like a ruddy sixteen-year-old. I can't get my words out properly.'

'You mean you have a stutter?' She teased.

'I have everything. I can't get you out of my head. Okay, I'm ruddy smitten and now I feel like a kid caught with my trousers down.'

She gave a girly giggle. 'Ooh too visual and too much information!'

'And too soon?'

What should she say? Play hard to get? No, bugger it. 'I'd say your timing's perfect. This is all very new to me as well. I've even started reading my daily horoscope.'

'As long as it doesn't say beware of men with lawnmowers. Seriously, Mia, I think we could be good together.'

She had pushed herself forward to the edge of her seat, holding her breath. Thoughts of *Bridget Jones' Diary* raced through her head; she was so tempted to punch the air and shout, 'Yes, yes, yes.'

'I think we could too, and it will be fun finding out, we just need to get to know each other better.' She swallowed hard. 'But let's not rush it, cupid seems to be on our side.'

'He does, doesn't he.'

The intercom buzzed. 'Damn. Someone's at the door.'

'Better get it, we'll talk tomorrow.'

She was loathed to end the call but said her goodbyes and rose to press the intercom button.

'Delivery for you.'

'Okay, bring it up.'

She waited a moment before opening the door to a man struggling with an enormous floral display. She signed his slip and asked him if he would mind carrying it in for her. He obliged, and she gave him some coins for his trouble.

'Drake, you are a very naughty boy.' The fragrance from the blooms of night-scented stock, white freesia, and miniature roses, filled the room. She looked closer, there were some flowers she didn't recognise – one favoured wisteria, with long cone-shaped heads and fleshy-leaved orchids. The heavy smell filled the room as she peeked between the blooms searching for the tiny envelope. What had Drake written? She pulled the card from its casing.

My dearest Mia, all is in the past.

There is nothing to forgive.

I am glad you are happy

Do something good with your life

and if our paths cross, it will be as friends.

Rufus

Tears welled and escaped her. She hugged the small card to her. Rufus had forgiven her. Such a mix of emotions in less than five minutes. She straightened her back, eyes settling once more on the urn. Only one thing more to do, fulfil her pledge to Constance. That was the easy part. Pinning Lisa down wasn't.

CHAPTER 53

THEY were sitting by a roaring fire in the George in Wraysbury, the smell of smoky wood and delicious aroma of food made her feel warm and relaxed. It was Drake's favourite gastro-pubs and Ben, the owner, was one of Drake's oldest friends. He joined them for coffee after their meal. He nodded and listened as Drake poured out his worries.

'Paul has tried to get me more involved in the office but it's not my thing. I enjoy getting my hands dirty, running the projects —'

'Don't forget cutting old ladies' hedges and carrying obnoxious women's suitcases,' Mia added cheekily.

Ben smiled at the exchange.

'Exactly. But if I don't keep ahead of it, we could lose a lot of money or, more importantly, our reputation.' He shrugged.

Ben tapped a hand against the table top. 'You are as bad as I am. How many times have you told me to delegate, get someone to organise, do the mundane stuff? How long have I known you? Since Uni, and you're still as pig-headed. Get some help. Sell it to Hilda you don't want her overdoing things, it's to help her. Then employ someone who can keep things steady 'til Paul's back. Liaise with him in hospital, his injuries don't stop him talking into a mobile phone do they?'

One of Bens staff flagged up the arrival of some regular patrons. ''Scuse me a moment.' He moved to greet some elderly customers, shaking hands with the man, and kissing the old lady's cheek, before taking her coat and escorting them to their table.

'Nice guy,' Mia said, watching Ben fuss around the old lady's chair.

'One of the best, but unlucky in love.'

'Really? You surprise me, he's very charismatic.'

Yep, great guy but a disaster with women. I wish he'd find one and settle down. He works far too hard.'

Ben approached, overhearing the comment. 'And you don't? Sorry to bow out, but I've got a big party in the function room, so you'll have to excuse me.' He bent and kissed Mia's cheek, squeezing Drake's shoulder. As he passed, he ducked down and stage whispered into Drake's ear, 'Don't let this one get away, she's gorgeous.'

'Don't worry I won't,' he said, throwing Mia a look that made her knees go weak.

They drove back into the hectic world of London traffic, chatting amiably about nothing in particular. Snuggling into the soft leather car seat with Drake driving felt so natural, the shared intimacy between them. The slow unveiling of emotions was addictive. There was no tip-toeing, they had begun a ramble. They were a new pairing, almost a couple, and she couldn't have been happier.

'What do you think about Ben's idea?' Drake asked.

'Getting someone in? It makes sense. You won't be weakening your business in any other area. It would take the pressure off you and ensure when Paul gets back to work, he's not wading through a mud-pie of admin.' She smoothed down her skirt. 'Sounds like you'll have to tread carefully though. Finding someone who doesn't want to take over the place and fluster Hilda won't be easy. You need someone with a sense of humour and a bit of cunning.'

'That's just what I was thinking.' He squeezed her hand. 'Can you start tomorrow? I know it's short notice, but I can't think of anyone better.'

'Me? No way. You've got to be joking.' She glanced at him. He didn't look like he wasn't joking.

'Why not? You know the delicacy of the situation, you know Paul, and can run things by him without upsetting Hilda. And I know you can run an office. It's a no-brainer. Oh, and one more plus… I know you're kind to little old ladies.'

She laughed. 'Bit of a salesman, aren't you?'

'It has been known.'

'Conman more like. Let me think about it.'

'Okay,' he grinned. 'You have about six miles till I get you home.'

'Don't be so pushy, I'm thinking.'

On the upside, she'd get to see him every day, but absence makes the heart grow fonder and she didn't want to do anything to jeopardise what they had going.

They stopped at traffic lights, he squeezed her hand again, looking at her expectantly. His smiling eyes fixing hers.

She melted. 'Okay. I'll do it but on several conditions.'

'And they are?'

'I'll do it for a week as a trial.'

'Okay.'

'You introduce me as a friend come to help you out because Hilda has so much to do without Paul.'

'Clever.'

'Yes, and less threatening than if you hired someone or get a temp in. And…Stop pulling a face.'

'I'm not, just preparing for something I don't like because so far, so good. And?'

'It's not bad, honestly. I was just going to ask if you'd go back to Sidmouth with me. I must let Constance find her resting place before Christmas.'

'Deal.'

'Oh, and I don't want paying.'

'No deal.'

'Then I won't do it.'

'Bugger you drive a hard bargain. Tell you what then, I'll pay for the hotel and dinner in Sidmouth.'

She gave a considered look. 'Yep. I think we have a deal.'

Drake pulled over towards her building.

'Just drop me off outside,' she said.

'You mean I can't come up?'

'No. I have to maintain a professional manner for my new position, and I can't have my boss taking advantage of me.'

Drake laughed a real belly laugh, shaking his head. 'You are something lady, you know that?'

She gave a cute shrug and winked. 'It's work in progress. Now go.'

She was grinning like a soppy kid at her reflection in the lift, but doubt was beginning to creep in.

Will familiarity breed contempt? Working in such proximity for a week, then the weekend in Sidmouth?

She had to make sure nothing ruined it.

CHAPTER 54

HILDA wore 50s style pointy glasses and dyed her hair an unconvincing black. She had a thick fringe followed by a bouffant. It reminded Mia of a jump at the Grand National. She looked apprehensive when Mia arrived, walking stiffly towards the inner office. The walls in between were glass panelled and Drake could be seen on the phone next door. As Hilda showed her into the main office, he waved a hand and she returned the gesture.

Mia took a deep breath. 'Erm, Hilda. I hope you don't mind me being here. I have no idea about landscape architecture, I'm better with window boxes, so I'll bow to your knowledge. I'm here to help, so give me anything you want – filing, tea making, photocopying.' She gestured around the two desks strewn with paper and unopened mail. Lever arch files labelled with bold marker pen filled two shelves. 'Goodness, I wouldn't know where to start.'

Hilda's tight frown showed no sign of relaxing. The old lady straightened.

'I know where everything is. I have my methods and I don't want anything changed.'

'Quite right. Tell you what, why don't you make a list of what you want me to do and I'll do it just it exactly how you like it.'

Hilda seemed unsure, her eyes darting from Paul's untidy desk back to Mia.

'I'll make the coffee, or is it tea you want? Then we can make a start. You better tell me about special cups, I know people have their favourites.'

The fact Mia was happy to take on tasks of an office junior seemed to change Hilda's attitude and her tight-lipped expression began to fade. By the time Mia carried in the tray and produced a packet of Hobnobs from her bag, the atmosphere had grown a tad warmer.

'What would you like me to do?'

'Well, better take in Drake's coffee. He'll be wanting it.'

Mia pulled a worried expression. 'I think you had better do it. He's used to you. I don't want to disturb him. He looks busy.'

Hilda looked pleased, fiddling with the cat broach pinned to her home-knitted cardigan.

'Yes, you're quite right. I know exactly what's needed. Now if you could sort out the papers into piles, bought ledger in one, sales in the other.'

Mia faked dumb. 'Do you mean what's to pay and what's to get in?' Hilda looked positively ecstatic, seemingly convinced the newcomer was not a threat.

The morning progressed well, and Drake came into their office at lunchtime.

'Hi, Mia, sorry I haven't had the chance to talk – a bit busy. How are you getting on?'

Mia kept her eyes on the task in hand, entering figures into a ledger. 'I'm not the person to ask, you'd better ask my boss,' she jerked a thumb in the direction of Hilda, almost feeling the glow of pride from the woman who had never considered herself a boss.

'She's picking things up very quickly.'

'You're a good teacher Hilda. Right, Mia, lunch at the pub?'

She swivelled on her chair, addressing Hilda. 'Is that what you usually do? I made a sandwich.'

Hilda looked flustered. 'Er I don't usually leave the office. I have my dinner when I get home.'

'You can share my lunch if you like,' Mia said, ' made plenty in case we had to work late.'

'No, no I have my snack, but thank you.'

'Looks like I've been blown out then.' Drake said, pretending to be put out. ' I have to go out anyway, so see you both later.'

Mia brought plates from the kitchen and they ate their lunch harmoniously. She kept the conversation light, asking where Hilda lived, was she married, did she have pets and what TV programmes did she like? By the afternoon, they were pals, with Hilda admitting she hated credit control, a job Paul usually dealt with it. So Mia hit the phones and had the promise of payment on the longest outstanding debts by close of play.

By Wednesday, Hilda was asking advice and allowed Mia to set up some spreadsheets to organise work rotas and soft copy files for each project. The office no longer looked like a war zone. Drake was absent a great deal of the time and Mia liaised with an incredibly grateful Paul on their progress.

At six o'clock the two woman tidied their desks and switched off their computers. Mia noticed Hilda had been quieter than usual. She hoped she hadn't overstepped the mark and upset her.

'Hilda, is everything alright? You haven't been your chatty self today.'

Hilda's bottom lip gave an involuntary wobble, she turned away.

'Oh, my goodness.' Mia put an arm around her shoulders. 'Have I done something to upset you? If I have, I didn't mean to. I'm very sorry.'

Hilda sniffed and searched up her sleeve for a handkerchief. 'It's not you, it's me.'

Mia pressed Hilda to sit, moving her chair to face her.

'Please don't be upset. Why don't you tell me what's wrong.'

Hilda opened her desk drawer and took out an envelope, it wasn't sealed. She handed it to Mia.

'Open it. It's my resignation letter. I wrote it three years ago, but haven't dared to hand it in. I'm too old and tired. I get flustered and make mistakes.' She blew her nose. 'Oh, the boys are truly kind, they never complain, but I'm seventy-three and it's all too much.' She raised her head, her watery button eyes fixing on Mia. 'This is a job for a younger person. My old-fashioned ways are a hinder. I stayed on for the boys because I promised Drake's father I would.' Her shoulders rose and fell. 'I'm so tired and the hours are too long.'

Mia smiled warmly. 'Then why don't you tell them? I'm sure they would have wanted to know, instead of you just struggling on.'

Hilda nodded. 'But I don't want to just leave them in the lurch. Paul always picks up the slack if I get behind. He never complains. And what would I do? I'd miss it so much.'

Mia leaned forward. 'Why don't you ask to go part-time? Part days, or maybe three days a week.'

Hilda shook her head. 'It's a full-time job and I'm not up to it.'

'Can you muddle on with me until Paul is back? Then I think it's time you asked. You've nothing to lose. Perhaps they could get in someone just to do the accounts, it would take a lot off you. I'm sure they'd go for it rather than lose all that knowledge and, well, loyalty.'

She brightened. 'Do you think so?'

'I do, and we have already streamlined some of the systems, so they'll be easier to manage and save you hours of paper filing.' Mia glanced out of the window. It was pouring with rain. 'Come on, let's go home. Tomorrow you can tell me what takes the longest to do and we'll see if we can devise a short cut.'

'A better way,' said Hilda, getting to her feet.

'Not a better way, just a different approach.'

'You are kind. I must admit I didn't want you here, you know. I thought you'd want to push me out. I didn't want to leave that way, not after all these years. But I can see Drake's fallen for you and that makes me happy. One less thing for me to worry about.'

'It's early days, but I like him too.'

This could work, it had to. She'd grown attached to the thumping in her chest every time Drake was near. Was this love? If Hilda could see it and Zannah too, why would she have any doubt?

CHAPTER 55

M IA had only just removed her wet coat when Drake rang. She recounted the conversation she'd had with Hilda. He seemed pleased with the result and was on his way to visit Paul, who was expected home at the weekend. He promised to discuss Mia's idea with him.

'Great job, Mia, thank you. I'll have to find some way of making it up to you.'

'I'm sure you will.' She gave a small giggle.

'Naughty,' he said in a wicked tone, 'but I've got bad news about the weekend.'

She couldn't stop herself – the disappointment, 'Oh no. You're not coming?'

'Nothing like that, I'd swim through fire to get there. Er, that may be a mixed metaphor? I'm sorry but I can't get you into your little box room. Hotel's fully booked except for two rooms in the courtyard – next door to each other.'

She didn't reply, not trusting herself to say don't bother with two, but then she would appear too eager.

'Look if it's a problem I can book the other hotel.'

'No. No problem.'

'Good, see you Friday. I'm —'

'Not in the office tomorrow, yes I know. Drive carefully, see you Friday.'

The chat she'd had with Hilda had made her home late, she had promised herself an early night after watching *Long Lost Family*. Drake had mentioned it in passing and she was inquisitive to find out what happened next and see people's reactions, comparing events to her situation.

The show had already started by the time she got in and she dipped in and out of the woman's conversation with Davina McCall whilst making herself some supper. There were always two stories, switching back and forth throughout the programme between Davina and Nicky Chapman. Mia compiled her salad ingredients with some prawns and glanced at the screen.

Nicky was talking to a watery-eyed woman called Bridie, his expression grave. He nodded his head, listening, as Bridie explained how she had been forced to give up her baby for adoption. It was the usual story of a baby conceived out of wedlock and an absconding boyfriend.

'Must have been dreadful for you. How long have you been searching?'

'On and off over the years but with no luck. I spent twelve weeks in the mother and baby home run by the Catholic church, it was awfully hard nursing my baby after she was born, knowing I was going to have to give her up. Sadly, the records for the home were destroyed long ago. But then recently, one of my aunts died and I discovered a box of old papers when we cleared her loft. We, my son Tim and I – I married his dad in 1980.'

The camera moved to the box on a nearby table, showing a stack of old photographs and papers. Bridie held up a biscuit-coloured paper.

'Inside was this.'

'The adoption papers,' Nicky offered.

'Yes. I don't know how she got them, but we have the name of the family who adopted my baby girl, but we've drawn a blank.'

'So, what *did* you manage to find out?' Nicky pushed.

'I discovered they were well-to-do. The adoptive father was a major in the British army.'

Mia almost dropped the olive oil.

'I'm not good at the computer that's why I came to you. I didn't like to ask my Tim, he has a busy job, but at least I know her name.'

'Always a good piece of information to start with,' Nicky said, his face serious. 'Tell me what you know.'

'Yes. Well, the family name, it's Croxley.'

'What?' Mia blinked. She shuffled to the edge of her seat. 'Oh, my God, this is more than coincidence. She must be looking for Georgina, she said she had her in 1971, It would be right. Gina's forty-two. Ruddy hell.' Her hands trembled so much she put down her knife and fork.

The camera cut to Nicky nodding. 'Unusual name, so something to go on.'

'Please find her for me. I just want to say I'm sorry, tell her I loved her.'

They cut to the adverts.

Mia sat back staring at the screen, a lump in her throat. Had Lisa felt the same way but knew where she was all along? Talk about coincidence. She and Gina were both about to discover their roots. She poured a glass of wine, annoyed with herself for finding an excuse and settled down to watch the rest.

The programme restarted with a recap of the other person's story and how Davina found their new relative, to discover they'd only lived five miles away.

'Yes, yes, love a happy ending, but get back to Bridie,' Mia shouted at the screen.

Finally, it was back to Nicky Chapman. The same recap of the story so far. Mia studied Bridie's features, the same flat forehead and oval face, there was a similarity. She concentrated on Nicky's words.

'Well, I'm delighted to tell you we've found her. The family name was double-barrelled, Croxley-Smith or Smith Croxley. Her name's still Georgina, and she recently moved with her husband to Australia.'

'Told you,' Mia said excitedly. 'Typical Gina, someone else did all the work.'

'And there's something else,' said a smiling Nicky. 'You have two grandchildren, a boy and a girl. Would you like to see a pho-tograph?'

'*Stupid question*, of course, she would,' Mia growled.

Bridie's face crumpled and Nicky moved forward and hugged her. The poor woman sagged with emotion.

'We've told her all about you, and she wants to meet you.'

In the background, a man appeared, who Mia presumed was Bridie's husband. Bridie held the photograph up for him and he took it, smiling, whilst giving her back a rub. Then more adverts. Mia rang Drake.

'Well hello.' Drake said in a voice that usually would have melted her, she ignored his tone pressing on, aware she had little time between the adverts.

'Are you at home? Put the TV on.'

'It's on. I was about to call you. *Long Lost Family.* It's Gina.'

'Unfortunately, yes. Poor Bridie. I feel sorry for her. Speak later.'

Mia tapped her nails on the worktop in agitation, waiting for the ad break to end. Drake said this was the bit that gave him goosebumps. Like a silent cheer for their happiness, as they reunited. But tonight was different, they knew the people involved, and she feared there'd be no happy ending for Bridie.

Gina's face came into view. There she was, Gina, her hair held back by a headband. Her expression was emotionless as Nicky explained her birth mother had been searching for her. He ran through the circumstances of her birth and the reason why she'd given her up. He bought out the photograph of Bridie and gave Georgina a letter to readout.

Gina showed no sign of emotion as Nicky asked the stock question: Bridie wanted to know if she'd been happy. Georgina was curt in her reply.

'Oh, she needn't have worried, I had a wonderful childhood. My father was a major in the British Army, I didn't want for anything,' she bragged. 'Being adopted by them was extremely fortunate. I never thought about life before them, they were my family.'

You bitch, poor Bridie to have that thrown in her face.

Next came the reunion. The aeroplane landing in Australia, then the drive to a lake. Bridie sat nervously on a bench, looking straight ahead at the flocks of wading birds. She had dressed smartly in a matching two-piece, obviously keen to impress. Gina approached from her left, wearing khaki three-quarter trousers, a blue shirt, and flip flops. It said it all.

'Nice to see you made the effort Gina,' Mia sighed, feeling hurt for Bridie.

She winced through the rest of the uncomfortable viewing, as Gina bragged about her life, dismissing poor Bridie's feelings. The last shot was of them walking around the lake and Bridie linking arms with her daughter.

There was always an update at the end typed onto the screen. Drake had told her to wait and read it.

There it was. It read, "since the initial meeting and Bridie's return to England, there has been no further contact." Georgina was quoted saying, 'she was pleased Bridie had found her but didn't feel the necessity to carry the relationship any further.' The last paragraph read, "Bridie is naturally disappointed but was pleased she has some happy memories of her trip and meeting daughter and grandchildren. She was glad Georgina had had a happy life and was settled in Australia."

Mia moved across the room and sat on the sofa, muttering to herself.

'Poor woman.' She shook her head sadly. 'Gina has no idea how lucky she is, at least she got to talk to her mother and got to hear the reason why she gave her up. You don't realise how lucky you are.'

Mia stared at the television screen. Gina hadn't improved since she'd last seen her. She was still hard and spiteful. There would only have been one reason she'd have agreed to meet Bridie: if she thought there was money in it.

The camera had taken the viewers into Bridie's small, neat flat, sparse in furnishings, abundant with knick-knacks.

'Not what gold-digging Gina would have been interested in. Gina who charged her mother £12 a week for her time to do the supermarket shop. At least I looked after Constance properly and, most of all, made her happy,' Mia murmured. Gina had no conscience, a bit like the man who sired her.

CHAPTER 56

M IA packed a weekend bag, placing Constance in the rucksack. 'This is positively the last time, I promise. Next stop Peak Hill.'

Drake needed a break, so she'd be the designated driver for this trip. She loaded her leased car and set off for the office. Hilda was in good spirits, having got her worries out in the open, she'd even purchased some iced buns to share at their mid-morning break.

Mia put her mobile on silent and plugged it into a charger underneath her desk. She must have a word with Drake about more power points – the two plug sockets had numerous extensions plugged into them, she worried about overheating and fire risk.

Drake had clients in for a meeting and Hilda sat in on it with her notebook handy. Mia felt a pang of envy. She was enjoying the role far more than she'd ever envisaged.

The meeting had concluded by lunchtime. Drake put his head around the door.

'Just off to Wonersh to check on progress at the Levingson's. Should be back by two-thirty and we can get on the road and beat the Friday rush hour. Are you sure you want to drive?'

'Absolutely, your turn to enjoy the countryside, for once.'

'In October?'

'Don't be a grumpy old man.'

'Hey, less of the old.'

Mia cleared her desk by two o'clock and was just about to shut down her computer when the intercom buzzed.

'Ah the electrician,' Hilda said, getting up to answer it and let him in. 'You have me so organised I was finally able to get around to internal projects. By Monday, we will have lots of lovely new power sockets.'

'What a clever idea,' Mia said, smiling to herself.

Drake had returned in good time and by three-fifteen they were on the road and chatting about *Long Lost Families*.

'Looks like you were lucky to be at boarding school,' Drake commented, 'Gina always came over such a goody-goody, dutiful daughter – sorry I don't mean to be rude.'

Before she could comment his phone rang.

'Yes Hilda, ah okay, I'll tell her. Yes, okay hang on.' He took his hand away from his ear. 'You left your phone behind and it has four missed calls from the same number, do you want her to call them back?'

'It's probably the agency after emergency cover, better let them know I'm not available. Yes, please Hilda,' she said, in a slightly louder voice.

'Okay, Hilda did you get that? Good thanks.'

A few minutes later Hilda called back. Drake said little except for, 'Can you text me the number?' A few miles further on he pointed out the motorway services.

'What did she say?'

'Hang on a mo, I'm parched, can we come off here?'

'Yes of course. We've made good time already.'

Steering the car into a parking spot at the Welcome Break services, she switched off the ignition. Drake touched her arm as her hand reached for the door.

'Don't get out. I got you to stop as I thought you might have had a job concentrating.'

She looked at him warily her brow furrowing in confusion.

'Don't panic.'

Her eyes widened. 'Don't say that or I will. What's going on?'

He swivelled in his seat to face her. 'I'm not sure if this news is good or bad. The calls to your mobile were all from Lisa Farrant.

And when Hilda said you were on your way to Sidmouth, she left her number, said to call you and say she'll meet you there.'

Mia blinked absorbing the words numbed by the revelation.

'Are you all right?' Drake said, put his hand over hers.

'Yes. Yes. I am. It's a bit of a shock that's all – my mother wanting a meeting. So this is a good thing. Isn't it?'

She searched his eyes for reassurance, he squeezed her arm. She swallowed, not trusting herself not to cry.

'And it's right it's in Sidmouth. It might be easier for her to explain when we're where it all started.' She grazed her teeth across her bottom lip, staring ahead. 'I just hope I can make some sense of it.' She turned her head back to face him attempting a smile. 'I'm glad that you came with me. It will help to have you to support me.'

'Goes without saying. This is a big thing for you – what do they call it? A life-changing event?' Gently, he reached across and tucked her hair behind her ear. 'So, are you afraid of hearing the truth?'

'No of course not, it's what I've wanted all along. Apprehensive would be a better choice of word.'

Another lie, I'm shit-scared but I don't want him to think me needy. It's embarrassing enough as it is. What if this meeting is as awful as Gina and Bridie's? Will I hear things I don't want to know?

CHAPTER 57

SIDMOUTH didn't have the same feel about it today. Even Drake's chatter had stilled as they approached the town. The bright lights glimmered along the promenade, but the night sea beyond look black and spiteful.

As they headed up the hill towards the hotel, she felt a sense of foreboding. Drake broke into her thoughts. 'Does it still feel like coming home?'

'Not really, but it still has magic about it.'

Drake shifted in his seat. 'I hope you'll still think that after tomorrow. I mean, I'm sure you will, and everything will be fine.'

'I wish I were as convinced as you, but after watching *Long Lost Family,* and poor Bridie's result with Gina, I'm not so sure.'

'Mm, tough one, but at least you already know Lisa and by now she knows exactly what you want from her. Anyway, we're here so *que sera...*'

Mia came to a halt outside the hotel.

'I have a memory of someone singing that to me as a little one. *Que Sera, Sera, whatever will be, will be.*'

'The future's not ours to see,' Drake finished the line. 'Very apt. My mum used to sing it with my gran after one Snowball too many.' He rested his hand over hers curling his fingers protectively. 'It will be all right you know.'

She turned to face him braving a smile but couldn't control the fear squatting behind her eyes. He must have noticed as he squeezed her hand even tighter.

'Come on, let's get you in and relaxed.'

Mia sat on the vast, modern bed in the courtyard feeling lost and longing for her usual little box room. In daylight, it gave her the comfort of the sea view and life going on below her in the town. At night, the moon piercing the indigo sky was like a hole in a familiar black sock.

Constance's urn sat beside the sofa at the end of the bed. Whatever happened here this weekend, Constance would not be coming home with them. It was Mia's promise and she'd keep it.

Even though Drake was just a few feet and some bricks away, she felt very alone. Rousing herself, she stripped off her day clothes, hoping a shower would warm her spirits. It didn't. She heard Drake's door slam, and as he tapped on her own she pasted on a smile, smoothed down the soft grey Angora sweater she'd teamed with a darker shade of trousers, rolled back her shoulders, and opened the door.

'Ready? Good. The wind's got up, let's get inside and get some food.' They hurried along the wooden balcony linking the courtyard rooms to the main hotel. Mia held her hair back from her face in the gusting wind.

The warm atmosphere of the hotel wrapped itself around them. Drake guided her to a spacious sofa facing the floodlit gardens and the glimmering lights of Sidmouth below.

'Gin and tonic?'

'Yes please.'

He left her side and strolled to the bar. When he returned, he sat close, protectively slipping an arm around her shoulder. The waiter appeared almost immediately, placing two heavy, ice-filled tumblers, and open bottles of tonic on the low table in front of them. He was about to pour but Drake stopped him.

'Fine thanks, I'll do that, and can we have a menu please?' The waiter had anticipated the request and had one clamped under his elbow, he passed it to Drake and left them.

'What do you fancy? From the smell of the food it's all rather good.'

'I'll have the rump of lamb with Dauphinoise,' she said without even glancing at it.

'Of course, I forgot, you know the restaurant well.' He waved over the waiter and gave their order before leaning towards the low table and pouring half a tonic in each glass.

'You're drinking?' Mia said with surprise.

'Don't look so shocked. I do now and then, especially if I know I'm not driving for a few days.'

'Am I getting you into bad habits?'

'I wish you would,' he said, giving her a boyish grin. 'Sorry, not the time or place.'

In reply, she put down her drink and snuggled into the crook of his shoulder, enjoying the warmth of his body, and began to unwind. He dropped a gentle kiss on the top of her head. The closeness of him was intoxicating, she wanted to stay like this forever.

'Can we not talk, just sip our drinks? Sorry, I'm a bit needy tonight. It's so unlike me.'

'Hush, no need to explain.'

'Thank you for being here.'

He stroked her shoulder, and they stayed like that until the maître d' approached to take them to their table.

As dinner progressed, her mood lifted. The light glow of a candle reflected in their red wine glasses set a romantic mood. The food was delicious, mouth-watering tender lamb, with the aroma of rosemary and garlic. She was glad they'd chosen the same meal – second-hand garlic was so unattractive as she hoped he'd kiss her goodnight. By the time they got to coffee, she noticed he was frowning.

'What's up, Drake, you seem uneasy?'

He took a sip of his coffee. 'Not uneasy, I never feel that in your company. I was just thinking about how honest you've been with me about your history. You deserve to know mine.'

She reached out for him as his eyes hooded with emotion.

'Please don't think you have to.'

He gave a nod and she noticed him drawing saliva into his mouth.

'I want to.'

She sat quietly waiting, he was right, it was his time to share now that he knew all about her..

'Neither of us was in a fit state to drive, but Lucy was stubborn and in my boozed-up state, I just crawled into the backseat and went to sleep.' He swept a hand through his hair. 'If I'd been less drunk and more adamant, two people would still be alive today.' Mia felt his pain as he revealed his story. The same story Helen told her, but this was the raw emotional version. 'So now you know it – warts and all.' He said softly as he sat back in his chair, clearly drained.

'Thank you for telling me. It's an awful thing to have happened. You look exhausted.'

Only now they both noticed the hovering staff in the empty restaurant keen to get to their beds.

'Sorry guys,' Drake apologised, as he signed the bill. The wind had dropped as they made their way outside to the walkway and back to their rooms. At her door, he took the key card from her hand and opened it for her. She turned to him, his eyes the colour of warm caramel, in the limited light.

'Do you want to come in?' She sensed him tense, his body was so close to hers.

'I want to, very much. But I won't, not tonight. I wouldn't want to take advantage, you're too vulnerable right now. Let's get through tomorrow.'

His words flowed over her, confirming his specialness. As their heads moved closer together, their mouths met in the deliciousness of warmth and passion. The desire for his skin against hers melted her insides. The kiss was soft and warm and, as they parted, it left her breathless and craving for more. His fingers released from the tangle of her hair to the nape of her neck, tracing down her shoulder, her arm, to her fingertips.

He took a step back as they parted, touched his mouth with his middle fingers, blew her a kiss goodnight, and walked away.

She stepped into her room and closed the door, launching herself onto the luxurious bed. She wrapped her arms around herself, trying to mimic the feel of his and, closing her eyes, she tried to recall every detail of his mouth on hers. Minutes later, reluctantly, she rose to get ready for bed, confident of a good night's sleep. It was then she noticed the envelope propped up against the mirror. Someone, perhaps Sam, had delivered it. She tore it open.

Dear Mia,

I will be at Connaught Gardens tea rooms from 11.00 tomorrow. And this time there will be no lies.

Lisa

The room squeezed together and bounced back like jelly as she repeated the words, 'This time there will be no lies.' Crossing her arms over her stomach, she closed her eyes and gently rocked. Tomorrow, all her questions would be answered and like it or not, she would finally know who she was.

CHAPTER 58

MORNING couldn't come quick enough. In her head, every possible scenario and never-ending conversations looped and swallow-dived to no resolvable conclusion. Even a run hadn't helped. She'd watched Drake eat a hearty breakfast while she barely managed a mouthful of toast. They sat closely together in the lounge. Drake had lain a selection of newspapers and magazines in front of her – she hadn't so much as turned a page. He placed his hand on her jiggling knee until she stilled it.

'And stop looking at your watch, it's still only just gone ten.'

'Sorry, I can't help it. I just want to get it over with. Do you think I should make a list of questions to ask?'

He replaced his coffee cup on its saucer, giving her a slow lazy smile.

'No. You're overthinking it. Just see what she's got to say. It won't be easy for her either, you know. She's probably feeling as anxious as you are.' Mia turned her head away, breathing heavily. 'Hey, none of that.' He reached out and brushed away a tear. She managed a wobbly smile. 'That's better, that's my girl.'

She fumbled for a tissue. 'Now I feel incredibly stupid, I hardly ever cry.'

'Come on, Mia, don't be so hard on yourself. This is probably the biggest thing that can ever happen to anybody. Perhaps you should cry more often. We all need a good blub sometimes. That's why they make films like *Love Actually* and *Four Weddings and a Funeral*. Hugh Grant's made a fortune out of making people cry.'

She couldn't suppress her smile. 'You always seem to find the right words. Perhaps I'll start calling you Mr Darcy.'

'God no, did you see him in *Bridget Jones' Diary*? Fights like a girl.'

'As did Hugh Grant. It was part of the attraction, submissive aggressive.' Her smile slipped as she checked her watch again, adding, 'He was more a lover than a fighter.'

'A matter of opinion,' he said as he drained the last of his coffee pushing the cup and saucer away from him.

'Drake you surprise me daily, I didn't have you down as a chick-flick man.'

'Oh, there's a lot you don't know about me,' he winked at her. 'A bag of Maltesers and a box of tissues on a wet Sunday afternoon. Nothing like it.'

She looked straight into his eyes. 'I never know when you're joking.'

'Ah, that takes time, years and years, but you'll get there in the end.'

'Will I?'

'If you want to.'

In a moment of terrible timing, Sam wandered over to them.

'Morning Missy, nice to see you back again. What do you think of the doing-up?'

'It's very nice Sam. The courtyard rooms are beautiful, but I do miss my little box room.'

'You won't recognise it by next stay.' Sam peered across the room towards the terrace, 'May get lucky with the weather for the next few hours. Tomorrow will be the best 'til Tuesday, I reckon.' His head jerked as his name was called. 'Better go, jobs to do. Have a nice day.'

'I wish,' Mia said getting to her feet.

Drake lifted her coat from the arm of the chair and held it out for her to slip it over her shoulders.

'Ready?' he said, hugging her.

'As I'll ever be.'

The closer they got to the tearooms, the more their pace slowed. Drake placed a protective arm across the small of her back.

'Do you want me to come in with you?'

'Thank you, a kind offer but I have to do this on my own.'

He leant forward and kissed her lightly on the lips. 'I won't be far away if you need me.'

She nodded and took a step back as his hands slid from her waist.

'Thanks, I'd better go.'

CHAPTER 59

Another hill. Always a hill, please may this be a sanctuary like the others. She spotted her straight away. It would have been normal to wave a greeting, but this wasn't normal. Lisa stood very still, silhouetted in the archway of the old tower wall. The low autumn sun made her body a dark outline against a blue sky. As the space between them shrank, step by step, Mia thought about Bridie and all the others seeking the truth and a sense of belonging.

Just feet away, Mia sucked in a gulp of air in an attempt to ward off the dizzy mix of apprehension. She must keep her cool, she told herself, but today she was in desperate need of the old Mia's armour.

She held out a gloved hand formally, Lisa took it, there were tears in her eyes.

Mia looked away.

'Let's get coffee,' Lisa said. Mia nodded and followed her into the café, where she ordered for them both.

'I'll get these,' Lisa said, taking her bag from her shoulder. Mia didn't object. They both stood awkwardly waiting for their drinks. 'Inside or out? I know it's cold, but it might be more...' She shrugged.

'Private,' Mia said quickly, looking away.

'Yes, probably.'

They each picked up their drink, Lisa was first to the door and held it open for Mia.

'Over there should be all right, it's out of the wind.'

They sat facing each other. Lisa broke the cavernous silence.

'I didn't mean to lie you know.'

'But you did anyway,' Mia said distantly.

'There was a good reason.'

'For you perhaps. I beg to differ.' Mia said fixing Lisa's eyes with her own.

Lisa bit her lip. 'Please don't be angry, Mia. Let me explain.'

'Can there ever be an explanation good enough for abandoning me?'

Lisa paused before answering, rolling her shoulders, she sat taller.

'Firstly, you were *not* abandoned. You were adopted, after being cared for and very much loved. You're not going to make this easy for me but hear me out. It's not what you think.'

Mia sat back in her seat. 'Go ahead. I'm all ears.'

'Firstly, Charles was a difficult man. He always got what he wanted.'

Mia's eyes widened as a small cry escaped her lips. 'Oh my God *no*!' She buried her head in her hands. 'You and him! I never considered that. It's just too horrible!'

Lisa slapped her palms on the table aghast.

'Will you just listen? Give me a chance. Stop jumping to conclusions. No, nothing happened to me and I didn't have an affair with the Major. And here's the biggest truth … I'm not your mother either.'

Mia jolted forward in her seat. 'But the birth certificate!'

'A lie, don't jump ahead. Just let me tell you from the beginning. As I said your *adoptive* father was a difficult man, but you knew that. Constance accepted the marriage was a sham. Charles chose her because he needed a good army wife. He ruled the household like a barracks. If anyone dared defy him there was hell to pay. He was on tour in Aden,

Cyprus, I can't remember, when Gina's adoption took place.' She warmed her hands on her coffee cup, before continuing. 'But before that, when he was away – sometimes three to six months at a time, Constance got lonely on her own so she would come down and stay with her older cousin, Elizabeth, in Sidmouth and that's where she stayed. Here she was free of him and had happy times. Elizabeth's house was huge.' She took a sip of coffee.

'Go on.'

'I will, there's no rush, let me tell it my way. Well, the Major just about consummated the marriage; then after that, he slept in his own room. Constance wanted a child and without him being in her bed he eventually he agreed to the adoption.' She looked away frowning, recalling her story.

'He needed Constance as a hostess and to attend functions and things army wives were required to attend. Even though Constance was much older than me we became firm friends or should I say allies. I came to live at Elizabeth's house a few weeks before Georgina was adopted.' She paused taking a tissue from her pocket and dabbed at her nose.

'Constance had been an only child, she knew nothing about babies, and Elizabeth was a spinster, that's why they employed me. The Major kept the adoption under wraps, he didn't want his virility under scrutiny. Constance was sent here for her supposed confinement, an old-fashioned word from an old-fashioned man. You saw the TV programme?'

'*Long Lost Family*, yes. Poor Bridie.'

Lisa took another sip of her coffee.

Mia jiggled her left knee. 'Go on. Don't stop now.'

Lisa nodded. 'As far as his army friends were concerned, Georgina was his daughter and he gave her a lot of attention when he was home, showing her off to his friends.'

'I know all of that, but what about me? If you're not my mother, who is?'

'Hold on a minute. You always were so impatient.'

Mia wasn't sure if she liked hearing that; it felt like a reprimand. 'I wouldn't call thirty-odd years impatient, would you?'

Lisa smiled, and Mia remembered the warmth of it, as tiny atoms of her past popped in her head.

'You're right, it's been too long.' She shifted in her chair. 'Constance loved it down here. As I said, she came back as often as she could get away with. Here, she could be free and enjoy life. And she certainly did. After a lot of persuasions, the major permitted a second adoption. God knows what we would have done if he'd said no. Anyway. That's it. That child was you, only you weren't adopted. The truth, Mia, is that Constance *was* your real mother. She gave birth to you here in the local cottage hospital.'

Mia's head reeled at this knowledge. The revelation felt like a blow to her body. She gasped, and her eyes filled with tears.

'She *was* my mother?'

Lisa nodded.

'Then she wanted me?'

'Very much, but she was terrified he might discover her secret. He almost did. Charles was away a lot, often for months on end, and he wasn't exactly discreet about his lady friends either. But Constance didn't care – she had you and Gina and the support of Elizabeth and Memmi.'

'I'm sorry I'm still trying to process this, who was Memmi?'

'Elizabeth's housekeeper. A wonderful woman. They lived in the cottage in the grounds.'

'They? I think I know what you're going to say but go on.'

Lisa's lips broadened, 'Memmi had a son Vikash.'

'Who worked on the railway?'

'That's right. Well, he also worked elsewhere, I'll tell you in a minute. Anyway, he and Constance fell in love. She became a different woman around him, happy and carefree. She loved festivals, dancing, swimming in the sea. Mutter's Moor was their special place.'

Mia spread her fingers wide and cupped her cheeks, slowly shaking her head from side to side.

'I can hardly believe what you're telling me. It's so alien. Const— my mother,' she corrected, her bottom lip quivering. 'She was my mother and she did love me.'

Lisa reached across the wooden slats and took Mia's hand.

'Oh, she loved you. As did your grandmother Memmi and Great Aunt Elisabeth. I have albums of photographs for you.'

Mia no longer felt the chill of the wind. She felt taller, whole, as if someone had just given her a new breath of life.

'Oh yes. I'd like that, it's my past, who I am, but why the adoption? Why were you named as my mother? How? I'm sorry, I don't mean to push you. I just want to know everything.'

'I know, and you will. Shall we get another coffee? I'm getting a bit of a dry mouth with all the talking. Let's go inside.'

They got up together and went inside, the warmth of the café making their cheeks flush. They discarded their coats and gloves and took a seat by the window.

Lisa looked out of the window and grinned. 'How about him, is he special?'

Mia followed her eyeline. Drake was making a bad job of browsing the gardens. It made her stomach flip.

'He is, yes. I have to admit, I never believed in all the cupid stuff, tingling and butterfly feelings, racing heart. But that's the effect he has on me.'

'Do you want him to join us?'

Mia hesitated. 'Er, no I don't think I do, not just yet. He's very patient. He'll be happy to wait.'

'Patient, as well as good looking. Great attributes in a man, so the novels tell me.'

'There's never been anyone in your life?'

'Not directly. Now, where did I get to? Oh yes, the adoption. When Constance discovered she was pregnant, Vikash was overjoyed, but she knew there was no way the Major would agree to a divorce. With him, it was all about saving face and control. Constance had raised the subject once before and he'd threatened to take Gina away from her – said he'd brand her as an unfit mother.'

Lisa paused.

'Poor Mummy.'

'Mm. Memmi wanted to take you in, but Vikash said it wasn't her decision to make. Somehow, Constance got the Major to agree to adopt another child. When you were born, you were gorgeous but not an English rose. Memmi and Elizabeth begged Constance to leave you with them and visit as often as she could. Constance registered with a local doctor under my name. There were no such things as computerised records in those days, so there was no fear of medical records not adding up. Vikash was named as the father and we both went to register your birth in Honiton.

'We had a little party afterwards, dressed up in our best clothes to mark the occasion.'

'Vikash wore a suit and a spotted tie.' Mia added.

'Probably, I can't remember the details. So, the wheels were set in motion for the adoption, with me posing as your birth mother.' Lisa paused to smile. 'It is such a relief to tell you, I've carried this all these years. Anyway, no room for sentimentality. Your mother and I travelled between here and Surrey when he was away. He was never interested in seeing the paperwork for you, he just signed where indicated.'

Mia couldn't help herself, wrinkling her nose in disgust. 'He was never interested in anything to do with me full stop. But why –'

'When he saw you, he demanded she got rid of you and adopted a fair-skinned child, but she wouldn't. Told him if he didn't let her keep you she'd make sure everyone knew that Georgina wasn't his, that he couldn't give her a child and why.' She fell silent.

'Was that when the abuse started?'

Lisa nodded. 'Mainly shouting at first, constant insults, the odd shove. He stayed away from home more often which suited us. I remember one day, he was watching you and Gina from his study. You were in the paddling pool, it was summer, and you were brown as a little berry, against Gina who was always pallid. He had one of his rages, told me not to let you out in the sun again. One day he came home unexpectedly. Memmi and Vikash had come for a visit, Vikash was playing with you. The Major went ballistic, threw them out of the house. Constance said they'd come for an interview as gardener and housekeeper. He berated her about even letting "darkies" through the door. Next thing we knew, he'd enrolled you at boarding school and you were gone. Constance begged him to change his mind, but he was having none of it. She cried for days. It was awful. After that, he left her alone and although Constance missed you, at least away he couldn't ill-treat you.'

'"A touch of the tar brush." That's what he said about me. It stuck, but I had no idea what that meant at the time. Yes, I was dark-skinned but no more than the Spanish and Italian kids at school.'

'He was the worst sort of racist. Back in the day when black men were called chalky Uncle Sam. He had Indian servants abroad, I suspect he didn't treat them well.'

'No wonder he made such a fuss when I came back to care for them...'

'Drink your coffee, it's getting cold.' Mia mock-frowned at the order. 'Sorry, old habits.' They both laughed. 'Once a nanny always a nanny!'

They sat across the table and Mia felt the affection that once bound them, returning.

'You have to know that Georgina wasn't all bad. She didn't know any different, he groomed her to be spiteful towards you, to gloat with the gifts he gave her. There was nothing we could do. I only stood up to him once.'

Mia leaned forward. 'What happened?'

'He sacked me.'

Mia crinkled her brow. 'So, you lost your job and Constance her ally.'

'Yes, in a way, but then I became a go-between. Mia, they loved you. Vikash even managed to secure a job at Chartley as a gardener so that he could be close to you.'

'Oh my God, really?' She rocked back into her chair, hand-stamped across her mouth, struggling to retrieve memories of faces from her schooldays. Was he the one who always waved – the one she often saw from the hill looking up at her? She saw the face, the one in the photograph, now it made sense.

'I had no idea. I grew up thinking I was unlovable, that no one wanted me. When all the time my father was just feet away.'

'Sadly, it was the only way one of them could watch you grow. So, you see, you were loved *very* much by them both.'

'But it was horrible. I built up a wall around me, I know that now.' Mia's voice dropped to almost a whisper, 'My life could have been so different. Why didn't someone tell me when I was older?'

'Your mother wanted to, but you were eighteen, you came home from Chartley and announced you were going abroad. She'd little control over you, all those years you'd been away, she was a broken woman with no fight left in her and there was Charles, who was delighted you had gone. I think by then she thought you were safer elsewhere. I'm sorry, I know it's a lot to take in.'

'You can say that again. I came here today full of anger, thinking you'd just dumped me. I wanted the truth, but I didn't expect this. I'm sorry. I thought you were a horrible person. But you were my mother's friend.'

Lisa's eyes filled with tears. Mia handed her the pack of tissues from her pocket.

'Please don't cry. You have nothing to feel guilty about.'

Lisa dabbed at her reddened cheeks. 'Don't make me out to be a martyr. I was paid well.'

Mia flinched. She'd not expected that sort of revelation.

'You see, my family were not well off. From the age of fifteen, I was the family breadwinner. My father was a drunk and womaniser, another hateful man. He knocked all of the confidence out of my poor mum. Like the Major did with Constance. When he sacked me, I...'

Mia leant across the table and held Lisa's hand.

'Enough, please. You don't have to explain, we were both victims of circumstance and I'm glad that she remembered you in her will. You look tired, is there much left to tell?' Lisa shook her head, 'Not really. At least you know now.'

'I still can't understand why she didn't leave him later on.'

Lisa dabbed at her nose, grimacing. 'Did you find the peacock bag? It was a gift from Memmi.'

'Yes, that's how I came to be in Sidmouth. Do you know it was that which caused her death? She tripped over it.'

Lisa stared into the distance. 'That bag has a lot to answer for. It was the reason Constance stayed with him. After you'd gone away the second time and without Vikash to watch over you, she got a little braver. Charles was retired from the army and was home a lot. One day he took the bag from her. She may have been little but she was a fighter, and nothing was going to separate her from that bag. They had a tug-of-war; him getting angrier and angrier, she refusing to let go. He just stopped and slumped into a chair. He couldn't talk, couldn't do anything, it was his first stroke. As much as she hated him she was honourable.'

'So, she stayed.' Mia said with sadness.

Lisa narrowed her brow. 'With Gina refusing to care for him she'd little choice. Guilt's a destructive thing.'

'Goodness,' Mia exhaled. 'Such a lot to take in. Do you mind if we leave it for today? I'm sure I'll have more questions tomorrow. Can we meet tomorrow?'

'Of course.' Lisa picked up her handbag, undid the catch, and produced an envelope. 'Here, I had these copied.'

Mia peeked inside.

'Tomorrow I'll tell you who's who and what was happening at the time. There's a lovely one of you as a baby with Vikash.'

'He sounds a very loving father.'

'Oh yes, he adored you.'

' I wish I'd met him.'

'He wishes that too... He's not dead Mia, you can meet him tomorrow.'

CHAPTER 60

DRAKE took her hand and led her back to the hotel. Mia was quiet, lost in thought.

'You don't have to tell me now if you don't want to,' he said, as he slipped his arm around her shoulder. 'Shall we go and order some lunch?'

'Thank you. It's all a bit fuzzy. I'm trying to get it into order.'

'You're not upset? Angry?'

'God, no. Far from it, but it's a long story. Do you mind if we go into town for lunch? I feel in need of a walk.'

Drake stopped and turned to face her, his eyes searching. It was Mia who moved forward to kiss him. As they parted, he showed an expression of smouldering relish.

'There, happy now?' she said, grinning. 'I'm okay, honestly. I have so much to tell you. I just feel I need a bit of a breather.'

'You didn't need to kiss me to get that.'

'Not even if I wanted to?'

'Well, in that case... Come on, let's go eat. This sea air makes me ravenous, perhaps I can have another kiss for dessert.'

Later, they left the café hand in hand and wandered onto the nearly empty beach, the wind whipping salty spray to their faces. It was past three o'clock and the daylight was fast being sapped from the sky.

'You look exhausted,' he said, squeezing her hand.

'I am a bit. I didn't sleep a wink last night. I almost got dressed at four to go for a walk.'

'On your own?'

'Yes. I wouldn't do it in London, but Sidmouth is far less threatening. When I opened the door it was raining, I'm such a wimp I went back inside.'

Drake chuckled. 'Nothing wimpy about you. You're one of the bravest women I know. Christ after all you've been through.' He guided her off the beach and back up the hill towards the hotel.

'Yes, well it's nearly all over,' Mia said, breathing deeply. 'One more day. I'm sorry, I'm talking in riddles. I haven't told you anything and it's mostly good news.'

The streetlights had begun to take on a glow. Drake came to a standstill, pointing above them towards Mutter's Moor, where the milky autumn sun was fading, leaving pink, orange, and purple scars across the sky.

'Red sky at night, Shepherd's delight,' he said pulling her tighter. They stood close together, admiring the warmth of colours, fighting against the approaching darkness.

'It feels like an omen.'

'Good or bad?'

'Oh, definitely good.' She tried to stifle a yawn.

'Come on. Up to your room, a few hours' sleep.'

'But I haven't told you what happened.'

'Another few hours won't kill me. You look dead on your feet. Get your head down for a few hours and I'll book a table for dinner around eight.'

'Old people take afternoon naps.'

'So do exhausted ones,' he said, lowering his eyebrows with concern.

She checked her watch. 'Fair enough, just an hour or so and then I'll tell you everything.'

They shared a lingering kiss at the door to her room. Within minutes of her sliding beneath the covers, she was sound asleep. Several hours later she woke feeling refreshed and slightly guilty that she'd not shared her news with Drake. Taking a lengthy bath, she dissected the shared knowledge. It made her feel different, whole. Soaping her arms recalling the detail. Dear darling Constance was her mother after all. And tomorrow, Lisa had promised, it would end in Sidmouth and she'd meet her father.

Mia ordered a bottle of champagne, two glasses, and found a quiet spot in the lounge to drink it.

Drake raised an eyebrow when he saw the champagne.

'Ah, so we're celebrating.'

She reached out and squeezed his hand. 'We are. And I apologise for leaving you hanging. It was selfish of me.'

His eyes fixed on hers. 'It wasn't selfish at all; I expect you had a lot to take in.' He popped the cork on the champagne and poured. Then raised his glass. 'Here's to a happy life and a new start.' They clinked glasses.

'Thank you, I couldn't have come this far without you.' She took a sip and relaxed back in her chair. Drake mimicked her movements.

'I think I'll start at the end, it's easier and a happy ending. Well, I hope so, after tomorrow.' He waited patiently while she gathered her thoughts. 'Can you believe it, Constance was my birth mother after all. I had both a Mum and Dad who loved me.'

'I can indeed. You're very lovable.'

She pulled a goofy face, placing a finger on his lips.

'Okay, I'll shut up.' He made a zip movement across his mouth, making her smile.

'So tomorrow, we'll say goodbye to Constance – Mummy,' she said feeling a warm glow as she spoke, 'And hello to Daddy. Vikash is my father, he still lives here.'

'No, really?'

'Yes, isn't that wonderful? It explains the obituary announcement and the wildflowers. Mutter's Moor was their special place, hence her final resting place. I suspect that's where I was conceived. Vikash, my father,' she said proudly, 'he got a job as a gardener at Chartley just to be near me. And all the time I was busy being a bitch to everyone who had nice loving families, he was there.'

Drake parted his lips to speak but changed his mind.

'Go on. You can ask me things, just butt in. God, I'm so happy.'

'Okay. Two questions. Firstly, why didn't she just get a divorce and marry Vikash? Secondly, why put Lisa's name down as your birth mother?'

'Because he would have got custody of Gina, she loved us both, she had to do what he said or lose her too. Lisa said he had his suspicions when he caught Vikash and Memmi visiting. Memmi was my grandmother. Anyway, he had one of his rages and threatened Constance that if she left him or wanted a divorce, he would see that she never saw either of us again. Lisa only skirted around that bit, but I get the picture. They both had something on the other; he was passing Gina off as his and Mummy threatened to expose him, not good for his male ego. Gina got to stay, his version of compromise. He wasn't interested in the details, so he never saw the birth certificate. I vanished abroad as soon as I left school, so Constance never got the opportunity to tell me.'

'God, that's amazing. I can't imagine what's going on in your head.'

Her shoulders raised as she filled her lungs then slid back again.

'I feel, well, sort of complete. Like a jigsaw with all the pieces. I'm all bubbly energy. I want to punch the air and shout.' She hugged herself. 'I'm so excited, tomorrow I get to meet my Dad.' Her eyes became moist.

'Hey, none of that.'

Her chin wobbled, 'I'm not sad. They're happy tears.'

He handed her a napkin. 'That's all right then. Come on, drink up, then let's get some food, while you tell me the rest.'

There wasn't much more to tell other than Lisa had texted to say she was with Vikash and they'd arranged to meet at Mutter's Moor car park the next day. They made their way back to their rooms, giggling like a pair of children. She stopped at her door, handing him her key card.

'Tonight, dear Drake, you can't deny me anything.'

He slid an arm to encircle her waist. 'Whatever you say, madam.'

'Well, I think you'll agree I'm not at all, er, vulnerable tonight?'

'Definitely not,' he said, trying to keep a straight face.

'So, you couldn't be accused of taking advantage of me, could you?'

His eyes twinkled in the light. 'I suppose not.'

In one swift move, he swept her into his arms, and they stumbled backwards into her room.

Drake raised a foot behind him and crooking the edge of the door with the tip of his shoe and kicked it, shutting out the world behind them.

CHAPTER 61

THE sky stretched out as far as she could see. A pinkish hue, fading to bluey-grey, meeting the horizon in a pencilled line. Sam had been right about the weather; it was a good day to say goodbye.

Mia stared out to sea, unable to lie in Drake's arms any longer, as wonderful as it felt. She breathed in the crisp, fresh air as day broke. And what a day it promised to be. After thirty-six years, she would reunite with Vikash, the father who'd loved her so much he'd taken a job to watch over her. She loved that idea, *watch over*. It seemed to wrap itself around her like a hug.

A noise behind her made her turn. Drake's head appeared around the door frame.

'What on earth are you doing outside at this time of the morning? Come back to bed.'

She glanced at her watch. 'It's gone nine, we've slept in.'

'Good, we needed it, you especially.'

She took one last look across the bay and followed him inside.

'I can't go back to sleep. I'm buzzing. It sort of feels like all my Christmases have come at once.'

Drake slipped under the covers, patting the space, 'I have that effect on women.' She half-smiled. 'Okay, I get the message. Your mind's elsewhere. I just thought I might be able to persuade you. Or do we class this as another vulnerable moment?'

In reply, she peeled off her dressing gown, and slid in beside him.

'I think I can spare you an hour or so,' she added, ' I'm full of unused energy so it's either you or go for a run...'

'Hey, I have feelings you know.'

'And very lovely they are.' She rolled on her side to face him, gazing into his eyes, just visible under his unruly bed-head. 'I'm sorry I'm so distracted but I do love you really.'

His body tensed against hers, cupping her chin towards him, his lips crushed against hers leaving her breathless.

'Now it's my turn for all my Christmases because I am very much in love with you too.'

She felt wrong-footed. 'I didn't mean to say...'

His eyes never left hers. 'That you loved me?'

'No. I mean yes. What I meant was, well, it was an expression. Shit now I've ruined the moment.'

A twitch at the corners of his mouth told her he was toying with her.

'Drake Quaid, stop teasing.'

He kissed her long and deeply, before pulling back.

'Now deny it,' he said.

'I can't.'

'Well then?'

She wriggled her hips closer. 'Okay. I have never said this to anyone in my life before, so I'd better get it right.' She dramatically cleared her throat. 'Drake, I have to tell you, that in all seriousness I am totally, unashamedly, in love with you.'

He tilted his head, softly kissing her eyelids. 'Thank you.'

She opened her mouth to speak but he silenced her with his.

Mia applied red lipstick then wiped it off again. It was important how she looked. Meeting the queen would be less nerve-wracking. Drake returned to his own allowing her time alone. Her skin still tingled from his touch. Nothing she'd ever experienced between the sheets had ever made her so content. She raised her arms and took a luxurious stretch.

That's the difference between sex and lovemaking. We're lovers and in love.

CHAPTER 62

'I'LL drive,' Drake said, taking the keys from her. Mia did not attempt to move. 'What's up? Come on don't look so worried. I promise it will all be fine.'

Mia ran her teeth back and forth over her bottom lip. Lowering her eyes, she held her hands as if clutching ski poles – her thumbs rubbing frantically along the sides of her forefingers.

Drake wrapped his arms around her. 'Nothing to be scared of and I'm with you all the way.'

She raised her head. 'I am scared, what if he doesn't like me?'

Drake smoothed her hair from her forehead. 'What if you don't like him?'

The confusion caused a frown, she shrugged out of his arms.

'Of course, I'll like him, he's my father. He cared about me.'

'Exactly, now come on, let's go and meet him.'

Drake drove the car up Peak Hill, turning into the stony car park at the sign that said Mutter's Moor.

'Mia, if you keep flipping that mirror up and down it'll fall off.'

'But do I look alright?'

'You look beautiful, the same as you did the last time you asked me.'

'Have we got time to nip back to the hotel, we got here very quickly, and I think I need the loo again.'

'Tell you what pop in the bushes and I'll keep watch.'

She stared at him in horror; he, in turn, quirked an eyebrow.

'Exactly, it's not urgent it's just nerves. Do some deep breathing.'

'I'm okay, sorry. I thought there would be more of a view from here,' she said scanning the car park. 'It's just a bit of common and some trees with a road running through it. It's not at all how I imagined it, you can't even see the sea.'

'I expect you can but we'll have to walk somewhere to their special place. Ah, this must be them.'

A small Fiat made its way slowly into the car park. Even though it was chilly her palms were tacky. Noisily she dragged the saliva from her mouth and swallowed.

'What if I don't know what to say to him?'

He squeezed her hand. 'You will, and he probably feels the same. Now go. I'll keep Constance company.'

She huffed a breath up her face as she climbed from the car. A smile broke her lips as she recognised him as the man she'd seen climbing the hill. She took a pace then another – faster. He held out his arms smiling. A sudden noise to her left, voices, the rustle of disturbed undergrowth. She stopped abruptly before she toppled into a stout man in a bobble hat.

'Morning,' he said raising his hand to his chest, 'you gave me quite a start.'

She mumbled an apology staring above the heads of the twenty or so walkers who had emerged from the wooded path and crossed in front of them. She waited for space, some room to get to him, her breathing rushed. Vikash her only focus. She rushed – half-ran, kicking stones from her path. In her head he would pick her up and spin her around, she was laughing and crying at the same time. She reached him; his leathered face wet with tears. They embraced, and somehow his smell was familiar. She snuggled into him feeling his bony body beneath his clothing and relaxed her grip. Neither spoke, they swayed and rocked. The sound of a nose being blown interrupted them.

'I wish Constance had been there to see that,' Lisa said.

'She is,' Drake said grinning as he approached them, waving the rucksack.

'How wonderful. The three of us together again. Hello, my beautiful daughter. I never thought I'd live to see the day.'

Mia's voice quavered as she spoke. 'He – Hello Vikash. Or may I call you Dad?'

He moved to her side, linking arms. 'If you are willing to call me Dad, I would like that very much. Let's walk.' He pointed with his shooting stick in the direction of the sea. 'Shall we?' They left the car park following the hikers' footsteps.

Mia threw a glance over her shoulder as the crossed the road. Lisa and Drake were following at a discrete distance. He raised a hand and waved.

As they walked, Vikash recounted stories about Mia's grandmother, Memmi. He had a long stride and Mia struggled to keep pace with him, but it felt right as if they'd known each other forever.

They passed through a gate leading onto heathland. White flint rocks poked their way through the surface of the grass. Mia's eye caught a dab of stubborn colour where some late wildflowers showed their heads between rough grass and thistle. A wooden signpost pointed out directions. One read Mutter's Moor, but it was in the direction they'd come from. She stopped.

'I think we're going the wrong way, it said Mutter's Moor that way.'

He patted her hand. 'That's right Mia, but I want to take you to our special spot. We didn't walk up the hill the way you drove. We came up the valley and across the top of the headland through Mutter's Moor then walked down the coastal path and home.' They stopped for a moment. 'Never get tired of that view.'

She could see why. The green of the land fell away to the expanse of sky and sea. Ahead at the end of the bay, the rich terracotta cliffs layered back like the ribs of a fan. In the other direction rising higher above them, evergreens dotted the hillside, dark green among the autumn golds of silver birch.

'This is where you began,' he said wistfully pointing to a narrow path that lead downwards and into a thicket of copper-toned trees. Mia fell into step behind him. 'Here we are,' Vikash said, coming to a stop. 'Your mother's top of the world.' He opened his shooting stick and perched on the leather seat. 'I can't get up this far nowadays. A few hundred yards past Jacob's Ladder is the best I can do.'

'I know, Dad, I watched you. You passed me one day when I was sitting on the cliff path. Then another time I watched you from my hotel window.' Her throat tightened. 'I think it's so sad that you could never be together. All of us, me too.'

His shoulders raised and fell. 'It was what it was. I watched you grow from a distance. I came to your aid when I could...that hateful woman,' He scowled.

Mia halted but he tugged her forward. 'You knew – about what happened?'

'Not for sure until I came across the evidence and destroyed it.'

'Thank you. You made it stop.'

'The other girls helped. You were such a pretty child and such a beautiful woman...'

'That must have been sad, just watching not being able to tell me.'

'No, not really. You were hurting and alone. One of us had to be with you and Constance had no choice. There was nothing to be done. Anyway, your sharp tongue protected you.' He chuckled. 'You get that from your Grandmother and your liking of hills from us.' I used to write to Memmi and tell her how you climbed that dammed hill so often.'

'I wish I'd met her.'

'You will, she's in the churchyard along with Elizabeth.'

She slid her arm around his shoulder. 'Was there never a time for us to be a family?'

'We were going to tell you when you left school, but you went away. Then Georgina got married and left home, Charles had the stroke and Constance felt obliged to stay. Oh, here you are,' Vikash said, glancing over Mia's shoulder.

'What a fantastic view,' said Drake, 'the moor, the bay, the sea, the cliffs ... amazing. No wonder it was your favourite place. It's stunning.'

'Constance used to have a little transistor radio that she brought here,' Lisa said. 'She told me how the two of you used to dance, without a care in the world.'

Vikash nodded his head in agreement. 'Couldn't now it's too overgrown.'

Lisa produced four plastic glasses and a bottle of champagne from her bag. Drake popped the cork and poured them all a glass and made a toast.

'To family and reunions and love.' They echoed his words then slipped into thought with only the rustle of the wind crossing from sea to land and the odd seabird's cry to disturb them.

A nod of the head from Mia was Drakes cue. He undid the rucksack and removed the urn. Vikash held out his hands and took it, holding it aloft before bringing it down to his lips. With one hand he unbuttoned his coat wrapping the urn against his heart.

Mia saw Drake look away as the old man closed his eyes and rocked. Lisa sniffed and dabbed at her eyes; Mia's tears fell silently, she stood by her father's side, letting him share the comfort of Constance. She'd said her last goodbyes, now it was his turn.

'It's time my love,' Vikash whispered. 'I hold you in my arms one last time before you fly into the wind and lay down forever in our special place.'

He handed the urn to Mia. 'Can you open it, please. My hands are not as useful as they were.'

She unscrewed the top and passed it back to him. He stepped forward holding the urn before him. Without warning, he began to sing, his voice thick and heaving with emotion.

It was so unexpected that Mia broke down. Drake came to her side as Vikash scattered Constance's ashes to the wind, then turned to hug his daughter.

'Don't cry, she is where she wished to be. You have been a good daughter.'

'That was so beautiful,' Mia said, dabbing at her face, 'the words, did you write them?'

'I wish I had, the sentiment is true, but it was Leonard Cohen. It's called "Dance Me to the End of Love". I'm not sure how accurate my version is. But Constance wouldn't have minded. I felt it appropriate, and it was one that your mother loved.' He smiled into her eyes. 'You're shivering, child. Time to go.' He folded his shooting stick and started back up the path. Calling over his shoulder, 'We should mark the occasion with a sherry, her favourite tipple.'

Lisa linked arms with him. 'I've booked us a table at the Bedford, I know you like the food there and I've brought the photo albums with me, so we can talk over dinner about happier times.'

Mia blew a kiss to the wind as Drake's arm encircled her waist. They moved off bumping hips as they trod the uneven pathway.

'That's it then. The end of the mystery. You lost your mum but found your dad. Very satisfying.'

'It is, and what a lovely song. Took me by surprise.'

'Me too, a bit of a Hugh Grant moment. So, what now? What's your next mission?' he asked as they took the broad path back towards the road.

'Change my name to Kumar I suppose. Croxley-Smith was always such a mouthful.'

He halted, turning her to face him.

'I've got a better idea, let's change it to Quaid.' Her eyes searched his, was he joking? He dropped to one knee, 'Mia, will you do me the honour of becoming my wife?'

There was a ripple of applause from Vikash and Lisa, who'd stopped by the kissing gate.

'Please say yes,' said Vikash smiling, 'If I'm to walk you down the aisle, you'll have to hurry up before I'm the one in an urn.'

'Well?' said Drake, still on one knee.

'Drake get up, the ground's all wet, silly. And yes, yes, I'll marry you.' He pulled her to him, kissed her and spun her off her feet. Her hair fanned out around her head like the feathers of a peacock.

'But do you think it's too soon?' She bit her lip. 'We hardly know each other.'

Drake rolled his eyes heavenward. 'Mia, I know every skeleton in your cupboard and you in mine. I love you. And you love me and if we don't want to end up like Vikash and Constance, we'd better get on with it.'

EPILOGUE

THEY'D picked the hottest time of day to climb Peak Hill. Mia insisted they didn't cheat by driving or take the bus. The group of three headed across the bracken path: the beautiful blue of the Meridian Sea beneath them.

'I wish we bought some water, it's far too hot,' Drake complained, wiping his brow.

'Don't worry we'll be in the shade soon, it's not far now.'

A few minutes later they'd reached their destination. 'It looks different with the undergrowth so lush,' she said placing the hand-tied bouquet of summer flowers on the ground. The baby blue ribbon lifted in the sea breeze.

'Nice touch that,' Drake said, 'using the ribbon to decorate Vikash's shooting stick with your flowers – a link between the two.'

'I thought it made him look quite jaunty as he walked me down the aisle.'

'And nice to see his tie back where it should be.'

Drake pulled out the second blue ribbon from his pocket. She tied it to the branch of a sapling as he lifted their sleeping daughter from her papoose. Mia took her expecting her to wake and complain but instead, she roused her huge brown eyes blinking in the sunlight.

'Mummy, I'd like to introduce you to Constance – we call her Connie for short; I hope you don't mind.'

Drake slipped his arm around Mia's waist. 'That's lovely,' he said, using his thumb to gently blot away a tear from Mia's cheek.

'We'll come back each year as she grows, Mother, I promise.' There was a beat of silence as Drake kissed the dark heads of both his girls. 'Well, my lovelies we have a wedding reception to attend. Let's get a move on and go celebrate.'

Going down was quicker than they expected, and they were soon back at the hotel and ready to cut the cake.

'Amazing wedding,' Zannah said, linking her arm through her husband's.

'Thanks to Vikash and Lisa,' a figure hovered in the background. 'Ah, not to forget Sam of course, who made the grounds look as best as they possibly could.'

Sam gave an awkward smile and moved away. It was strange to see him in a collar and tie, he'd been so much of her journey, she couldn't leave him out.

Vikash touched her arm and guided her a few paces away. 'My beautiful Maureen.' Mia pulled a face. 'Memmi helped us choose it.'

'Because it was Lisa's second name, and she made it possible.'

'No. That was a coincidence. We chose the name because of its meaning – different in many countries - much loved, in Gaelic, star of the sea, in Latin. In Hebrew or Egyptian, it means a drop of the sea - bitter or beloved. In Vietnamese it means beauty. Now you see how apt the choice of name was.'

Mia rearranged her face to an apology. 'I wish I'd known. I'd have carried it with pride.'

Vikash chuckled. 'Like I have you. The pride of my heart.' He walked a little further away. 'Are you happy with the arrangement?'

'I am. I think it's right Lisa moving in with you. Mummy wouldn't have minded. You both need someone to look after and I suspect she's always been a little bit in love with you.'

'We are friends, and now will be companions. Without Lisa, Constance could never have kept you and we would have lost you forever.'

They turned to a voice from behind. 'Not making my wife cry, are you?' Drake said holding Connie out to Vikash who welcomed her into his arms.

'Tears spent at a wedding are tears of joy. And we couldn't be happier.'

Mia suspected that the "*we*" wasn't him and Lisa, but he and Constance. All together in one place. Mutter's Moor would be held dear to them all and she would see to it that Connie came to it regularly and understood its great importance.

Accident of Fate

Having escaped a difficult past, Joanna Lane meets gallery owner Marcus Tierney and falls in love. When they adopt baby Adam, they set in motion a chain of events that opens a Pandora's box.

Lizzie Owen is growing up in a dysfunctional family when a terrible accident leaves her in the hands of the charmer, Liam Riley.

Ava and Imogen Chase are mother and daughter. Ava, a world-renowned artist, takes Liam Riley as a lover. Imogen has had her sights on Liam from an early age and her compulsive obsession with him becomes more sinister as time passes.

As love and lives converge, Joanna finds herself caught between loyalty and integrity, as she battles to unravel secrets, for the sake of her family's happiness.

Every link in the chain of events leads straight back to one person... Liam Riley.

What happens next? … Accident of Birth

Accident of Birth

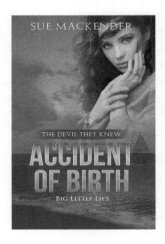

Sasha Chase must flee her sociopathic boyfriend Adam Tierney. Her only hope is her grandmother Ava Chase, but she lives in Malta. Can Sasha get there without Adam finding her before it's too late? They have done a terrible thing and she knows she will be punished for it.

Motorway cop Ned Wilson has seen all sorts of carnage on the M25 but what he's not expecting to find is a new-born baby girl abandoned in a crashed bread lorry. More importantly – what has happened to the baby's mother?

Adam Tierney has tried cashing in on his father Liam Riley's good looks but has lost everything and it's all Sasha's fault. Wherever she is, he will find her.

About the Author

Sue Mackender sold her successful recruitment business after 29 years to follow her lifelong passion for books and begin a new career as a writer. Sue is often termed as a Grit-Lit writer of Commercial Fiction. She places her heroines in impossible situations where they need to fight their corner to survive.

Her first two novels Accident of Fate and Accident of Birth have been firm favourites with Book Club readers. She has also been published in America in the Chicken Soup for the Soul anthologies.

The Girl on the Hill is Sue's third novel. In 2019 Sue was awarded the coveted Katie Fforde bursary.

Sue lives with her husband in Surrey.